Where Did
All the Men Go?

WOMEN IN CROSS-CULTURAL PERSPECTIVE

Sue-Ellen Jacobs, Series Editor

This series presents ethnographic case studies that address theoretical, methodological, and practical issues in basic and applied fieldwork; it also includes cross-cultural studies based on secondary sources. Edited by Sue-Ellen Jacobs, the series aims to broaden our knowledge about the varieties and commonalities of women's experiences. One important focus of the series is on women in development and the effects of the development process on women's roles and status. By considering women in the full context of their cultures, this series offers new insights on sociocultural, political, and economic change cross-culturally.

In This Series

Where Did All the Men Go? Female-Headed/Female-Supported Households in Cross-Cultural Perspective, *edited by Joan P. Mencher and Anne Okongwu*

Balancing Acts: Women and the Process of Social Change, *edited by Patricia Lyons Johnson*

Sanctions and Sanctuary: Cultural Perspectives on the Beating of Wives, *edited by Dorothy Ayers Counts, Judith K. Brown, and Jacquelyn C. Campbell*

Where Did
All the Men Go?

Female-Headed/Female-Supported Households
in Cross-Cultural Perspective

EDITED BY

Joan P. Mencher and
Anne Okongwu

Westview Press

BOULDER • SAN FRANCISCO • OXFORD

*To all the women struggling to
maintain female-headed households*

Women in Cross-Cultural Perspective

Copyright © 1993 by Westview Press, Inc.

Published in 1993 in the United States of America by Westview Press, Inc., 5500 Central Avenue, Boulder, Colorado 80301-2877, and in the United Kingdom by Westview Press, 36 Lonsdale Road, Summertown, Oxford OX2 7EW

Library of Congress Cataloging-in-Publication Data
Where did all the men go? : female-headed/female-supported households
  in cross-cultural perspective / edited by Joan P. Mencher and Anne
Okongwu.
     p. cm.—(Women in cross-cultural perspective)
  Includes bibliographical references.
  ISBN 0-8133-8540-7
  1. Women head of households—Cross-cultural studies.   2. Poor
women—Cross-cultural studies.   I. Mencher, Joan P., 1930–   .
II. Okongwu, Anne.   III. Series.
HV1444.W44   1993
305.4—dc20   92-39725
                                                                             CIP

Printed and bound in the United States of America

The paper used in this publication meets the requirements
of the American National Standard for Permanence of Paper
for Printed Library Materials Z39.48-1984.

10   9   8   7   6   5   4   3   2

Contents

Preface

Although Female-Headed/Female-Supported households have been discussed a great deal by policy makers, they have only recently come to engage the attention of social scientists. The available literature is widely scattered, and focused on only one society. Very little is known about the diverse forms of these households or the diverse strategies they follow in order to survive.

The papers in this book are an outgrowth of two symposia, one held at the American Anthropological Association meeting in the fall of 1986 and a larger one held at the 12th International Congress of Anthropological and Ethnological Sciences (IUAES) in Zagreb, Yugoslavia. We are especially grateful to our fellow social scientists from all over what was then Yugoslavia for making that conference a possibility. The day-long session on Female-Headed Households was jointly sponsored by the Commission on Women and the International Womens Anthropology Caucus (IWAC).

This book has been long in reaching fruition. Without the steady encouragement and hard work of editing provided by Franklin C. Southworth, it would have been impossible. His careful reading and useful comments on every article greatly improved the clarity of the book. His deep concern for the issues involved was reflected in the questions he posed and the suggestions he made.

The main title for this book, Where Did All the Men Go? was originally the title for the article by Anna Lou Dehavenon in this volume. Because we felt it applied to all of the articles, we asked her permission to use this title for the book and she graciously agreed. We are indebted to her for this extremely provocative title.

We also thank Regina Caulfield for help with typing and collating parts of the manuscript.

We hope that the work will prove useful not only to academics, but more importantly to policy planners in improving the quality of life for these women and their families.

Joan P. Mencher
Anne Francis Okongwu

1

Introduction

Joan P. Mencher and Anne Okongwu

This book examines female-headed/female-supported households in a wide variety of local contexts and links them to wider economic, social, and political processes. In the process of doing this, it focuses on the importance of culture and the ways in which culture interacts with race (and/or caste), class and gender in defining the experience of women who have the responsibility of supporting their households.

The idea for this book emerged from two symposia run by the editors, the first at a meeting of the American Anthropological Association in 1986, and the second at the International Congress of Anthropological Sciences in Zagreb in 1988. It grew out of the awareness of the importance of female-headed/female-supported households worldwide, their frequent correlation with poverty, and at the same time a sense that they differed significantly in different parts of the world. The papers should be viewed as a series of case studies from different regions of the world that highlight the ways in which female-headed/female-supported households function, their diverse strategies for survival, and the differences and similarities between these households and the more traditional male-headed/male-supported households. The articles highlight both the similarities and differences between these different types of households.

Throughout the world we find a wide variety of situations in which women provide the main source of economic support for their households and often, though not always, function as the "head of the household". Such situations are found across cultural, national, class, racial and ethnic boundaries. Each of the essays here takes up a specific aspect of this general situation. Taken together they inform us of the wide range of cultural variability among female- supported households around the world.

The title of this book -- *Where Did All the Men Go?* -- derives from the analysis of the structural conditions facing female-headed households both in the

United States and elsewhere. For the United States the role of the state, in formulating eligibility criteria for various types of essential subsidies, acts as part of the household survival strategies to separate men from their families. Thus the lack of adequate employment for semi-educated males forces them to take jobs in the secondary labor force which are insecure and from which they are often laid off. Such jobs provide little or no fringe benefits, and often mean that in order for their families to survive they cannot live together.

This title is also relevant for the southeast African case discussed by Apeadu where men are often forced to work far from home (in the mines, on tea-estates, etc.) and in effect create female-headed households. Male migration for work not only leaves female-headed households at home, but also creates a situation in which rural women (whether in their traditional villages or in refugee camps) assume full responsibility for household survival on a day-to-day basis.

We are not arguing that families are always better-off if there is a male in the household. As Blumberg's article shows, in many instances where women hold "purse power" children may be better fed and/or better educated, even where the households are poorer.

While the papers are in many ways quite disparate, they share several recurring themes and concerns. Thus for example many of the papers deal with the question of how households and the women who head them manage to put together a support package for their families. The issues raised in the papers are not always easily comparable, yet taken together we hope that the volume will stimulate discussion and a movement toward a better theoretical understanding of the general phenomenon.

At the present time, the interest in and concern about households solely or largely supported by women is not only theoretically significant, but also directly related to some of the major economic and policy issues confronting Third World nations, as well as many countries in the developed world. As such, this topic is at the center of a number of raging debates about the importance of the work that women do. This is a matter that concerns not only social scientists, but even more importantly, development planners and activists.

There is a great deal of baggage associated with the concept of headship that needs to be broken down and analyzed because it includes a number of sometimes overlapping and sometimes discrete elements. Previously, it had been implicitly assumed that all of these elements were congruent with a single "head", i.e. that all of the attributes associated with headship resided in a single person. However, as a result of the past 15 to 20 years of research in which closer attention has been paid to the activities of various members of households and families in a wide variety of societies, we have come to recognize the distinction between household and family, and to pay closer attention to what members of households and families actually do. Thus we recognize that people can make major economic contributions to households without even being present in the household, and also that different responsibilities connected with headship may be dispersed among different family members.

There are four major aspects of headship: (1) authority or power, (2) decision-making, (3) sources of economic support, and in some instances (4) control over and possession of children in case of divorce or death. These present a multi-dimensional picture that has come from explorations of "female-headed" households, and of women in a wide variety of "male-headed" households. Each of these aspects is found to be discrete in some societies or situations. For example, a man might be the head of the household in terms of power or authority, yet within the household he might consider it beneath him to get involved in decisions involving household management (as noted for many traditional, large, joint families in some parts of India in the late 19th. century); at the same time his decision-making power outside the household might be limited to his own domain of economic or political activity and not include that of his wife or the female world. (For example, in some parts of India it was the women who negotiated a son or daughter's marriage.)

Okali and Sumberg note that West African women tend to be more independent in their "use of money than in other aspects of decision making." (1986:180). They go on to note that in one study by ICLA "alley farmers claimed that their spouses took most decisions--even those connected with the sale of their own animals (ibid)." Jones in talking about the Cameroons notes that women have complete control over any cash that they might have, thus any cash received from rice farming can be used for consumer goods if they so desire (1986:113), and Guyer notes that:

> in the southern Cameroon cocoa belt. . . the woman has the right and responsibility to provide staples for the family diet while the man earns his primary income from cocoa. With respect to cocoa production the woman's labour is "exogenous" to the household head's decision making. But the relationship of her activities to his activities is "endogamous" to the household defined in a general sociospacial fashion. . . . In Africa, it still matters precisely who has resources to allocate. Men and women have different resources - as well as different constraints on their choices, different responsibilities to meet with their incomes and different possibilities for spreading the risk of failure. (1983:96-97).

When analyzing the concept of headship, it is clear that the same individual does not necessarily fulfill all of the functions traditionally associated with headship in the west and in Asia. Nor is the same pattern found in all households within a given population even in the west, or parts of Asia such as India, though there may be general patterns observable. In the past, traditional societies tended to have less diversification in patterns than colonial and contemporary societies. Nonetheless, where data exist we find that even the traditional societies exhibited some degree of variation. Thus it may be useful to dissect each of the four main categories of headship into their respective components, and to discuss them in terms of the multi- dimensional picture that has emerged from work done during the past two decades.

While most of the literature, both before and since 1980, has investigated questions of (1) family form, (2) definitions of what constitutes a family and/or a household, and (3) variations in domestic organization, much less attention has been paid to the question of headship even in individual societies, not to mention cross-culturally. With the growth of the women's movement, the "female-headed" household has come to be recognized not as an undesirable anomaly which should not exist, but as commonplace in many societies across the world. It is recognized further that there has been a significant increase in the number of these households during the past 10 to 20 years, though perhaps the numbers might have been underestimated earlier. We have come to understand that they also existed earlier on even in some traditional societies, and that a large number of socio-cultural, ideological, economic, and political factors have played a role in the formation of female-headed households at different points in time and under varying historical conditions.

The issues of what constitutes a "female-headed" household is often confusing and not always directly related to the problems confronting women. A household primarily supported by women can for example have a formal male head who is either (1) too old or too infirm to work, (2) unemployed, (3) living away from the household because of migration, and not sending much money home because of low wages or unwillingness, (4) a polygamous husband who expects each wife to provide for herself, (5) a man who simply refuses to support the household, (6) a farmer who only produces cash crops which provide for occasional luxury items and for the man's status-producing activities, but does not feed the family, (7) a man who is primarily involved in political or religious activities for which he receives little compensation, or (8) as in some societies such as the Ashanti in Ghana, a man whose major obligations are to his sister's children rather than to his own.

Female-supported households also include families supported by an unmarried or widowed daughter, and children supported by mothers or grandmothers who have migrated out and left the children behind to be reared by other kin, who rely on outside remittances not only for the school fees or support of an occasional child, but for the maintenance of the entire household.

The factors responsible for women assuming prime responsibility for the economic support of households include: (1) death of a spouse, father, or other responsible male; (2) migration of the male for employment (it has been noted that female migrants are far more likely to send back large proportions of their earnings than males; Prescod-Roberts 1980); (3) high male unemployment; (4) divorce, abandonment or separation; (5) residence with another wife in another location—for example, a man living with one wife in an urban area and another in the rural area and refusing to give economic support to the rural wife apart from her access to the land; and (6) culturally prescribed role behavior.

Each one of these situations has a different kind of social response in a particular cultural context, so that a woman who is divorced might receive a different response from the local community than a woman who has never married and has children. Thus we must look at the social, economic and political context in which the community is responding to women who find themselves in the situation of being either the sole or the main support of a given household. It is important to examine the conditioned responses of family, friends and the state to these women. Further, in addition to variations in the responses of the community and state to women who support their households, the international economic and political context in which they conduct these activities changes the contours of their experience (Bolles:1983, Nash:1983, and Safa: 1983).

Global Dimensions

There has been a rise in female-headed households globally, and this increase has been accompanied by international concern. Why the increase? Why the concern? The papers by D'Amico, Abraham, Castro, Dehavenon and Singh all focus on the gender, race, class and ethnic dimensions of the contemporary global economy and the vulnerability of women and households to shifts in economic, social, political and military policies. These policies force changes in (1) the amounts of money women need to feed households, (2) the possible sources of income generation which exist (e.g. agribusiness can destroy subsistence food production, and international policies favoring export of high-tech industry can also reduce local level employment opportunities), (3) opportunities for housing and education (e.g. as a result of cutbacks to meet debt payments), or the appropriation of land for mining, tourism, or the like.

The size, shape and activities of households and their members need to be seen against this larger backdrop -- as responses to war, refugee status, urbanization and contractions in demand for unskilled labor -- and the ways in which these forces and events differentially affect women, men and children of various racial, ethnic and class groups, and how they affect the interactions and relationships among them.

Researchers working in a broad range of societies have illustrated the importance of analyzing contemporary families within both their national and international contexts. (See Baca Zinn and Eitzen 1990, Nash 1981, Meillassoux 1981, Sanjek 1982, Wallerstein 1984.) This literature demonstrates through linking of their analyses of households and families to wider social, economic and political forces a useful way of understanding the range of factors that condition household composition, family organization, standard of living, income generating strategies and life chances of family members.

Specifically, this work suggests that: (1) the particular ways in which a nation is incorporated into the world economic system shapes the contours of the opportunity structure within a particular social context, (2) the level of development and internal structure of the state, including the range and types of subsidies to citizens, importantly conditions the strategies employed by families to gain access to the essentials of life; (3) within each social context, it is necessary to give careful attention to the historically and culturally specific ways in which structures of inequality manifest themselves at a given point in time, and the impact of these on differential incorporation into the opportunity structure, access to life-sustaining resources as well as current and future life chances of family members.

The use of this type of macro-framework in the study of families proves useful in alerting researchers to the multiple variables that condition contemporary family life. Further it adds a dimension to micro-studies that acts to circumvent the limitations inherent in attributing the behavior of individuals solely to cultural or intra-family dynamics.

The Local and Cultural Context

Diverse local and cultural contexts may serve to inhibit or encourage the formation of female-headed households. We are concerned with the circumstances under which this type of household emerges, whether due to male migration, the desertion of women by their husbands or mates, widowhood, the inability of males to earn a living, male drug abuse, other problems connected with urbanization, female choice (see Castro on Brazil); and with the stages of women's lives at which these occur. Some examples from the chapters that follow include: Abraham, who notes that for female-headed households to give way to nuclear ones in Curacao, men must not only earn more, but women less. Is this true of other places? Garcia notes that under certain circumstances females in Colombia and Brazil may prefer to live without a male in the household. Another important set of local conditions considered in the papers is the role of state structures and how they affect and are affected by local economies in determining access to formal and informal income, to housing, to shelter, and to health care and benefits. Dehavenon discusses these questions in great depth for the United States.

In considering the genesis of female-headed households, it is important to include men along with women in the discussion of gender, the better-off along with the poor in the discussion of class, and whites along with blacks (and other minority groups) in the discussion of race. As Burnham has made clear for the U.S., the feminization of poverty thesis is flawed because it looks only at gender, and not at how the consequences of gender are experienced differently in different racial and class groupings. This point is argued both in the papers by Okongwu and Dehavenon. The latter paper devotes a large part of the discussion of female-headed households in New York City to answering the question, "but where are the men?"

Some important differences which emerge cross-culturally about the ways in which female-headed households come into being include beliefs and practices concerning the generation, disposal and control over income and resources; that is, differences among (1) those societies in which women generate, but do not control, resources or income, (2) those in which women generate, dispose of and control resources or income, and (3) those in which women control household expenditure but do not generate income. From a theoretical point of view, Blumberg deals with this question in detail in her overview.

Beliefs about sexuality and control over women's sexuality also shape the kinds of households which are formed in response to external conditions. For example, as shown in Islam's paper on Bangladesh, the combination of war and gender ideology created female-headed households where they did not exist before.

The different articles also point up different attitudes towards women bearing children out of wedlock. The articles by Okongwu, Castro, and Dehavenon note that in the west, including Latin America and the Caribbean, single women, especially poorer single women in the 1990s, often have children, whereas in the Middle East (Saunders) and Asia (Mencher and Islam) this is extremely rare. Castro's paper about Brazil indicates that this is the single main reason for the rapid increase in the number of female-headed households in recent years where teenage pregnancies, married men having more than one family, and a greater age for marriage all play a role in household formation.

In Asia and most of Africa there is a tendency for females to marry soon after puberty. Indeed, in the vast majority of old world societies (though not all), there is today and has been in the past an intolerance for any female having a child out of wedlock. If a girl were to become pregnant, the only alternatives have been: (1) abortion; (2) an immediate rushed marriage to anyone, not necessarily the father of the child in question, just to hush things up (often it can be an older man, a widower, or someone with some deficit that precludes his getting an unsullied wife); (3) in some cases killing of the girl by her own kin, (4) infanticide, (5) abandoning the child or giving it for adoption-- all done secretly. Above all else, no one must know that the girl was pregnant before having a legitimate father for her child. On the other hand, there is often a great disparity in age between husband and wife, and thus, most female-headed/ female-supported households are the result of male death. Following this in frequency (which varies from region to region and country to country in the old world) are desertion, divorce and male employment away from village or town (with visits as frequent as once a month to as rare as once in three or four years). While these factors also play some part in the west, perhaps the single most important reason in many western societies is pregnancy outside of wedlock. Second in order of importance is desertion.

The Household Level

The book also considers the definition of what is meant by the concept of headedness: see the papers by Dehavenon, Mencher, Okongwu, and Singh, all of which deal with which men are present, why and for how long, what resources are utilized, what activities are engaged in, and what features and which dimensions are important. Blumberg's article in particular, and those by Dehavenon and Okongwu, also deal with the history of the female-headed/female-supported household, as well as how and why this form has been considered important in social analysis, and why it is currently generating great interest. Singh's article indicates how important it is to provide programs specifically aimed at the poorest of these households, recognizing at the same time that not all of them are among the poorest of the poor. This issue is also discussed in Mencher's article.

In the United States, discussion has focused on the question of why and how and with whom women get pregnant, and not on how they manage afterward. For example, the "Right to Life" movement is really concerned with the right to the biological event of *birth*, not the *quality of life* that comes after. In the United States the birth of children "out of wedlock" is seen as the genesis of the poverty of these households, rather than the conditions which make sustaining the lives of children so difficult for unmarried women, who are often poor, unskilled, etc. Yet it is the "afterbirth" conditions under which sustenance of children occurs that reproduce and enhance the inequalities of gender, race and class.

This approach to the analysis of female-headed households was most clearly demonstrated in a 1965 government publication by D.P. Moynihan which still is quoted by policy makers and planners: *The Black Family: A Case for National Action*. This book represented a watershed in stimulating debates that have created a foundation for the misconceptualization of female-headed households. One wonders if it occurred to Moynihan or others who think as he does that if the inequalities of gender, race and class did not exist, female-headed households would be viable regardless of the "match" between the circumstances of biological reproduction and those of the ongoing reproduction and sustenance of children after birth. For as Burnham points out, adding an unemployed or unemployable male to a household does not guarantee its rise from poverty, and as Dehavenon documents, may even lessen its chances for access to vital services.

The articles by D'Amico-Samuels, Okongwu, Abraham, Blumberg and Dehavenon make reference to discussions of parenting roles in the West Indies and the United States, noting the differences between *owning* (claiming biological parenthood), *caring* (doing the actual, daily domestic work of rearing children), and *minding* (assuming financial responsibility for a child). These roles may adhere in one person alone or be spread among different individuals and households. But the separation between biological parenting and the activities involved in sustenance are clearly delineated. The class, race and gender position of individuals who take on aspects of these sustenance activities has everything to do with the viability of the household and the life chances of the children in it. While these may vary greatly from one part of the world to another, and clearly the situation in Asia and Africa differs greatly from that of the United States and the Caribbean, nonetheless the role of socio-economic class is crucial. A poor woman left with no other earning adult to look after small children is in a very different position from the middle-class woman in the same situation.

The effect of migration in promoting the existence of female-headed/ female-supported households is also an important consideration. Yet processes like migration are affected by different types of employment structures for men and for women both within the nation as well as internationally. They determine who migrates and the amount of remittances to the household. In some cases the amount might be of major significance for daily life, but in other instances the remittances might only provide for the rare purchase of a luxury or the reroofing of a house, not for day-to-day maintenance. Migration also affects the activities involved in daily reproduction of the household, preparation of children for adult roles and domestic organization. For example, if a West Indian or African mother migrates to an urban area or abroad to work as a domestic, leaving her children in the care of a female relative, this has different implications for domestic family organization than if a father migrates leaving his wife and children behind. Or, if a local or international company recruits female labor where employment opportunities for males are limited, this might mean that mothers have greater direct access to the cash economy than fathers. Depending on the cultural context and range of income-generating strategies available to men, this situation will have different types of implications for family organization and family life as well as male-female relations (Safa 1981, Mies 1982).

This book stresses the importance of analyzing the experiences of women supporting their households within the context of their integration into the local, national and international economic and political system and relates this to national and local class structure as well as culturally defined sex/gender systems (Rubin 1975, Davis 1981).

Conceptualizing families as social units which hold both human and material resources, it may be seen that in both the developed and underdeveloped world each family (here equated with household) has developed a series of strategies to insure its survival and reproduction. These include (1) combining work in the formal and informal sector; (2) agriculture and trade; (3) obtaining help from both natal and affinal kin while simultaneously generating income or food through their own economic activities; (4) combining resources from the state with self-generated resources including paid or unpaid work, etc.; (5) relying completely on resources from the state and personal networks. The contributions of children vary from society to society and within societies between households, based on socio-economic class and other cultural variables. In some instances contributions of children, even very small children, can be critical. The small girls working in the Sivakasi match factories in southern India are an example in point since some of them may be the only source of cash income in their households for at least part of the year. In places like Accra in Ghana young girls may be the main salespersons for their mother's prepared foods.

Policy Planning

Two of the articles deal primarily with policy planning the one by Singh and the one by Dehavenon and Okongwu, but many of the other papers, such as those by D'Amico, Mencher, Castro, and Blumberg, point to policy concerns and some possible solutions. All of the papers ask which policies provide women with *viable choices* for sustenance of themselves and their kin. An important component of this discussion, given the global factors discussed above, is to what extent gender, race (or caste) and class-structured inequality are built into the kinds of development and fiscal policies being pursued today by governments? Though none of the papers offer definitive solutions, Singh's discussion of ILO programs in South Asia does offer some possible models for emulation.

This information in this volume is expected to serve both scholars and policy makers. Our intention in presenting these studies to the public is to provoke concern and stimulate interest in this extremely varied and widespread phenomenon. We believe that without paying attention to the roots of female-supported households, any attempts to deal with the phenomenon either intellectually or from a practical standpoint are likely to prove superficial and ineffectual.

References

Bolles, Lynn. 1983. "Kitchens Hit by Priorities: Employed Working-Class Jamaican Women Confronting the IMF," in Nash and Fernandez-Kelly (eds.) *Women, Men and the International Division of Labor*. Albany: State Un. of New York Press, Pp. 138-160.

Burnham, Linda. 1985. "Has Poverty Been Feminized in Black America?," in *The Black Scholar*, March/April, pp. 14-24.

Caufield, Mina Davis. 1981. "Equality, Sex and Mode of Production" in G. Berreman, (ed.) *Social Inequality: Comparitive and Developmental Approaches*. Academic Press, New York 206-212.

Guyer, Jane. 1986. "Intra-Household Processes and Farming Systems Research: Perspectives from Anthropology," in (J. Moock ed.) *Understanding Africa's Rural Households and Farming Systems*. Boulder, Col. Westview Press pp. 92-104.

Jones, Cristina. 1986. "Intra-Household Bargaining in Response to the Introduction of New Crops: A Case Study from Northern Cameroon," in (J. Moock ed.) *Understanding Africa's Rural Households and Farming Systems*. Boulder, Col. Westview Press. pp. 105-123.

Mies, Maria. 1982. "The Dynamics of the Sexual Division of Labor and Integration of Rural Women into the World Market," in Lourdes Beneria (ed.) *Women and Development: The Sexual Division of Labor in Rural Societies*. New York. Praeger Publishers. pp. 1-28.

Moynihan, Daniel P. 1965. *The Negro Family: A Case for National Action*. Washington, D.C. Office of Policy Planning and Research, U.S. Dept. of Labor.

Nash, June. 1983. "The Impact of the Changing International Division of Labor on Different Sectors of the labor Force," in Nash and Fernandez-Kelly eds. *Women, Men and the International Division of Labor*. Albany: State University of New York Press, Pp. 3-38.

Nash, June and M. P.Fernandez-Kelly (eds.). 1983. *Women, Men and the International Division of Labor*. Albany: State University of New York Press pp. 138-160.

Okali, C. and J.E. Sunberg. 1986. "Sheep and Goats, Men and Women: Household Relations and Small Ruminant Production in Southwest Nigeria" in J. Moock (ed.) *Understanding Africa's Rural Housholds and Farming Systems*. Boulder, Co. Westview Press. pp. 166-181.

Prescod-Roberts, Margaret. 1980. *Bringing It All Back Home*. Bristol, England. Falling Wall Press.

Rubin, Gayle. 1975. "The Traffic in Women: Notes on the Political Economy of Sex," in Rayna R. Reiter (ed.) *Towards An Anthropology of Women* New York, Monthly Review Press. pp. 157-210.

Safa, Helen. 1983. "Women, Production and Reproduction in Industrial Capitalism: A Comparison of Brazilian and U.S. Factory Workers," in Nash and Fernandez-Kelly eds. *Women, Men and the International Division of Labor*. Albany, State University of New York, Pp. 90-116.

2

Poverty Versus "Purse Power": The Political Economy of the Mother-Child Family III

Rae Lesser Blumberg

Introduction

In 1977 and 1978, I published papers on "the political economy of the mother-child family" (Blumberg with Garcia 1977; Blumberg 1978) in which I formulated five conditions under which female-headed units might emerge, become prevalent and persist. Although I noted that these conditions would most *frequently* obtain among the poor in wage labor societies, they were phrased to apply to other groups as well, e.g., single working women in developed societies who choose to raise a child without a husband.

A major goal of the papers was to show that the mother-child family was structurally/economically based and widely distributed around the world, rather than something linked to race, specifically being "ethnically Negro", as alleged by Murdock and Wilson (1972). At the time, the literature on woman-headed homes still focused primarily on their disproportionate prevalence among blacks in the United States and the Caribbean.

Today, there is more awareness that such units are increasing in both developing and developed countries (Bruce and Lloyd 1992; Buvinic 1990; Folbre 1991a, 1991b; Rosenhouse 1989), and among diverse ethnic groups in the U.S., Europe, Latin America, the Caribbean, Africa and parts of Asia.[1] There are now even data showing that although women-headed households are most frequently encountered among the poor, not all are poorer than male-headed units (Gupta 1989).

How well have the five conditions fared since 1978? I suggest that they appear to help account for the increased incidence and geographic spread of woman-headed units in general, and *mother-child households* in particular. Since the two previous papers were written, I have been working on two gender theories which could broaden the explanatory power of the five conditions:

1. a general theory of gender stratification which purports to apply to

all human societies at all points of our history, and to all levels from micro to macro (Blumberg 1984); its central proposition is that the most important (although not the sole) predictor of the level of gender stratification is the relative control of economic resources by the men and women involved;

2. a still-evolving theory of gender and development which links women's relative control of economic resources to the wealth and well-being of both nations and families, and to the success of planned development projects that rely on women's labor (Blumberg 1988a, 1989a, 1990a, 1991a, 1991b).

In this paper, I cull some hypotheses from these theories to supplement and improve the predictive power of the conditions. In particular, I add hypotheses indicating potentially positive consequences for family well-being when the household head is a woman vs. a man, especially when level of income is controlled.

Specifically, I shall suggest that at any given income level, when women are in control of income and the household unit, their spending patterns often provide for better child nutrition and health, and for more - and more even-handed - emphasis on the education of boys and girls. These child welfare effects are so strong, I propose, that they often have been found even when women-headed units proved dramatically poorer than their male counterparts. My final addition to theory concerns economic and structural conditions influencing the prevalence of the "non-isolated mother-child family." I consider three basic forms: (1) the extended (often three-generation) residential unit built around a woman and her child(ren); (2) mother-child families enmeshed in flexible networks of sharing and exchange; and (3) mother-child families where the woman is a polygynous co-wife with a dwelling separate from the male head or other wives. They arise under different circumstances, but do have two commonalities. On the one hand, they seem to emerge under certain structural, rather than cultural, conditions. On the other, they represent three degrees of isolation of the mother-child unit, with the extended unit the least isolated and the mother-child polygynous unit the most. Beyond these three, we can talk of mother-child units that, indeed, are structurally isolated. Different policy implications follow.

The paper is organized as follows: First, the five conditions are reviewed. Second, an update is given on the literature, on issues ranging from the patterns of distribution of these households world-wide, to the varying definitions being proposed. Third, the additional hypotheses are drawn from my theories and added to the conditions. Fourth, evidence is marshalled for these hypotheses, showing that sometimes there are *positive* consequences from living in such units, even when they are poor. Fifth, the material on the "non-isolated mother-child family" is presented. Finally, conclusions and policy implications are discussed.

Five Conditions for the Emergence, Prevalence and Persistence of Woman-Child Families

Condition I: That the unit of labor, the unit of compensation, and the unit of property accumulation be the individual, independent of gender.[2]

Condition II: That females have independent access to subsistence opportunities. This condition is a function of (1) the existence of *viable* economic opportunities open to women[3] through (a) their own work, (b) their economically productive children to whose labor or compensation they have access, (c) inheritance, and/or (d) state-provided welfare; and (2) women being permitted, and in fact, *able* to head a separate residence and control property.[4]

Condition III: That subsistence opportunities open to females can be reconciled with childcare responsibilities. If women's work can be carried on simultaneously with childcare responsibilities, Condition III is satisfied. If not, paid childcare might be used, or formation of the mother-headed unit might be postponed until young children can be cared for by a sibling old enough to do so, and/or some other childcare agent, or until no young children are left; and/or until the woman can arrange sufficient income from a working child, property, inheritance, and/or state welfare to permit her to stay home.

Condition IV: That a woman's subsistence opportunities from all sources in the absence of a male head not be drastically less than those of the men of her class.

While these four conditions, and female-headed households, can arise among better-off women in developed societies and among rural women horticulturalists in sub-Saharan Africa, they are most prevalent among poor groups that can be characterized as surplus labor in wage-labor societies. There, such units are expected to be most *persistent* to the extent:

Condition V: That the political economy of the society produces and profits from a surplus labor population, and that the female-headed unit successfully reproduces the surplus labor population to the benefit of those who control the political economy.[5]

In short, the conditions alert us to look for:

1. the demand for female labor in the society's major productive activities;
2. the compatibility of these activities with simultaneous childcare responsibilities;
3. the compensation received by women for their participation in production - both (a) in absolute level, and (b) as a relative proportion of the compensation of the men of their class; and
4. the level and availability of alternate sources of income aside from the women's own earnings, such as welfare, children's contributions, etc.

The literature that has emerged since the late 1970s does not treat the fifth condition extensively, so for reasons of space it will not be further dealt with in this paper. Conversely, there have been many studies on women-headed households in most corners of the globe since then, and they do *not* seem to provide negative evidence for the first four conditions. Rather, the conditions appear to be quite useful, for example, in illuminating the uneven geographic distribution of female-headed households that has been uncovered by subsequent research. In particular, the low rates of women-headed units in the countries running from North Africa and the Middle East through Pakistan, India and Bangladesh can be seen as predicted by the conditions (see "An Update of the Literature" below). In contrast, much higher rates have been found in northwestern Europe, the United States, and Canada on the one hand, and the Caribbean, Latin America and Sub-Saharan Africa on the other. In these countries, the data indicate that the conditions are more (and increasingly) likely to be filled.

Let us now review what has happened to each condition since the late 1970s and how this may affect patterns of female headship.

Condition 1: That the unit of labor, the unit of compensation, and the unit of property accumulation be the INDIVIDUAL, independent of gender

The first condition is more prevalent today than in the late 1970s, with the notable exception of rural China.[6] Elsewhere, fewer sons, daughters and even wives labor *solely* as unpaid family help. Empirical studies find little confirmation in much of the Third World, especially Sub-Saharan Africa, for the still-prevalent view of the household as a monolithic income-pooling entity that can be described by a single production function (Becker 1981). Instead, men and women, and senior and junior members, have at least partially separate income streams and at least partially separate expenditure responsibilities (Blumberg 1988a, 1991a; Dwyer and Bruce 1988). In much of Africa, in fact, men and women maintain largely "separate purses" (Staudt 1987; Blumberg 1988a). Finally, land reform has individualized land tenure (often to women's disadvantage, however) in numerous Third World countries: except for some types of pastures, holdings are much less likely to be held by a corporate kin or village communal group. In sum, many forms of economic individualism have increased in the last 15 years, and all of them facilitate female headship.

Condition II: That females have independent access to subsistence opportunities

One aspect of the second condition (II.1[a]) also has become much more prevalent since the first two papers were written: more and more women are earning market income. According to Sivard (1985:12), women's participation in the labor force has increased at twice the rate of men's since 1950. In addition to women's greater involvement in the formal labor force, they are heavily involved in the burgeoning informal sector in most parts of the Third World.[7] And the informal sector has grown explosively since the late 1970s. So more women than ever have the potential for maintaining a separate household.

Also, we now have considerable data showing that income-earning children in a variety of countries are more likely to turn over income to the *mother* than the father (e.g., Kusterer et al. 1981, Blumberg et al. 1989 on Guatemala; Blumberg 1992a on Ecuador; Segalen 1986 on England; Wolf 1991 on Java). This fulfills II.1(b), that women have access to the earnings of offspring.

In contrast to women's much increased access to market income (II.1[a]) and, apparently, children's earnings (II.1[b]), there has been little change in II.1(c), women's access to inheritance. There has been some reform of family law codes, mostly in women's favor. But there is not much evidence beyond the occasional court case that women have been able to tilt *de facto* traditional practices in patrilineal systems that restrict their inheritance from fathers and/or husbands. For most women heads, it has not been a comfortable inheritance that enabled them to form their own household, either in the late 1970s or now.

But there has been a definite *decrease* in another aspect of condition II since then: state welfare systems (II.1[d]) have shrunk in most of the world during the 1980s. This has been true not only in the United States, where welfare, as measured in constant dollars, has been dropping steadily for more than a decade (Dentinger 1991), but also in debt-ridden Third World countries forced into "structural adjustment" austerity programs as a condition for further aid. Most of these have sharply cut their social budgets (i.e., welfare, health care, education). Potential women heads can count on fewer government transfer payment "eggs" in their basket of survival strategies. But the drop in welfare has not reduced female headship; earned income seems more critical.

Concerning women's ability to head a separate residence (II.2), housing is probably tighter today than 15 years ago in most Third World countries. This is a potentially inhibiting or delaying factor. But overall, condition II is more likely to be fulfilled today. This is *mostly* due to the steep rise in II.1 (a), women earning income via both formal and informal sector pursuits.

Condition III: That subsistence opportunities open to females can be reconciled with childcare responsibilities

This can be via women's work that is compatible with childcare, or via paid childcare, or a delay in formation of the unit until childcare agents (including the woman herself) are available (that is, until the woman finds childcare-compatible work), or until the children are older.

Childcare-Compatible Pursuits. As noted, the informal sector has been expanding explosively around the Third World; in most of Latin America and the Caribbean, Africa and Southeast Asia, women comprise the majority of the sector's smallest-scale microentrepreneurs. One of the hallmarks of such informal sector pursuits is the fact that they can be undertaken with children in tow; Boserup (1970, 1974) notes that children's labor can increase the mother's income in many of these ventures. So for an increasing number of women in the informal sector, they can combine income-generation with childcare and female headship.

Paid Childcare. At the other end of the spectrum, paid childcare is a growth industry in all the developed countries, where women's share of the labor force has jumped dramatically in the last 15 years.[8] If they can afford it, potential women heads in these countries have more options than before for daycare, hence fulfilling condition III.

Mutual Aid. And, finally, for poorer women who cannot take their children to work and cannot afford commercial daycare, the situation is presumably about the same as 15 years ago. Women rely on informal social support networks of nearby or co-resident kin or kin-like neighbors. Here, one childcare agent can solve the problems of a number of women who need to work. Or these women can rely on their older children to care for younger siblings. They may have to delay forming a female-headed unit until they can arrange these kinds of childcare support, which is one reason that data from a growing number of studies on female-headed households also show that they are likely to be somewhat older than male heads.

Women heads also are more likely to have extended family living in the house than their male counterparts (references will be presented in "Non-Isolated Mother-Child Families" below). Thus they have more potential access to resident childcare agents. Moreover, the data further indicate that women heads are likely to be considerably older in the extended units. Where this is a "grandmother family," she may not be the principal support, but is given the title of head because it is her home, and/or for reasons of respect of elders.

Adding up these various trends, we can conclude that fulfilling condition III is somewhat more likely now than ever before.

Female Headship in Extremis. But filling condition III is not the definitive limiting factor in the creation of female headship; in this sense, it may be considered the weakest of the conditions: economic factors generally outweigh childcare considerations in the formation of mother-child families. Thus, world-wide, millions of women with no choice leave tiny children alone when they desperately need to make a living in activities that are not childcare-compatible (this is discussed in "Non-Isolated Mother-Child Families" below).

Summing up the changes discussed for conditions I-III, we find more instances where these first three conditions are met. Under the circumstances, the rise in female headship documented by the recent studies should come as no surprise.

Indeed, in the group that registers the highest proportion of female-headed households ever encountered in the literature, the filling of conditions I-III is clear: among the residents in the low-income Mathare Valley in Nairobi, Kenya, where 75 percent of the women brew and sell illicit beer, a staggering 60-80 percent of the households have women heads (Nelson 1978, 1979 cited in Clark 1984). There, poverty combines with women earning their own informal-sector income in a country with a tradition of separate management of domestic units by polygynous co-wives. These women rely on informal social support networks, largely involving their female kin, for childcare and economic aid. Nelson suggests that these women brew beer despite its unpredictable income not only because they have few alternatives, but because it brings more income than working as a barmaid or domestic servant, and can be brewed and sold at home, and thus combined with child-care responsibilities (Clark 1984:351).

Condition IV: That a woman's subsistence opportunities from all sources in the absence of a male head not be drastically less than those of the men of her class

One aspect of condition IV does not seem to be more *or* less prevalent: the gap between male and female earnings is about as wide in most places now as 15 years ago. Where women make about half as much as men, we cannot expect women-headed households to have more than about half the income of their male counterparts. After all, they lack the higher earnings of a resident adult male, and any subsidiary earners are likely to earn less than an adult male by virtue of gender and/or age. Is, say, half of male household heads' income so "drastically less" that the formation of female-headed units is discouraged? Apparently not. Women heads presumably get to allocate their own income, children's contributions and transfer payments. It is well-documented that men often hold back a considerable fraction of their earnings for personal consumption (Blumberg 1988a, 1991a give overviews; case studies include Chant 1985 on Mexico; Mencher 1988 on India; Pahl 1989 on England and Roldan 1988 on Mexico). Thus, women heads' lower income may not be *that* much less than that actually used for family maintenance in many male-headed units.

We also cannot ignore the possibility that more men will leave now that more women are earning income: once they know that their wives have access to enough income to scrape by, they may feel less compulsion to remain (Folbre 1991b). But overall, the documented fact that female headship is becoming more prevalent indicates that whether the unit was formed by her choice or his exit, it exists. This is a *de facto* indicator that women's earnings from all sources are *not* so drastically inferior as to make female-headed household formation an irrational, or very short-lived, act.

Moreover, there is evidence that more female-headed units form when there is a shrinking of the gap between male and female resources *coupled with an increase in women's absolute income*. This represents a subset of the cases covered by condition IV, but there is evidence that in many parts of the world, especially in western industrial countries, it is a growing subset.

As a first example, a study discussed in my earlier paper bears repeating:

> Farley analyzed U.S. government data on race, income and female-headed household formation from 1950-1968. He found that during this time, *African-American women increased their real incomes faster* than whites of either gender, or African-American males. Specifically, income of non-white women (almost all of them black) rose 260% between 1950-1968; that of non-white males rose only 160%. Concomitantly, while proportions of *female-headed households* rose for all races during the 1960's, the rise was *fastest among African-American women* (U.S. Department of Labor 1973). Farley also shows that it was among younger black women 15-34, and even more so in the age group 35-44, that rates of family headship increased the most. Moreover, this rise in female-headed units did not seem to reflect a deinstitutionalization of the husband-wife relationship among blacks (counter to the assertions of the "Moynihan Report" (Moynihan 1965).[9] This is because the surge in female headship was *not* achieved by a reduction in the proportion of non-white married men heading families; that figure, in fact, increased somewhat. Rather, the women establishing female-headed households were those who previously would have had to live with relatives

in order to survive without a spouse, but now had sufficient earnings to go it alone (Blumberg: 1978).

Second, there are increasing numbers of adult women earning enough to choose and support single motherhood. Recently this form of mother-child familism exploded into public controversy in 1992 when Vice President Dan Quayle criticized Murphy Brown (a fictional independent, affluent TV journalist) for choosing to have a baby as a single mother. Even 15 years ago, this would have been socially far less acceptable. Now, support groups already are springing up, such as Single Mothers by Choice.

In socioeconomic terms, what we might call the "Murphy Brown mothers" are considerably better off than teens who deliberately choose single motherhood but rely on welfare or family to keep them afloat if they attempt female headship. There are as yet no quantitative studies, but voluntary single motherhood appears to be on the increase among U.S. women whose income is both (1) high enough in absolute terms to support themselves and a child, and (2) not drastically below counterpart males in relative terms.

A third example comes from Ghana and exemplifies the other side of the coin: women from a group characterized by high rates of female headship and economic autonomy clinging to matrimony as a result of a great rise in their husbands' relative and absolute earnings. Among the Akan peoples of Ghana, descent is matrilineal, residence matrilocal, conjugal ties weak, and women's relative economic resources and autonomy high. Oppong (1974:116) lists three factors as underlying women's traditional autonomy: (1) their income-generating work outside the home; (2) their matrilineage membership, with its rights to property, residence and inheritance, and (3) their rights to choose their husbands and initiate divorce (the latter right frequently exercised).

In her fascinating study of marriage in a sample of the elite top civil servants and their wives, Oppong found that the women put up with a level of male patriarchal behavior, including adultery, that never would have been tolerated in the matrikin homeland. But although these women were usually fairly well educated as well as employed outside the home, it was to their husband's job, and not their own efforts or their matrikin's wealth, that they owed their luxurious standard of living. This included large government-supplied homes, cars, and other perquisites of their husband's rank.

Not surprisingly, they lived conjugally with their husbands, an unusual practice in the traditional system. Since both spouses tended to be migrants separated from their matrikin, women's three sources of autonomy were no match for their husbands' material advantage. In the typical case, (a) the wife's moderate education (few of the women were university graduates) and outside job provided vastly inferior income and "perks" to those of her husband; (b) the economic resources and status of her distant matrikin could not provide anything close to her lifestyle as the wife of a senior government official; and (c) unlike the village situation, where a woman who divorces usually can easily enter an equally good new marriage (if she so chooses) even after early youth, the top official's wife has no chance to marry as exalted a personage if she divorces him. (Many other women would be eager to replace her.) So these women remained in their marriages in a neolocal conjugal household in which legally they were not entitled to inherit any part of their husband's property (which goes to his matrikin).

There are few places on earth where the traditional property system is so favorable to women as among the Akan of Ghana; also, the wives of top government officials are a numerically minute group. Statistically, the more important story is that many more women are earning market income not drastically below that of their male counterparts, and sufficient to support female headship. Below, it is proposed that under these circumstances, more women *voluntarily choose* to go it alone with their children. Here, however, we can conclude from world trends that even without a dramatic shrinkage of the male-female income gap, more and more women are fulfilling conditions II and IV as they begin to *earn* appreciable income.

Overall, in fact, we can conclude that the states of affairs specified by the five conditions have, in the majority of cases, become more prevalent over the last 15 years. And while illustrative evidence is no substitute for more rigorous study, we can further conclude that we have found no empirical or logical reason to discount the conditions as predictors of the increased prevalence of women-headed households that has, in fact, occurred in recent years.

An Update of the Literature

Prevalence/Geographic Distribution

When I wrote the first two papers, the geographic/ethnic focus on units headed by New World black women was so great, that it was important to document that female-headed families had been observed world-wide. My list included Adams's (1960) statistics on female-headed families in Central and South America; Geertz (1959) on Java; Calley (1956) and Smith and Biddle (1975) on part-Aboriginal Australians; Kay (1963) on Tahiti; Aginsky (1947, 1949) on Pomo Indians; and Boyer (1964) on Mescalero Apaches.

Including female-*centered* as well as female-*headed* families broadened the list to include European families with a resident male but female-centered interaction patterns: See Lopreato (1965) on South Italian peasants and Young and Wilmott (1957) on East London.

In fact, female-headed vs. female-centered families were then the focus of a definitional debate. Whereas female-headed households were characterized by the absence of a resident male head (making the woman the actual head), the term "female-centered household" described the interaction pattern, without regard to whether a male head was absent or even whether the woman was important in the family control structure. The main commonality was that both types were discussed as most frequent among the poor.[10]

What has happened since? First, the geographic/ethnic debates have moved on to new ground. Buvinic, Youssef and Von Elm compiled the first comprehensive statistical examination of female-headed households in 1978 and found significant proportions of female-headed households in many parts of the Third World (excluding North Africa, the Middle East and South Asia). As it happens, these are precisely the countries where the conditions are least likely to be fulfilled, since women have much lower access to market income than in, say, Latin America and the Caribbean or sub-Saharan Africa, and the social constraints against a woman living without the protection of a man are strongest.[11] Earlier, in fact, Abu-Lughod (1975) pointed to just these low female-headship countries in her critique of Eames and Goode's (1973) contention that matrifocal families are a near-universal, rational and functional "coping response" to urban poverty. She noted that their data covered mainly Latin America and secondarily sub-Saharan Africa, with only spotty and anecdotal coverage for the rest of the world. Moreover, "the entire Muslim world is ignored (or misinterpreted) all the way from North Africa to Pakistan, perhaps because it refutes the thesis of matrifocal family."

If we focus on women's economic role, as specified in the conditions, the low incidence of female-headed families "all the way from North Africa to Pakistan" is understandable. Women's current rates of participation in formal production is very low. Further, these countries' traditional economies involve dry (rainfed) plow agriculture and/or large animal herding. The former predominates. World-wide ethnographic evidence based on the full 1170-society Ethnographic Atlas (Murdock 1967), or more refined sub-samples (Murdock and White 1969), shows that women play a more limited role in production in both dry plow agriculture and large animal herding. Moreover, the prevalent property and kinship systems give women very limited access to inheritance or other resources on which to base "a home of one's own."[12]

The most recent geographic overview is Folbre's (1991a). She notes the rise in women-headed homes in the United States, Canada, and northwestern Europe, where they now comprise over 20 percent of all households. (Indeed, in the United States, Sweden and Denmark, mother-child families comprise over 20% of all families with children under 18 [Folbre 1991b:18].) In these areas divorce, separation, and widowhood account for most female-headed units. Although these units are maintained largely by women's income, it is *mother-child* units in the United States that fare least well, since transfer payments and enforcement of men's child-support obligations lag behind, especially compared to northwest Europe.

Folbre (1991b:16) also points out that female headship is much higher in the United States than in many European countries, which provide not only more generous public assistance to women with children, but also more policies that aid intact nuclear families. (Many of these European countries' benefits and children's allowances are rooted in pronatalist efforts to reverse declining birth rates; see Folbre 1991b.) In the United States, female headship has continued to rise since 1975, even though benefit levels of Aid to Families with Dependent Children (AFDC) have declined dramatically (Garfinkel and McClanahan 1986; Dentinger 1991). The reason, according to the conditions, is that more American women are in the paid labor force and thus able to head families. It is thus work, not any "perverse incentives" of AFDC that discourage marriage (Murray 1984)[13], that has spurred female headship.

Folbre also finds that "many countries of the Caribbean, Latin America, and Sub-Saharan Africa...are...at or above 14 percent" (1991a:11-12); indeed, in certain countries, such as Jamaica and Barbados, women head about 40% of all households (ibid.:18).

As Kennedy (1992) points out, however, the urban/rural locus and the reasons for the increase in female headship differ in Latin America vs. Africa. In Latin America and the Caribbean, rural-to-urban migration primarily by single women, plus rising adolescent fertility, have led to an increase of urban, often poorer, female-headed households (CEPAL 1985; Buvinic 1990). By contrast, in sub-Saharan Africa, female headship results from male migration as well as widowhood, and is mainly a rural phenomenon. Moreover, such units are not always poor (Kennedy 1992; Kennedy and Peters 1992).

Folbre goes one step farther historically in tracking the antecedents of female headship: she traces the low rates of legal marriage in the Caribbean and Latin America and the high rates of male off-farm migration in Africa to the impact of colonialism. She notes but does not explain why female headship is so much less prevalent in South Asia, especially Pakistan, which also endured colonialism.[14] She argues that the level of economic development is not the explanation for the difference, since the Caribbean countries have such high rates of female headship, while Japan and South Korea have some of the world's lowest levels of households headed by separated/divorced women.

In sum, Folbre (and Kennedy) focus more on description than explanation. In contrast, the conditions would predict that in the countries where Folbre finds the highest rates of female headship, women's access to income is highest and social constraints against a woman maintaining an independent household are lowest.

The following discussion relating to the incidence of women-headed households includes additional variables such as culture and subsistence strategies that are useful in understanding some of the reasons for high and low incidence cross-culturally.

Definitions of Female Headship

The definitional debates also have moved on to new issues. First, there is now a distinction between *de facto* and *de jure* female headship. For example, Kennedy and Peters (1992) classify households as *de facto* female-headed if the male head is absent more than 50 percent of the time. Their research in Kenya and Malawi found *de facto* female heads who do not receive regular remittances from the absent husband to be even poorer than women (e.g., widows) who are the actual heads. In contrast, a study in Ghana (Lloyd and Brandon 1991) found that married women whose husbands resided elsewhere were significantly better off (because of remittance income) than separated, divorced or widowed women heads, whose children had no legitimate claim on any male's income.

Second, it is now recognized that definitions of female headship are asymetrical: such units almost invariably lack an adult male, but male-headed units almost invariably have one or more adult females (see, e.g., Bruce and Lloyd 1992).

Bruce and Lloyd also introduce a third definitional innovation: they note that defining households as bounded economic units is more descriptive of male than female economic reality. Especially for poor woman-headed households, economic survival may depend on participation in a "sharing network" of extra-household economic and social exchange. The structural-economic reasons for this are discussed further under "Non-Isolated Mother- Child Families" below. Here, however, let us note that these networks have been found in many places. Stack 1974 describes one such network for poor black women in Urbana, Illinois; Peattie 1968, Brown 1975 and Stavrakis and Marshall 1978 discuss parallel situations for poor women in Venezuela, the Dominican Republic and Belize, respectively. Clark 1984 and Nelson 1978, 1979 also found significant use of informal networks by women household heads in Kenya.[15]

Fourth, Folbre (1991a) discusses the definitional and measurement problems of current definitions used in national censuses. The U.S. Bureau of the Census has scrapped the old "household head" nomenclature in favor of "householder" (the person in whose name the living space is owned or rented), but continues to tabulate "female householders, no spouse present" in order to maintain statistical continuity. Although the United Nations soon began to recommend the "householder" terminology, most Third World countries retain the "household head" title for the person "recognized as such." To get a lower bound estimate of households maintained by women alone, Folbre would exclude households where a woman was designated head but was legally or consensually married (not separated).

Folbre does not mention it, but this definition also provides a lower bound estimate of units where the woman head is presumed to play the lead role in decision-making. The fact that most female heads also are presumed to control the allocation of (at least) the income they themselves bring into the household leads to the consideration of headship, income control and family well-being.

In fact, women's economic support has emerged as a main definitional issue in delineating households where women take primary responsibility for family maintenance. Some authors advocate as a measure the number of hours of market work spent in support of the household. Rosenhouse (1989), for example, measures hours of market work (including goods produced at home but excluding housework). Applying this definition to the Living Standards Measurement Survey (LSMS) data from Peru increased the proportion of female-headed households to approximately one-third, vs. only 17 percent when the definition involved self-reported headship. Others use income contributed (e.g., Korale 1988 for Sri Lanka; Mencher, this volume, for India), and refer to women-*supported* units.

What many of these studies are looking for is a definition of female headship that serves as an index of control over allocation of household resources. At issue here is the extent to which family members, especially children, may be better off living in female-headed units where the woman does not have to cater to male authority in allocating expenditures for food, education and other indicators of well-being. The implicit question is, given that women-headed households tend to be considerably poorer, can there be any benefits from having a lower income controlled by a woman? This question will be considered in the discussion of additional hypotheses about the impact of women-headed households below.

There is now considerable data showing that woman-headed units are generally (but not universally) poorer than male-headed ones. Two recent overviews of the literature are Gupta 1989 and Buvinic 1990. First, Gupta 1989 found female-headed households to be poorer in 33 out of 45 studies reviewed; Third World regions represented included Africa, South Asia, Latin America and the Caribbean (LAC), and Turkey. Second, Buvinic 1990 found that women-headed households were overrepresented among the poor in 19 of 22 LAC studies.

Before tackling the empirical evidence on whether children are *ever* better off living in female-headed households, let us introduce the additional hypotheses taken from my theories, which propose that under certain circumstances this should be the case. The hypotheses also provide an additional rationale for why such units are most prevalent among the poor.

Additional Hypotheses About the Impact and Incidence of Women-Headed Households

These hypotheses are derived from my theories of gender stratification and gender and development. They rest on the increasingly common assumption in the literature on mother-child families that a woman who is a head of and *not* living with a common-law or legal husband bears primary responsibility for allocating income brought in by her, or contributed to her.[16]

Impact Hypotheses

H1: Income-controlling women, including women household heads with provider responsibilities, tend to hold back less for themselves than male counterparts.

H2: Income controlled by women with provider responsibilities, including women household heads, will tend to be spent more single-mindedly on family well-being, especially children's nutrition, health and education, than income controlled by counterpart men.

More specifically:

H2a: Within levels of income, children will be better nourished in female-headed than male-headed households, *ceteris paribus*. (There is significant evidence that in male-headed households, mother's income is a stronger predictor of children's nutrition than father' income; see below and Blumberg 1989b for references.)

H2b: Where women have "purse power," either by being a female household head or outearning their husbands, there will be less favoritism toward boys' education i.e., women will promote education for *both* daughters and sons.[17]

Incidence Hypotheses

H3: The greater incidence of female headship among the poor is based on the generally *inverse* relationship between social class and: (a) the proportion of women who are economically active and (b) the proportion of household income they provide.[18]

H4: The greater the amount and proportion of a woman's resources relative to counterpart men, the more likely it is that *she* initiates female headship.[19]

The Impact of Gender of Household Head on Well-being

H1: Do women heads hold back less for their personal consumption? The evidence on this for *wives* vs. husbands indicates that this is generally the case (Blumberg 1988a, 1991a and Chant 1985:642 give overviews; see also Mencher 1988 on South India; Roldan 1988 on Mexico City).[20] There is some evidence that *women heads* also spend less on themselves. First, Chant's own data showed that whereas just over half (12) of the male heads in her in-depth sample kept as much as 50% of their income for personal use, "female heads, alternatively, seem to contribute *all* their wages to family welfare" (ibid., emphasis added).

Second, women are much less likely to hold back income for the purpose of spending it on the consumption of alcohol. In Malawi, for example, a detailed comparison of expenditure patterns showed that female-headed households spent 25-50 percent less on alcoholic beverages than male-headed units (Peters and Herrera 1989; Kennedy and Peters 1992). Similarly, a recent study in Jamaica found that female-headed households spent a significantly smaller income share on alcohol (Louat, Grosh and van der Gaag 1991). These data parallel research in the Cote d'Ivoire (Hoddinott and Haddad 1991) concerning differential spending of female- vs. male-controlled household income: they found that a doubling of income under female control would lead to a dramatic decline in spending on alcohol (-26%) and cigarettes (-14%).

H2: Do income-controlling women spend a higher percentage of their earnings on children's nutrition, health and education? That women heads spend a higher proportion of their income on children's well-being is fairly well documented (for an overview, see Blumberg 1988a, 1989b, 1991a; see also Chernichowsky and Smith 1979; Folbre 1991a; Greer and Thorbecke 1986; Kennedy 1988).

One must be careful here, however, to take Engel's Law into account. In 1857, the German economist proposed that the proportion of income spent on basic necessities was inversely related to income (Houtthaker 1957). Since women-headed units are frequently poorer than households headed by men, income must be controlled, which many studies fail to do.

One study did, in fact, compare how much men and women contributed vs. how much they earned: Mencher's research on South India (1988). As it turned out, in one of 10 Kerala villages in Mencher's random sample, women and men earned the same income, but women contributed 91 percent of their income to household survival, vs. men's contribution of only 76 percent. This is an important finding. It provides clear-cut evidence that (at least in this case) women's family-centered spending pattern is not merely an artifact of Engel's Law.

Two other studies have relevant data concerning expenditure patterns in female-headed households. First, Chant's (1985) data showed a much more even-handed income distribution in female-headed families, so that despite lower family income, women-headed units' members were actually *better off* than those in men-headed homes. This gender-linked spending pattern has consequences for children's nutrition, as specified below for H2a.

Second, a study in Malawi (Peters and Herrera 1989) focused on comparisons of male- and female-headed households. The authors measured various types of woman-headed units, including some fairly well-off households receiving remittance income from migrant husbands; they found that *most* female-headed households spent a higher proportion of their money on food. This, too, indicates that women's spending patterns cannot be explained by Engel's Law alone.

Studies linking gender of head and children's education are treated under H2b. Time and space constraints prevented a literature search for difference in spending on children's health care as a function of gender of household head. Nevertheless, it is relevant that in a study of 504 rural households in Kenya's Nyamza District, children in women-headed units (both *de jure* and *de facto*) had lower incidence of illness (Kennedy 1989; Kennedy and Cogill 1987). All in all, the above data have turned up nothing that contradicts the basic proposition that women with provider responsibilities, if in control of income, spend more of it on children's basic needs (Blumberg 1988a; Dwyer and Bruce 1988).

H2a: Are children in women-headed units better nourished (especially if level of income is controlled)? Some studies find that female-headed households eat better regardless: e.g., two studies in Jamaica reported that units under women's headship ate foods of higher nutritional quality (Horton and Miller 1989; Louat, Grosh and van der Gaag 1991).

But it must be emphasized once again that in order to compare the nutritional level of children in families under male vs. female headship, it is essential to control for income, and many studies do not. One study that did, Engle's (1989) study of 302 urban mothers in Guatemala, included both female heads and wives of male heads. She controlled for income and found that women heads spent a greater proportion of their income on food for children.[21]

Overall, studies from many countries around the world show a positive link between women-headed households and child nutrition. First, four studies involving rural poor included in von Braun and Pandya-Lorch 1991 are relevant. In two, children were *less* likely to be *malnourished* in female-headed units (von Braun and Wiegand-Jahn 1991 in Rwanda; Vosti and Witcover 1991 in Brazil). In the other two studies, children's nutrition was *no worse* than in male-headed units (Edirisinghe 1991 in Sri Lanka; Kumar 1991 in Bangladesh), even though the female-headed households were poorer.

Second, Kennedy's extensive literature review (1992) finds that the studies for Africa, and some of the studies for Latin America and the Caribbean (LAC), show better-nourished children in female-headed units. She does not give enough details to make it clear whether the LAC studies that find to the contrary controlled for level of income. And it is control of income that seems to be at issue.

Blumberg (1988a, 1989b, 1991a) summarizes studies which show that mother's income (or subsistence production) is a better predictor of children's nutrition than father's income. These include Kumar 1978 on Kerala, India; Stavrakis and Marshall 1978 on Belize; Senauer 1988 on the rural Philippines;

Kennedy and Cogill 1987 on southwestern Kenya, and Tripp 1981 on northern Ghana. Johnson and Rogers 1988 find this same pattern for a national sample of families in the Dominican Republic; they discovered that the effect was most pronounced in the lowest income quartile.

Similarly, in Rwanda, when male- and female-headed units were compared, holding income constant, households headed by women consumed 377 more calories per adult equivalent per day, and once again, the effect was strongest in the lowest income groups (von Braun et al. 1990). Kennedy and Peters' research in Malawi and Kenya (1992) also found that the proportion of income controlled by women, in both male- and female-headed households, had a significant positive impact on caloric intake. In both countries, Z-scores indicating child malnutrition were significantly lower in the various categories of female-headed units (even the poorest, *de facto* ones) than in male-headed households. Parallel findings have been found in the United States: A national study of the WIC program (a food subsidy program for low-income women and children under three years of age) found that when males are present, the children's height for age was lower (Rush, Horvitz and Seaver 1986).

Additionally, as noted above, women's control of food (not just income) also enhances nutrition: in Gambia, the share of cereal production controlled by women added 322 more calories per adult equivalent per day (von Braun et al. 1989).

The most spectacular findings on the impact of female- vs. male-controlled income on child nutrition come from Engle's (1992) study of a random sample of 294 children and their families from two Guatemalan industrial towns south of the capital. She found that the higher the percent of the total family income the mother *earned,* the higher the nutritional status of the children, on all nutrition measures. For fathers, the proportion of income *contributed* was the best predictor. Bruce and Lloyd 1992 recast Engel's regression findings very dramatically, noting that the attainment of an additional half a standard deviation of height for a child would require $11.40 per month if earned by the mother and *$166* per month if earned by the father.

H2b: Are women with "purse power" (either by being a female head or outearning their husbands) less likely to favor boys' education? Prior to the study to be presented here (Blumberg et al. 1992), only two studies seem to have explicitly explored gender of head and children's education[22]. First, Chant in her study of shantytown dwellers in Mexico found that:

> in female-headed families there tended to be less discrimination shown towards female children, and girls were given opportunities equal to those of boys. In fact, female family heads stressed the need for girls to have education, should they be deserted by their future husbands (Chant 1985:646).

Second, Botswanan children in female-headed households were found to receive more education than children in male-headed households (Kossoudji and Mueller 1983). But since Botswana is one of perhaps three countries in the world where women have higher educational attainment than men (Sivard 1985), and parents' education is usually found to affect children's schooling attainment, the result cannot be clearly attributed to gender and/or gendered control of income. Further muddying the explanatory waters, female-headed households had fewer productive assets, so that the value of their children in home production was reduced. Under those circumstances, women-headed units sending their children to school would experience less loss of income.

A New Quantitative Study of "Purse Power" and Education

In contrast, in our analysis (Blumberg et al. 1992) of a random sample household survey for Santiago, Chile, there is no doubt about the role of both male-female control of income and gender of household head in affecting the education of boys and girls. In preview, we found that whereas there was significant favoritism toward boys' schooling in male-headed units, this favoritism vanished when the children lived in one of the following types of households: (1) female-headed ones, or (2) those where the woman outearned her husband.

The data come from the 1987 CASEN II national household survey of Chile.[23] We drew a subsample from the data for the capital city, Santiago, consisting of all households with at least one boy or girl of high school age, thirteen to nineteen. The sample obtained includes 1,609 households with 8,515 individuals, among whom are 2,519 boys and girls aged thirteen through nineteen. In 86% of the cases, these 2,519 are sons or daughters of the household head and/or spouse. Another 7% were grandchildren; the remainder include various "other family" and non-family members.

Seventy eight and four tenths percent (1,976) of these teenagers live in male-headed households and 21.6% (543) in female-headed units. As is often found in studies comparing heads by gender, the female heads proved a little older and less educated than male heads (female heads average 48.4 years of age vs. 45.7 for male heads and 42.3 for their wives; female heads average 7.65 years of schooling vs. 9.42 for male heads and 8.83 for their wives). These slight differences pale in comparison with the income gap, however: Female heads have only *half* the income: 12,200 (pesos), vs. 24,000 (pesos) for male heads.

Defining women with "purse power." The first group consists of wives who outearn household-head husbands: 9.4% (185) of the teenagers in the sample live in male-headed households where the wives earn *more* than their husbands. The second, and more relevant group for this paper, consists of the 543 teenagers (21.6% of the total sample) living in *female-headed* units. Especially important are the 476 (83% of those in women-headed households) who live in homes where the woman has *no mate* who might dilute her power to allocate resources. (Unexpectedly, 67 teenagers (14%) live in female-headed units with a man listed as the common-law or legal spouse of the woman head. In 13 of these 67 cases (19.4%), the female head outearns her non-head spouse; in 54 cases, he outearns her.)

Gender of Head and Schooling Rates. In male-headed households, boys proved significantly more likely to go to high school (83.6% attend) than girls (79.0% attend). Although female-headed units earn only half the income, 72.9% of their boys go to high school, and 76.7% of their girls.

There are two points to note here. First, the figure for the boys' advantage in male-headed households is statistically significant but the girls' advantage in female-headed households is not. Second, although women heads' teenagers are somewhat less likely to go to high school, the difference in attendance is nowhere near as pronounced as the difference in male- vs. female-headed units' incomes. The women heads clearly have to prioritize education higher to come so close to the male-headed households' rates with half the income.

"Purse Power" Ends the Favoring of Boys' Education. Clearly, women with "purse power" tend to be more *even-handed* in the treatment of boys and girls. Consider this contrast, for example: Among male heads, the gap between boys' and girls' education *widens* both with husband's increasing income and with increasing amounts by which he outearns his wife. In comparison, when we look at female heads by income quartiles, in the lower three quartiles there were *no* significant differences in the percentages of their boys vs. girls attending high school. In the top income quartile of female heads, there was a significant favoring of girls' education, but even here it was not as pronounced as the extent of boys' schooling advantage among men heads in the top income quartile.

The data offer other insights on the impact of "purse power":

First, we followed up the unexpected finding that 67 of the teens lived in female-headed units where a man was identified as a resident husband (legal or common-law)[24] by comparing spouses' income and its impact on boys' vs. girls' schooling. As noted, in 54 of the 67 instances, the man earned more than the female head.[25] In this small group, significant favoritism toward *boys'* education was found - the only such instance among woman-headed households.

Second, as predicted, in male-headed households, favoritism toward boys' education did not disappear unless the wife earned *more* than the husband. This provides empirical support for my hypotheses about "discount factors" that result in a woman getting "less than a dollar's worth of economic power for every dollar she brings into the household" (Blumberg 1984, 1991a; Blumberg and Coleman 1989).[26]

Specifically, in the still relatively patriarchal Hispanic culture of Santiago,

Chile, women face a combination of structural and ideological barriers that erode the leverage they get from contributing earned income to households. In particular, enough remains of the traditional Latino dictate that "the woman is for the house" (*la mujer es para la casa*) that a woman who "goes out to the street" (*sale a la calle*) to earn income is engaging in culturally questionable behavior. She would be compounding her "sins" if she then engaged in hard bargaining to extract every bit of power from her earnings. According to England and Kilbourne (1988), that is unlikely anyway, given that women are not socialized to bargain vigorously for power with intimates.

As predicted, then, wives had to earn *more than equal income* to eliminate the significant favoritism toward boys' education: boys remained advantaged in male-headed households where the woman earned an amount *equal* to her husband's.[27]

Unfortunately, we had too few cases to see if there were any women heads with resident husbands and equal earnings. It would have been interesting to see if the woman's title of household head meant that equal earnings were enough to gain equal education for her girls, or whether she, too, would need to *outearn* her mate.

Even without such an analysis, our findings clarify the issue: female headship seems to owe its positive and even-handed effects on children's welfare to the fact that most women heads are more clearly in control of income and thus have greater say in household decisions. Where a women head did not have "purse power," i.e., had a husband who outearned her, boys were favored; but where wives outearned male heads, equal education for both genders resulted.

The Incidence of Women-Headed Households

H3: Is the frequent finding that female headship is most common among the poor due to the inverse relationship between social class and 3(a), the proportion of women who are economically active? I have argued against considering poverty a cause in and of itself, in the absence of the other conditions, and have used the low incidence of woman-headed units in the countries stretching from North Africa through South Asia as evidence that poverty alone need not result in female-headed households.

This hypothesis argues the other side of the coin: female headship is more prevalent among the poor because this is where more women are economically active (often driven by necessity; see Blumberg 1990a for references). This fulfills condition II, that women have access to viable subsistence activities. Also, as stipulated by 3(b), the proportion of household income earned by women is inversely related to social class, i.e., the gap between women's and men's earnings tends to be lowest among the poor (Blumberg 1990a). This fulfills condition IV, that women's earnings not be drastically less than the men of their class. In short, poor women have a two-condition "head start" toward female headship in most societies.

Both local gender culture and level of economic opportunity for women then intervene. Where both severely constrain women's ability to earn income, as in the North Africa-Middle East-South Asia region, female headship rates are lowered even among the poor. But the example of the Quichua Indians of highlands Ecuador (spelled Quechua in Peru and Bolivia) shows another scenario: an ethnic culture that promotes economic activity and control of resources for women while insisting on the couple as the basic unit for social adulthood. Among these Indians, well-off peasant women are as likely as much poorer ones to be economically active in cultivation, pastoral activities, handicraft production and market trade (Alberti 1986; Blumberg and Colyer 1990; Hamilton 1992); both are equally *un*likely to become female heads due to separation, desertion or divorce (Blumberg and Colyer 1990; Blumberg 1990c, 1991b). Among neighboring mestizos, however, both women's economic activity and headship are negatively correlated with social class, i.e., highest among the poor (Alberti 1986; Blumberg 1990c). World-wide, there appear to be few groups like the Quichua, who are ethnic or cultural exceptions to the widespread fact that women's economic activity, relative parity of earnings and headship all are inversely related to social class.

H4: Is it true that female headship is more likely to be at the woman's initiative the greater the amount and proportion of her resources? First, by "greater amount," I mean that a woman earns more than what is required for mere physical survival for the members of her potential household. In my theory of gender stratification, I argue that people get more economic power from allocating surplus than from mere subsistence. In no society, for example, is it acceptable to withhold food from hungry children. This is why poor women, who may contribute such a high proportion of household income, often have so little power. In other words, they have almost no degrees of freedom in allo-cating their income: it all goes for minimal survival needs and so cannot be used for leverage and control.

Second, the "proportion of her resources" referred to is in comparison with the men of her class. Thus far, I have found only qualitative evidence in support of this proposition.

For example, Chant's random sample (1985) included only those who *owned their own homes*. This indicates some surplus, rather than mere subsistence, income. She found that in as many as one-third of the cases, the woman-headed unit was formed by *female* initiative:

> This is a significant minority, given that it is difficult for the female partner to initiate a separation for a number of reasons. Not only is it unlikely...that women can earn enough money to support their families, especially when the children are young, but also there are

social stigmas attached to being a single parent in Mexico (Chant 1985: 647).

Similarly, Kusterer et al. 1981 found that about one-fifth of the sample of women employees of the ALCOSA agribusiness processing plant in Guatemala had changed their domestic arrangements more to their liking. Their principal reasons were to get away from abusive husbands or fathers. These women worked long hours during the 8-9 month "high season". And because the firm (the wholly-owned subsidiary of a U.S. multinational) paid the government's rarely honored minimum wage and overtime rates, women working in the ALCOSA plant earned quite a lot of money by local standards. They made perhaps three times as much as a market trader or domestic (women's main alternative occupations), and as much as a male urban factory worker or local farm family. These women could support themselves, if they chose. A number so chose, stressing in interviews that their new household arrangements were at their own initiative. What is significant here is that these women had an income not only high enough to provide more than mere subsistence, it was not drastically less than the men of their class.

Condition IV, let us recall, stipulates that female headship is more prevalent where women's income from all sources is not drastically less than counterpart men's. The further refinement discussed in this paper is that with higher absolute levels as well, more women would *seek* to head their own households.

Non-Isolated Mother-Child Families

Bruce and Lloyd (1992) suggest that defining households as bounded economic units is more descriptive of male than female reality. The literature on diverse types of mother-child families shows that they are likely to be embedded, to varying degrees, in kin-based arrangements that enhance their survival chances, despite generally much lower income. Here, I propose that three quite diverse types of units can be seen as representing different degrees of "non-isolated mother-child families."

These are: (1) the extended (often three-generation) residential unit built around a woman and her children; (2) mother-child families enmeshed in flexible networks of sharing and exchange; and (3) mother-child families where the woman is a polygynous co-wife with a dwelling separate from the male head or other co-wives. I suggest that these three types share two main commonalities. First, they represent three degrees of isolation of the mother-child unit, with the extended household the least isolated and the mother-child polygynous unit the most. Second, they are more the result of structural-economic arrangements than childcare considerations or cultural desiderata.

They also involve one important difference. The first two types are generally poor. Both band together, on a voluntary basis, with others--mostly women--in roughly the same situation for the purpose of economic survival. The third type does not involve economic cooperation between women. It is most common where in-marrying polygynous co-wives are important producers and live with their *husband's male kin*. Housing her and her children separately from other wives helps prevent a producer alliance that might threaten male dominance (Blumberg with Garcia 1977); instead, it encourages her *individual* accumulation.

Let us further explicate these three types:

1. Extended Mother-Child Families:
Poverty and Economies of Scale

The mother-child unit is *least* isolated in the extended (often three-generation) residential unit built around a female head and her children. Many times, these are "grandmother families," with the oldest woman bearing the title of head even when she is not the main economic support of the household. Studies in a wide variety of countries show that female-headed households are more likely to have extended family living in the house than male-headed ones (overwhelmingly, consanguineal kin). These include Blumberg with Garcia 1977 on Venezuela; Blumberg et al. 1992 on Santiago, Chile; Chant 1985 on Mexico; Clark 1984 on Kenya, and Smith and Biddle 1975 on Australian part-Aboriginals.

Structurally, such units tend to be even poorer than non-extended mother-child families (e.g., Blumberg et al. 1992). All indications are that they are much more likely to emerge for economic survival reasons than childcare considerations. As Friedl 1975, Blumberg 1984 and Huber 1991 all argue, women are more likely to accommodate their childcare to their economic tasks than vice versa; and the poorer they are, the more childcare takes second place to the activities needed for economic survival.[28]

Similarly, women heads living with extended kin gain economies of scale of consumption and, more often than not, contributions to the household budget from extra earners, as well as more in-house childcare agents. Here, the units are benefitting from the positive side of the extended mother-child family.

Nevertheless, these units are sometimes extended in ways that spread poverty more than resources. Extended women-headed units also may be more likely to take in dependents with no other options: the very young, the old and/or the sick. Only a small elite in Third World countries are covered by social insurance (old age support, family allowances, health care); these are typically public employees and urban formal sector wage earners (Folbre 1991a). Extended female-headed units are among the least likely to receive such benefits. Rather, they tend to *offer* them, as "kin-keepers of last resort".

2. Mother-Child Families in Sharing Networks:
Smoothing Out Uneven Resources

Here, one critical variable is added to account for this form of non-isolated female-headed units: *unpredictable fluctuations of sometimes scarce resources lead to sharing and exchange*. This has long been demonstrated in the literature on hunters and gatherers (Lee and DeVore 1968 and Sahlins 1965 provide early overviews). Such networks also have long been found among various marginal groups in the U.S. (Stack 1970, 1974; Lombardi 1973; Valentine 1968, 1970) and around the world (e.g., Calley 1956 on Australian part-Aboriginals; Brown 1974 on the Dominican Republic; Peattie 1968 on Venezuela).

Lombardi (1973) showed mathematically how such redistribution smooths out fluctuations in net available resources: it spreads risks.[29] He also demonstrated empirically, via an input-output analysis, that sharing was what prevented one U.S. welfare family from going below his zero point three times in a single month. (Zero meant no money, no food in the house, and nothing to pawn.) Sharing, of course, undermines individual accumulation. Mother-child units in sharing networks survive but their children have no money for extras.

The Kindred of Viola Jackson vs. the Colleagues of Murphy Brown. Carol Stack's studies (1970, 1974) about the "kindred of Viola Jackson" exemplify both the extended and the sharing network patterns. Her study took place in Urbana, Illinois in the late 1960s just after the plant that had been the main (and best) employer of poor blacks closed. Extended household composition changed quickly and adaptively, with various kinds of doubling up and shifting of children. The sharing network smoothed out the unexpected fluctuations in resource availability vs. needs. Somehow, despite adversity, all the children were cared for. But getting ahead was almost impossible when needy kin and near-kin held claims to any surplus income another network member was able to acquire. In short, the economic functions of the shifting residential and network arrangements were paramount, and put both ceilings and (shaky) floors on the fortunes of participants.

The non-isolated mother-child familism prevalent in the "kindred of Viola Jackson" (the matriarch) contrasts sharply with the middle-class networks depicted for the unmarried TV character, Murphy Brown, in the controversial television show where she gave birth. With minimal relations with her far-away natal family, she was shown as succored by her colleagues, and coached in a Lamaze delivery by her house painter. This was emotional, but not financial, support. And she is seen as neither living, nor sharing economically, with kin. One can posit that the rising ranks of more affluent heads of mother-child units, e.g., the "single mothers by choice," tend to be similar to the mythical Murphy Brown. Here, the main burden of single headship is emotional and logistical, as opposed to struggling to survive. This is apparently less likely to lead to collective strategies.

3. The Political Economy of the Polygynous Mother-Child Unit

Blumberg and Garcia, in their 1977 paper, attempting to show that race has nothing to do with the mother-child family, undertook part of their analysis only *within black Africa*. The idea was to demonstrate that it is a set of structural conditions, not race, that leads to separate mother-child dwelling/management units. But the same data also indicate that the system whereby co-wives pursue a semi-isolated, rather than collective, strategy to raise their fortunes and their children's prospects arises from the conjunction of the self-interest of two sets of actors: the women and their husbands' male kin.

Polly Hill's (1969) study of Hausaland in Northern Nigeria was the first to emphasize that under this system, men and women have a great deal of economic autonomy, and women sometimes become richer than their husbands. Co-wives often cooperate to share housework, childcare, and the sexual services of a common husband, but they very rarely cooperate or share economically. With their individual dwellings and, typically, granaries, they maintain their own microenterprises.

Here is a summarized version of the three main structural conditions where we expected mother-child residence to be most common *within* Africa: (1) where women are important producers, and (2) are concentrated by general polygyny (3) in the home territory of the husband's kin (i.e., marital residence with husband's male kin, and/or patrilineal descent). Because of a coding artifact in the Ethnographic Atlas (the source of our data), all the societies with mother-child residence have general polygyny.

Moreover, 71% of all African societies in the Ethnographic Atlas have mother-child residence. Nevertheless, when we examined the relationship between women's contribution to production and mother-child residence within Africa, the (significant) gamma was the same as world-wide (0.46). In fact, the within-Africa relationship remained significant (0.59) even after three additional controls were introduced: residence with husband's kin, extensive hoe horticulture as the dominant subsistence base, and the highest level of brideprice. The last two variables indicate the value of women to the husband and his kin group: horticulture is the most feminized of the world's modes of subsistence (Murdock 1967; Bryson 1981). And a high level of brideprice is associated with a high subsistence contribution of women: men are paying for a woman's value as a *producer*, rather than as a *re*producer (Blumberg 1984).

There might well be a convergence of interest on the part of *both* the woman and the husband's kin group in giving her the measure of independence represented by "a home of one's own." For the husband's kin group, there is the desirability of ensuring that her strategic resources (e.g. labor) remain within the group while reducing the likelihood of her allying with others in a similar structural situation (e.g. the other co-wives in the household or village). For example, when co-wives have been able to unite, as among the Lovedu, where they are cousins (Murdock 1949), they have gained important powers; Lovedu women, for example, control marriage and have considerable economic independence and leverage.

I am suggesting that the husband/male kin's interest is in reducing women farmers' opportunities to form producer alliances. Therefore, it seems eminently logical (from the perspective of these men) that the two most common organizations of production in African hoe horticulture are (1) the farming of scattered individual plots by individual women (e.g., Kaberry 1953), and, less frequently, (2) centralized activity under direct male supervision.

For the woman, separate mother-child residence represents a gain in autonomy vs. living with other co-wives under the husband's roof. It also facilitates individual accumulation of property. Even in patrilineages, women retain lifelong obligations to natal kin, and try to keep them up because this maximizes their potential access to important kin group *economic resources* (e.g., crisis aid, inheritance of the occasional plot), as well as emotional support. It also means that--at least temporarily--"she can go home again." The greater economic autonomy for a woman represented by a separate mother-child residence gives her more ability to accumulate and allocate her own resources as she sees fit.

The prevalent African system of "separate purses" means that income flows and expenditure obligations can be considered "his, hers, and theirs." A co-wife and her husband will have a few joint obligations (e.g., both may contribute to the schooling of their mutual children). But for the most part, the woman producer focuses her economic activities and exchanges on her own microenterprise, children and natal kin. This takes place even though she lives in her husband's compound, and discharges a marital obligation to do some farming for him. In return, she gets use rights to plots for her own farming, the right to market the surplus, and is able to share domestic tasks with co-wives. In short, her mother-child family is non-isolated in that it is partially embedded in two different kin exchange networks, her husband's and her natal family's. But both groups together seem to give less aid for her children than women heads get in either extended kin households or sharing networks.

Conclusions and Policy Implications

Data accumulated during the 1980s and early 90s indicate that the hypotheses I originally developed in 1977 and 1978 as well as the conditions discussed at the beginning of this paper continue to be strongly supported by empirical evidence. This paper has attempted to supplement and improve the predictive power of the conditions and to indicate that consequences for family well-being when the household head is a woman can be positive if the level of household income is controlled for.

The importance of female control over income or "purse-power" in influencing the lives of children, especially female children has also begun to be documented cross-culturally as far as nutrition and health are concerned and at least for Latin America when it comes to education. Whether this holds for the education of girls in Africa and Asia remains to be investigated empirically.

This paper has argued for a series of conditions under which female headship is most prevalent. It also has made a limited argument that children can be better off (as, obviously, can their mothers) in a woman-headed unit, even when it is poorer. It has *not* argued, however, that female headship is better for children's welfare across the board: economic, social and psychological consequences of the absence of the husband-father preclude that.

Data presented above has demonstrated the importance of mothers having direct access to male wage and/or labor. This suggests the need for policies that would *emphasize men's financial obligation to children* would undoubtedly help many overcome hardship and privation (Bruce and Lloyd 1992; Folbre 1991a, 1991b). Given the gender gap in earnings, it is literally true that many women "are only a husband away from poverty." Getting a husband is a much more likely way for a U.S. woman to get off welfare and out of poverty than getting a job (Dentinger 1991).

For the moment, such policies are most discussed in developed countries. In part, this is because the state does not have the money or machinery to enforce paternal responsibility in Third World countries. An exception might be the small group of men working in the formal sector, a portion of whose wages could be attached. However small these groups may be, it can be argued that even the mere adoption of such policies would begin a process of shifting the climate of opinion and, ultimately, practices. This may be true even when a particular government cannot devote more than token resources to enforcement of men's obligations to support their children. Still, it will take a good deal of time for such policies to be adopted, and, ultimately, vigorously implemented.

Meanwhile, we are left with the policy implications that flow from the fact that women heads are more likely to both earn and control income than wives, and that important consequences flow from income under women's vs. men's control. The most important is that a woman's income comes with a built-in "synergy bonus": that which is not used to assure the performance of her main economic activities and enterprise(s) will be spent more single-mindedly on the children's well-being. This frequently will mean that the children will be *better nourished* than those in male-headed units, even when the latter have higher income. It may also mean that the mother will be more *even-handed in education*, hence advantaging her daughters' schooling beyond what would be the case in male-headed households, especially those not too far above her in income.

It is known that women's education is perhaps the most important determinant of lowered infant mortality and decreased fertility (see extensive literature review in Blumberg 1989b). It is also known that fertility has a strong negative impact on national income growth (Hess 1988). Therefore, the more education-focused spending priorities of most women heads (and other women with "purse power") might have consequences for the wealth and well-being of their nations for generations to come. This is especially so since they will tend to promote their girls' schooling along with their sons'; and females (still) have 100% of the babies.

Considerable data exist to show that women microentrepreneurs, small entrepreneurs and small farmers are at least as good at what they do, controlling for resource levels, as counterpart men, and they are better at paying back loans (Blumberg 1989b). There is a policy implication that flows from all this. Providing women in these fields (especially women heads) with a level of assistance in planned development programs proportionate to their representation in the target group will reap a "synergy bonus": the women will generate not only economic benefits for themselves and their countries, but also well-being benefits for their children and their children's (fewer) children.

Targeting women farmers in sub-Saharan Africa, where they raise up to 80% of locally grown food (Saito and Weidemann 1990), would be especially fruitful. At one fell swoop, this can help alleviate the worsening African food crisis. In no other area do the people (women) who are the principal agricultural producers get less development help with their farming, and in no other area is fertility as high. Those women farmers *need* the extra children: with more men migrating and creating de facto or de jure female-headed units, and more children in school, they are desperately short of labor. The problem is compounded by environmental degradation, which also makes it more time-consuming to bring water, fuelwood and fodder. The additional children help provide their mothers with water and firewood, child and animal care, and many other productive tasks. More children mean that a woman farmer can earn a living now, but intensify the problem for the next generation. Meanwhile, the food crisis continues to worsen: per capita food production keeps falling farther behind increases in population growth (Blumberg 1988c, 1989a, 1989b, 1992b).

Helping African women farmers also could benefit their daughters. First, the total of those who are (1) *de facto* or *de jure* household heads and (2) polygynous co-wives with separate dwellings and, often, separate farming ventures, in many places represents a majority of rural households. Second, sub-Saharan Africa shares with the countries of North Africa-Middle East-South Asia the largest gap in boys and girls' schooling rates (Sivard 1985). Third, it is not subjugation that keeps these girls out of school; instead, it often is their mothers' needs for their labor, with mother-child units typically having the greatest unmet labor needs.

Furthermore, girls help in a wider range of tasks than boys and receive a lower rate of return for education, so given limited funds for school fees/expenses, boys' schooling is privileged. If the mothers received help with farming and availability of water and fuelwood, the resultant labor time saved could mean that more girls would have more time for school (Blumberg 1989b). While the relationship between schooling and fertility is not as strong in sub-Saharan Africa as elsewhere, it still is substantial (United Nations 1987). In sum, helping women farmers could affect not only agricultural productivity (and ease pressures on the environment), it also could help increase girls' schooling and decrease the world's highest fertility rates.

The final policy implications flow from the degree of isolation of poor mother-child units. The *less* isolated they are, the more they share economic and childcare resources. This helps the short-term survival of their children but may mean that the resultant sharing helps assure that their children have less chance for social mobility. The policy implication for poorer countries is that mother-child units should be given preference for aid that helps the children remain in school (books, uniforms, transport allowance). In more affluent countries where the threshhold level of education for getting above poverty is higher, the assistance must extend to college education.

The *more* isolated the mother-child unit, the more the absolute level of the woman head's resources determines the outcome. Children are most at risk if female heads are both isolated and poor.[30] This is where the most urgent policy response is needed. The mother-heads may be isolated because they are recent migrants or have violated local mores. In poor countries, scarce daycare places and social welfare aid should give preference to such units. In more developed countries, if the mothers are getting welfare and are able and willing, programs that support their own education and training to levels that will lead to above poverty-level jobs should be explored. Such programs should subsidize childcare where necessary. They also should target non-isolated mother-heads. Aid of this type should help pay for itself by reducing both extant welfare loads and the likelihood of another generation in poverty.

In conclusion, the best world-wide policy recipe for now would seem to combine three main ingredients:

(1) promoting non-resident fathers' responsibility to provide support for their children, which would also increase their stake in responsible fertility behavior;

(2) enhancing the access to income of women in general and women heads in particular, including assuring that development assistance goes to women microentrepreneurs and farmers in proportion to their representation in the target population, and

(3) providing aid that helps poor female heads to further the schooling of both girls and boys.

Notes

1. One no longer finds studies attributing mother-child units to either African survivals (Bascom 1941; Herskovits 1937, 1941, 1943, 1947; Matthews and Lee 1975) or the lingering effects of plantation slavery (e.g., Campbell 1943; Frazier 1939; Henriques 1953; Myrdal 1944; Powdermaker 1939). Remaining explanations encompass social pathology (including the irresponsibility and desertion of many poor men), cultural diffusion, and survival strategies of the poor in capitalist economies (Clark 1984).

2. Women rarely emerge as heads of families where families are the unit of labor, and/or compensation is paid to the male head, and/or family property is corporately held.

3. If female-headed units are not viable, they are short-lived. Either they split up or are reabsorbed into some other unit (e.g., the woman's parental home) or they do not survive. Whereas welfare systems have been available in only a few societies, starvation has occurred periodically in many - even now.

4. In cities where housing is especially scarce, unmarried women with children might remain in the parental home although otherwise able to leave, as Buvinic (1990) found in Santiago, Chile.

5. To the extent that a society's political economy is controlled by external (e.g., extranational) factors, the size of any surplus population and the extent to which it is internally beneficial to the society's elite become independent of their wishes. Where condition V is fulfilled though, regardless of state rhetoric, few programs that successfully reduce poor woman-headed families will be undertaken in the absence of a change in the structural conditions.

6. There, work points accruing to the individual are being displaced by state-fostered household-based farm production, with the wife once again serving as unpaid labor for the husband-head.

7. Earnings and benefits may be lower than in the formal, measured labor force, but informal sector activities are often more compatible with simultaneous childcare (i.e., condition III, discussed below).

8. Paid daycare is also rising in some developing countries as well, particularly where the ranks of middle class working women swell while the pool of cheap domestic help shrinks. In Swaziland, for example, in a study of micro/small enterprise, a woman member of the multitudinous royal family described the soaring growth of her day care cum minivan pickup service (Blumberg 1991c).

9. Moynihan's controversial report clearly considered the rise in female headship among poor urban blacks as a growing social cancer. In his words: "at the center of the tangle of pathology is the weakness of the family structure. Once or twice removed, it will be found to be the principal source of most of the aberrant, inadequate, or antisocial behavior that did not establish, but now serves to perpetuate, the cycle of poverty and deprivation" (1965:30). Moynihan saw the growing rate of formation of woman-headed households as a self-perpetuating, accelerating trend that had outstripped unemployment statistics and other economic causes of family breakup. Many social scientists and blacks criticized his report as a "blame the victim" analysis.

10. Nancy Solien de Gonzalez further distinguished two female-centered family forms: the "consanguineal" and the "matrifocal." The "consanguineal" is a "coresidential kinship group which includes no regularly present male in the role of husband-father. Rather, the effective and enduring relationships within the group are those existing between consanguineal kin" (1959). In some consanguineal families, the mother's brother or other male uterine kin may be the family head and/or pretty well run the show (as among the matrilineal Nayar of India; see Gough 1952).

In contrast, "matrifocality" is: "a general tendency to emphasize the mother as the stable figure and decision-maker within the family as well as an emphasis upon her kinsmen over those of the father and his kinsmen" (1970) - a definition broad enough to type Young and Wilmott's East London families as matrifocal, despite their male heads.

11. Women have restricted rights to inheritance in much of both North Africa-Middle East-South Asia and sub-Saharan Africa. But sub-Saharan women have much greater access to income via farming and/or own-account trading, so they can more easily become heads.

12. Nevertheless, that it is the productive base and property/kinship system - and not Islam - that seem to be the key to the low rates of fulfillment of the conditions in these countries is illustrated by the case of Java. It has had centuries of Islam and yet even this strong dose of "patriarchal religion" failed to eliminate women from their traditionally important role in production (in irrigated paddy rice agriculture and own-account market trade; Vreede-de Stuers 1967; Stoler 1977). Nor did Islam change the bilateral kinship and inheritance systems which give women access to rice land and other resources (Wolf 1991).

13. Folbre 1991b turns Murray's conservative attack on women on welfare upside down: she argues that we can consider policies that relieve men of obligations for supporting children as "perverse incentives;" among other things, they make male responsibility in fertility control more problematic (Oppong 1987).

14. Kennedy (1992:9) notes that female headship is increasing in South India. It is relevant, in terms of the conditions, that South India is the area of India where women have long traditions of economic activity.

15. Buvinic (1990:5), to the contrary, claims an erosion of traditional support networks for urban Latin America and the Caribbean but provides no data or references.

16. One study, by Chant (1985), involving a random sample of 244 low-income "owner households" in three Mexican shanty towns, found that female-headed units formed "when children were older and participating in wage-earning activities" (1985:644), and had more democratic decision-making patterns than male-headed households. But there was no suggestion that women did not control income allocation decisions affecting family well-being. To the contrary, "[m]any female heads stressed that they were financially better off once their husbands had died or deserted because they could then plan their budgets more efficiently for the week ahead. Many women who lived with volatile husbands stressed that they could never budget effectively because of the variable amount that their husbands gave them for 'housekeeping' each week" (ibid.:642).

17. One exception are the Muslim Hausa women in northern Nigeria who need their non-secluded preadolescent daughters to hawk the wares they produce in their compounds, and who resisted the 1976 Universal Primary Education act (Schildkrout 1984; Blumberg 1988b).

18. The main exceptions to H3 are ethnic/cultural, as will be discussed below. For example, among the Quichuas of highlands Ecuador, women from better-off peasant families are as likely to be economically active as those from poorer ones. Also, because one must almost invariably be married to be accorded social adulthood, female-headed households are rare except for the occasional elderly widow (Blumberg and Colyer 1990; Blumberg 1990c, 1991b).

19. Folbre (1991a:31) argues the converse: that "as children become more expensive, the temptation for men to default on the responsibilities of parenthood increases; their propensity to do so depends, among other things, on family law and public policy."

20. One study, however, (Engle 1992), did not find that mothers contributed a higher percent of their income to household expenses than fathers in the same family. Some of the other studies may have compared men and women's earnings vs. contributions without comparing actual couples, so further clarification is needed.

21. Since female units are usually poorer, not controlling for income may be behind the fact that some research finds units under female headship to be worse off, especially in Latin America and the Caribbean (Buvinic 1990). Perhaps the most drastic manifestation of a mother-child family being worse off is its having higher infant mortality. In Wood's (1989) study of headship and infant mortality in Brazil, the bivariate relationship showed that women heads' families had more deaths. He also found that units with female heads had less than half the income of male-headed ones. In the full regression model, however, which introduced 11 variables, including mother's education and labor force participation, region, race, and access to sewage, water and Social Security, the relationship between female headship and higher infant mortality vanished. Wood concluded that the higher deaths in women-headed units were not due to female headship per se, but to their lower education, income, and living standards.

22. Although my study of men and women microentrepreneurs in Quito and five secondary cities of Ecuador did not always get the headship status of women sampled, the qualitative data showed that women (especially those identified as heads) emphasized education for daughters at least as much as for sons (Blumberg 1990d).

23. The 1987 population of Chile consisted of 2,891,138 households totalling 12,568,556 individuals. CASEN II surveyed 22,734 households with 97,136 individuals. The Santiago sample consisted of 5,867 households with 25,342 members.

24. We suspect that most are common-law boyfriends who moved into the houses of their lovers, but we have no way to test this.

25. Following Ross's advice (1987), we used a *difference* score between husband-wife earnings, vs. a ratio score. Ross argues that a ratio score makes unrealistic statistical assumptions.

26. There are two types: (1) *Macro-level discount factors*, usually negative, measure how male-dominated and repressive of women are a country's economic, political, religious, legal, and ideological systems. (2) *Micro-level discount factors* can be either negative *or* positive: e.g., if a woman is less committed to the relationship and more sexually attractive (two of the micro-level discount factors), her leverage from any income earned would be *enhanced*. Other micro-level discount factors which can raise or lower a woman's power from any income include the man's perceived need for her income, gender role ideology, and even assertiveness.

27. Women's income increases their "voice and vote" in various household decisions, but it appears that different household decisions and practices require different levels of relative and absolute income for women to gain greater leverage. Roldan (1988) found women earning over 40% of income to have much more say in fertility decisions. This study implies that women need more than 50% of income to eliminate the preference of sons' education over daughters'. Other research and hypotheses indicate that it may take even *more* to get husbands to participate equally in housework and childcare (see propositions and references in Blumberg 1991a) to get parity in housework, I have suggested, means that the woman has been earning more than half the income for some time, that there is surplus income to allocate, and that the husband is ideologically committed to sharing such work equally.

28. In areas where women are important in farming, for example, they may stop cooking hot meals for their children during peak periods. Among the poorest in paddy rice areas, more babies die during rice transplanting season, when women work dawn to dusk to get all the seedlings transplanted in time.

29. In fact, he used the same equation (for the damping of a sine curve) that actuaries use in their calculations of expected losses which set the basis for insurance rates.

30. Anecdotal evidence from Venezuela indicates that, when rural-urban migration was once again allowed after Perez-Jimenez (1948-58) was overthrown, armies of street children (shoe-shine boys, parking boys, etc.) soon emerged as the end product of a two-stage process. First, a family came to the city but the husband could not support them and left. Second, the isolated wife-head proved unable (or unwilling) to hold the oldest boy. The mother and remaining children lived in misery. Such outcomes are probably not rare for poor, isolated mother-child units in poor countries.

References

Abu-Lughod, Janet. 1975. "Review of Eames and Goode (1973)." *Contemporary Sociology* 4:448.

Adams, Richard N. 1960. "An Inquiry into the Nature of the Family." Pp. 30-49 in *Essays in the Science of Culture*, edited by Gertrude E. Dole and Robert L. Carneiro. New York: Thomas Y. Crowell.

Aginsky, B. W. and E. G. Aginsky. 1947. "A Resultant of Intercultural Relations." *Social Forces* 26:84-87.

---------- 1949. "The Process of Change in Family Types: A Case Study." *American Anthropologist*

46

51:611-14.

Alberti, Amalia M. 1986. *Gender, Ethnicity and Resource Control in the Andean Highlands of Ecuador*. Ph.D. dissertation. Stanford University.

Bascom, W. R. 1941. "Acculturation Among the Gullah Negroes." *American Anthropologist* 43:43-50.

Becker, Gary S. 1981. *A Treatise on the Family*. Cambridge, Mass.: Harvard University Press.

Blumberg, Rae Lesser. 1978. "The Political Economy of the Mother-Child Family Revisited." Pp. 526-75 in *Family and Kinship in Middle America and the Caribbean*, edited by Arnaud F. Marks and Rene A. Romer. Curaçao and Leiden, Netherlands: Co-publication of the Institute of Higher Studies in Curaçao, Netherlands Antilles, and the Department of Caribbean Studies at the Royal Institute of Linguistics and Anthropology at Leiden, Netherlands.

----------. 1984. "A General Theory of Gender Stratification." Pp. 23-100 in *Sociological Theory 1984*, edited by Randall Collins. San Francisco: Jossey-Bass.

----------. 1988a. "Income Under Female Versus Male Control: Hypotheses from a Theory of Gender Stratification and Data from the Third World." *Journal of Family Issues*, 9(1):51-84.

----------. 1988b. "The Half-Hidden Economic Roles of Rural Nigerian Women and National Development." Draft. Washington, D.C.: The World Bank, Women in Development Division.

----------. 1988c. "Gender Stratification, Economic Development, and the African Food Crisis. Pp. 115-137 in *Social Structures and Human Lives: 1986 American Sociological Association Presidential Volume in Honor of Matilda White Riley*, edited by Matilda White Riley, Beth Hess and Betting Huber. Newbury Park, CA: Sage.

----------. 1989a. "Toward a Feminist Theory of Development." Pp. 161-199 in *Feminism and Sociological Theory*, edited by Ruth A. Wallace. Newbury Park, CA: Sage.

----------. 1989b. *Making the Case for the Gender Variable: Women and the Wealth and Well-Being of Nations*. Washington, D.C.: Agency for International Development, Office of Women in Development.

----------. 1990a. "Gender, Control of Household Income and Planned Development: 20 Hypotheses." Draft. Washington, D.C.: GENESYS/Agency for International Development, Office of Women in Development.

----------. 1990b. *Gender and Agricultural Production Systems in Latin America and the Caribbean: Diversity, Commonalities and Change*. Draft. Rome: Food and Agriculture Organization of the United Nations.

----------. 1990c. "Gender and Development in Ecuador." Quito: United States Agency for International Development.

----------. 1990d. "Gender and Microenterprise in Ecuador." Chapter 2 in *Enterprise and Development in Ecuador's Informal Sector*, edited by John Magill. Washington, D.C.: Development Alternatives, Inc./Agency for International Development.

----------. 1991a. *Gender, Family, and Economy: The Triple Overlap*. Newbury Park, CA: Sage.

----------. 1991b. "Women and the Wealth and Well-being of Nations: Macro-Micro Interrelationships." Pp. 121-140 in *The Macro-Micro Link, 1989 American Sociological Asssociation Presidential Volume in Honor of Joan Huber*, edited by Joan Huber. Newbury Park, CA: Sage.

----------. 1991c. "Gender and Small Business Development in Swaziland." Draft. Mbabane: United States Agency for International Development.

----------. 1992a. "Gender and Ecuador's New Export Sectors." Draft. Washington, D.C.: GENESYS/Agency for International Development, Office of Women in Development.

----------. 1992b. *African Women in Agriculture: Farmers, Students, Extension Agents, Chiefs*. Morrilton, AR: Winrock International Institute for Agricultural Development. Development Studies Series.

Blumberg, Rae Lesser with Maria Pilar Garcia. 1977. "The Political Economy of the Mother-Child Family: A Cross-Societal View." Pp. 99-163 in *Beyond the Nuclear Family Model*, edited by Luis Leñero-Otero. London and Beverly Hills: Sage.

Blumberg, Rae Lesser and Marion Tolbert Coleman. 1989. "A Theory-Guided Look at the Gender Balance of Power in the American Couple." *Journal of Family Issues* 10(2):225-250.

Blumberg, Rae Lesser with the assistance of Maria Regina Estrada de Batres and Josefina Xuya Cuxil. 1989. "Work, Wealth and a Women in Development 'Natural Experiment' in Guatemala: The ALCOSA Agribusiness Project in 1980 and 1985", in *Women in Development: A.I.D.'s Experience, 1973-1985, Vol. II. Ten Field Studies*, edited by Paula O. Goddard. Washington, D.C.: Agency for International Development, Center for Development Information and Evaluation.

Blumberg, Rae Lesser and Dale Colyer. 1990. "Social Institutions, Gender and Rural Living Conditions." Pp. 247-266 in *Agriculture and Economic Survival: The Role of Agriculture in Ecuador's Development*, edited by Morris D. Whitaker and Dale Colyer. Boulder, CO: Westview Press.

Blumberg, Rae Lesser, Viviane Brachet-Márquez, Fernando Cortés and Rosa Maria Rubalcava. 1992. "Women's 'Purse Power' in the Household: Reducing Favoritism Toward Boys' Schooling in Santiago, Chile." Paper presented at the meetings of the American Sociological Association, Pittsburgh, August.

Boserup, Ester. 1970. *Woman's Role in Economic Development*. New York: St. Martin's Press.

----------. 1974. "Employment and Education: Keys to Smaller Families." The Victor-Bostrum Fund Report No. 18, Spring.

Boyer, Ruth M. 1964. "The Matrifocal Family Among the Mescalero: Additional Data." *American Anthropologist* 66:593-602.

Brown, Susan E. 1975. "Love Unites Them and Hunger Separates Them: Poor Women in the Dominican Republic." Pp. 322-332 in *Toward an Anthropology of Women*, edited by Rayna Reiter. New York: Monthly Review Press.

Bruce, Judith and Cynthia Lloyd. 1992. "Beyond Female Headship: Family Research and Policy Issues For The 1990s." Draft. Presented at the Workshop on Intrahousehold Resource Allocation: Policy Issues and Research Methods, February 12-14, 1992, International Food Policy Research Institute, Washington, D.C.

Bryson, Judy. 1981. "Women and Agriculture in sub-Saharan Africa. Implications for Development (An Exploratory Study). *Journal of Development Studies* 17(3):29-46.

Buvinic, Mayra. 1990. "The Vulnerability of Women-Headed Households: Policy Questions and Options for Latin America and the Caribbean." Paper prepared under the auspices of The Population Council/ICRW Seminar Series on Determinants and Consequences of Female-Headed Households.

Buvinic, Mayra, Nadia Youssef and Barbara Von Elm. 1978. "Women-Headed Households: The Ignored Factor in Development Planning." Washington, D.C.: Agency for International Development, Office of Women in Development.

Calley, M. 1956. "Economic Life of Mixed-Blood Communities in Northern New South Wales." *Oceania* 26:200-13.

Campbell, A. A. 1943. "St. Thomas Negroes - A Study of Personality and Culture." *Psychological Monograph*, No. 55(5).

CASEN II: Encuesta de Caracterización Socioeconómica Nacional. 1987. Santiago de Chile: Presidencia de la República, Oficina de Planificación Nacional (ODEPLAN) and Universidad de Chile, Facultad de Ciencias Económicas y Administrativas.

CEPAL. 1985. "Análisis Estadístico de la Situación de la Mujer en Paises de America Latina a Traves de las Encuestas de Hogares," LC/R.418 (Sem. 2412).

Chant, Sylvia. 1985. "Single Parent Families: Choice or Constraint? The Formation of Female-Headed Households in Mexican Shantytowns," *Development and Change* 16(4):635-656.

48

Chernichowsky, Dov and Christine Smith. 1979. *Primary School Enrollment and Attendance in Rural Botswana*. Washington, D.C.: The World Bank.

Clark, Mari H. 1984. "Woman-headed Households and Poverty: Insights from Kenya." *Signs: Journal of Women in Culture and Society*. 10(2):338-54.

Dentinger, Ann. 1991. *AFDC Households with Heterogeneous Preferences and the 1988 Family Support Act*. Ph.D. dissertation. University of California, San Diego, Department of Economics.

Dwyer, Daisy and Judith Bruce. 1988. *A Home Divided: Women and Income in the Third World*. Palo Alto: Stanford University Press.

Eames, Edwin and Judith Garnick Goode. 1973. *Urban Poverty in a Cross-Cultural Context*. New York Free Press.

Easton, Nina J. 1992. "Life Without Father." *Los Angeles Times Magazine* June 14.

Edirisinghe, Neville. 1991. "Income and Employment Sources of the Malnourished Rural Poor in Kandy District, Sri Lanka." Pp. 139-144 in *Income Sources of Malnourished People in Rural Areas: Microlevel Information and Policy Implications*, edited by Joachim von Braun and Rajul Pandya-Lorch. Working Papers on Commercialization of Agriculture and Nutrition, No. 5. Washington, D.C.: International Food Policy Research Institute.

England, Paula and Barbara Stanek Kilbourne. 1988. "Markets, Marriages and Other Mates: The Problem of Power." Paper presented at the Conference on Economy and Society, University of California, Santa Barbara, May.

Engle, Patrice L. 1992. "Influences of Mother's and Father's Income on Children's Nutritional Status in Guatemala." *Social Science and Medicine*, in press.

----------. 1989. "Mother-Headed Households: Consequences for Children in Guatemala," paper presented at Population Council/ICRW Seminar II on Female Headship and the Consequences of Female Headship and Female Maintenance, February 27-28, 1989.

Farley, Reynolds. 1970. "Family Types and Family Headship: A Comparison of Trends Among Blacks and Whites." Paper presented at the meetings of the American Sociological Association.

Folbre, Nancy. 1991a. "Women on Their Own: Global Patterns of Female Headship." In *The Women and International Development Annual*, Vol. 2, edited by Rita S. Gallin and Anne Ferguson. Boulder, CO: Westview Press.

----------. 1991b. "Mothers on Their Own: Policy Issues For Developing Countries." New York/Washington, D.C.: The Population Council/International Center for Research on Women.

Frazier, E. Franklin (1939), *The Negro Family in the United States*. Chicago: University of Chicago Press.

Friedl, Ernestine. 1975. *Women and Men: An Anthropologist's View*. New York: Holt, Rinehart and Winston.

Garfinkel, Irwin and Sara S. McClanahan. 1986. *Single Mothers and Their Children. A New American Dilemma*. Washington, D.C.: Urban Institute Press.

Geertz, Hildred. 1959. "The Vocabulary of Emotion." *Journal for the Study of Interpersonal Processes* 22:225.

Gonzalez, Nancy Solien de. 1959. *The Consanguineal Household Among the Black Carib of Central America*. Ph.D. dissertation. University of Michigan.

----------. 1970. "Toward a Definition of Matrifocality." Pp. 231-43 in *Afro-American Anthropology: Contemporary Perspectives*, edited by Norman E. Whitten Jr. and John F. Szwed. New York: Free Press.

Gough, Kathleen. 1952. "A Comparison of Incest Prohibitions and the Rules of Exogamy in Three Matrilineal Groups of the Malabar Coast." *International Archives of Ethnography* 46: 82-105.

Greer, Joel and Erik Thorbecke. 1986. "Food Poverty Profile Applied to Kenyan Smallholders." *Economic Development and Cultural Change*. 35(1):115-141.

Gupta, Geeta. 1989. "Female-Headed Households, Poverty and Child Welfare", Paper presented at the Population Council/ICRW Seminar Series on Determinants and Consequences of Female-Headed Households. New York, April.

Hamilton, Sarah. "Women's Management of Agricultural Production Capital in the Central Ecuadorian Highlands." Paper presented at the meetings of the Society for Applied Anthropology, Memphis, March.

Henriques, Fernando. 1953. *Family and Colour in Jamaica*. London: Eyre & Spottiswoode.

Herskovits, Melville J. 1937. *Life in a Haitian Valley*. New York: A. A. Knopf.

----------. 1941. *The Myth of the Negro Past*. New York: Harper & Brothers.

----------. 1943. "The Negro in Bahia, Brazil: A Problem in Method." *American Sociological Review* 8:394-404.

Herskovits, Melville J. and F. Francis. 1947. *Trinidad Village*. New York, A. A. Knopf.

Hess, Peter. 1988. *Population Growth and Socio-Economic Progress in Less Developed Countries: Determinants of Fertility Transition*. New York: Praeger.

Hill, Polly. 1969. "Hidden Trade in Hausaland." *Man* 4(3).

Hoddinott, John and Lawrence Haddad. 1991. "Household Expenditures, Child Anthropometric Status and the Intrahousehold Division of Income: Evidence from the Cote d'Ivoire." Washington, D.C.: International Food Policy Research Institute.

Horton, Susan and Barbara D. Miller. 1989. "The Effect of Gender of Household Head on Food Expenditures: Evidence from Low-Income Households in Jamaica." Paper presented at Yale Conference on Family, Gender Differences and Development.

Houtthaker, H. S. 1957. "An International Comparison of Household Expenditure Patterns, Commemorating the Centenary of Engel's Law." *Econometrica* 25:532-551.

Huber, Joan. 1991. "A Theory of Family, Economy, and Gender." Pp. 35-51 in *Gender, Family, and Economy: The Triple Overlap*, edited by Rae Lesser Blumberg. Newbury Park, CA: Sage.

Johnson, F. C. and B. L. Rogers. 1988. "Nutritional Status in Female-headed Households in the Dominican Republic." Paper presented at the International Conference on Women, Development, and Health. Michigan State University, October 21-23.

Kay, Paul. 1963. "Aspects of Social Structure in a Tahitian Urban Neighbourhood." *Journal of Polynesian Society* 72:325-71.

Kayberry, Phyllis. 1953. *Women of the Grassfields*. London: HMSO.

Kennedy, Eileen. 1988. "The Significance of Female-Headed Households in Kenya." Paper prepared for joint ICRW/Population Council Seminar II on Consequences of Female Headship and Female Maintenance, Washington, D.C., February 27-28.

----------. 1989. *The Effects of Sugarcane Production on Food Security, Health, and Nutrition in Kenya: A Longitudinal Analysis*. IFPRI Research Report 78. Washington, D.C.: IFPRI.

----------. 1992. "Effects of Gender of Head of Household on Women's and Children's Nutritional Status." Paper presented at the workshop on The Effects of Policies and Programs on Women. Washington, D.C.: International Food Policy Research Institute.

Kennedy, Eileen T. and Bruce Cogill. 1987. *Income and Nutritional Effects of the Commercialization of Agriculture in Southwestern Kenya*. Research Report No. 63. Washington, D.C.: International Food Policy Research Institute.

Kennedy, Eileen and Pauline Peters. 1992. "Household Food Security and Child Nutrition: the Interaction of Income and Gender of Household Head." *World Development*, Summer. (In press.)

Korale, R. 1988. "Statistics on Economic Support and Female Headship of Households from Sri Lanka Censuses and Surveys." Paper presented at the Joint Population Council/ICRW Seminar Series, Concepts and Classifications of Female-Headed Households: Implications and Applications for National Statistics, New York.

Kossoudji, Sherrie and Eva Mueller. 1983. "The Economic and Demographic Status of Female-headed Households in Rural Botswana," *Economic Development and Cultural Change*

31(4):831-859.

Kumar, Shubh K. 1978. "Role of the Household Economy in Child Nutrition at Low Incomes: A Case Study in Kerala." Occasional Paper No. 95. Ithaca: Department of Agricultural Economics, Cornell University.

----------. 1991. "Income Sources of the Malnourished Poor in Rural Bangladesh." Pp. 155-161 in *Income Sources of Malnourished People in Rural Areas: Microlevel Information and Policy Implications*, edited by Joachim von Braun and Rajul Pandya-Lorch. Working Papers on Commercialization of Agriculture and Nutrition No. 5. Washington, D.C.: International Food Policy Research Institute.

Kusterer, Ken, Maria Regina Estrada de Batres and Josefina Xuya Cuxil. 1981. *The Social Impact of Agribusiness: A Case Study of ALCOSA in Guatemala*. Washington, D.C.: Agency for International Development. A.I.D. Special Evaluation Study No. 4.

Lee, Richard B. and Irven DeVore. *Man the Hunter*. Chicago: Aldine Publishing Co.

Lloyd, Cynthia and Anastasia Brandon. 1991. *Women's Role in Maintaining Households: Poverty and Gender Inequality in Ghana*. New York: The Population Council, Research Division Working Paper No. 25.

Lombardi, John R. 1973. "Exchange and Survival." Paper presented at the meetings of the American Anthropological Association, New Orleans, November.

Lopreato, J. 1965. "How Would You Like to be Peasant?" *Human Organization* 24:298.

Louat, Frederic, Margaret Grosh and Jacques van der Gaag. 1991. "Welfare Implications of Female-headship in Jamaican Households." Washington, D.C.: The World Bank.

Matthews, Lear and S. C. Lee. 1975. "Matrifocality Reconsidered: The Case of the Rural Afro-Guyanese Family." Paper read at the Fourteenth International Sociological Association-Council for Family Research Seminar, Curaçao.

Mencher, Joan. 1988. "Women's Work and Poverty: Women's Contribution to Household Maintenance in Two Regions of South India." Pp. 99-119 in *A Home Divided: Women and Income in the Third World*, edited by Daisy Dwyer and Judith Bruce. Palo Alto, CA: Stanford University Press.

Moynihan, Daniel Patrick. 1965. *The Negro Family: The Case for National Action* (The Moynihan Report). Washington, D.C.: U.S. Department of Labor, Office of Policy Planning and Research.

Murdock, George Peter. 1949. *Social Structure*. New York: The Macmillan Company.

----------. 1967. "Ethnographic Atlas: A Summary." *Ethnology* 6:109-236.

Murdock, George Peter and Douglas R. White. 1969. "Standard Cross-Cultural Sample." *Ethnology* 8:329-69.

Murdock, George Peter and Suzanne F. Wilson. 1972. "Settlement Patterns and Community Organization: Cross-Cultural Codes 3," *Ethnology* 11:254-95.

Murray, Charles. 1984. *Losing Ground: American Social Policy, 1950-1980*. New York: Basic Books.

Myrdal, Gunnar. 1944. *An American Dilemma*. New York: Harper & Brothers, 2 vols.

Nelson, Nici. 1978. "Female-centered Families: Changing Patterns of Marriage and Family among Buzaa Brewers of Mathare Valley." *African Urban Studies* 3(Winter):85-104.

----------. 1979. "Women Must Help Each Other: The Operation of Personal Networks among Buzaa Brewers in Mathare Valley, Kenya." Pp. 88-98 in *Women United, Women Divided: Comparative Studies of Ten Contemporary Cultures*, edited by Ann Caplan and Janet Bujra. Bloomington: Indiana University Press.

Oppong, Christine. 1974. *Marriage Among a Matrilineal Elite*. London: Cambridge University Press.

----------. 1987. "Responsible Fatherhood and Birth Planning." In *Sex Roles, Population, and Development in West Africa. Policy-Related Studies on Work and Demographic Issues*, edited by Christine Oppong. London: James Currey, Ltd.

51

Pahl, Jan. 1989. *Money and Marriage*. London: Macmillan.

Peattie, Lisa R. 1968. *The View from the Barrio*. Ann Arbor, MI: University of Michigan Press.

Peters, Pauline and G. Herrera, with Thomas Randolph. 1989. "Cash Cropping, Food Security, and Nutrition: The Effects of Agricultural Commercialization among Smallholders in Malawi." Final report to AID, NIPD. Cambridge, Mass: Agency for International Development.

Powdermaker, Hortense. 1939. *After Freedom: A Cultural Study in the Deep South*. New York: Viking Press.

Roldan, Martha. 1988. "Renegotiating the Marital Contract: Intra-household Patterns of Money Allocation and Women's Subordination among Domestic Outworkers in Mexico City." Pp. 229-247, in *A Home Divided: Women and Income in the Third World*, edited by Daisy Dwyer and Judith Bruce. Palo Alto, CA: Stanford University Press.

Rosenhouse, Sandra. 1989. "Identifying the Poor: Is 'Headship' a Useful Concept?" Living Standards Measurement Study Working Paper 58. Washington, D.C.: The World Bank.

Rush, David, Daniel G. Horvitz and W. Burleigh Seaver. 1986. "The National WIC Evaluation; An Evaluation of the Special Supplemental Food Program for Infants, Women and Children" Vol. 5, Instrumentation. North Carolina: Research Triangle Institute.

Ross, Catherine E. 1987. "The Division of Labor at Home." *Social Forces* 65(3):816-833.

Sahlins, Marshall D. 1965. "On the Sociology of Primitive Exchange." In *The Relevance of Models for Social Anthropology*, edited by Michael Banton. A.S.A. Monograph I. London: Tavistock Publications; New York: Praeger.

Saito, Katrine A. and Jean Weidemann. 1990. "Agricultural Extension for Women Farmers in Africa." Washington, D.C.: The World Bank. Policy, Research and External Affairs Working Papers.

Schildkrout, Enid. 1984 "Schooling or Seclusion Choices - for Northern Nigerian Women." *Cultural Survival Quarterly* 8(2).

Segalen, Martine. 1986. *Historical Anthropology of the Family*. Cambridge: University of Cambridge Press.

Senauer, Benjamin. 1988. "The Impact of the Value of Women's Time on Food and Nutrition." Department of Agricultural and Applied Economics, University of Minnesota. Draft.

Sivard, Ruth. 1985. *Women - A World Survey*. Washington, D.C.: World Priorities.

Smith, Hazel M. and Ellen H. Biddle. 1975. *Look Forward, Not Back*. Canberra: Australian National University Press.

Smith, Raymond T. 1956. *The Negro Family in British Guiana*. London: Routledge & Kegan Paul.

Stack, Carol D. 1970. "The Kindred of Viola Jackson: Residence and Family Organization of an Urban Black American Family." Pp. 303-12 in *Afro-American Anthropology: Contemporary Perspectives*, edited by Norman E. Whitten, Jr. and John F. Szwed. New York: Free Press.

----------. 1974. *All Our Kin: Strategies for Survival in a Black Community*. New York: Harper & Row.

Staudt, Kathleen A. 1985. *Agricultural Policy Implementation: A Case Study from Western Kenya*. West Hartford: Kumarian Press.

----------. 1987. "Uncaptured or Unmotivated? Women and the Food Crisis in Africa." *Rural Sociology* 52(1):37-55.

Stavrakis, Olga and Marion Louise Marshall. 1978. "Women, Agriculture, and Development in the Maya Lowlands: Profit or Progress?" Paper presented at the International Conference on Women and Food, Tucson, Arizona.

Stoler, Ann. 1977. "Class Structure and Female Autonomy in Rural Java." In *Women and National Development: The Complexities of Change*, edited by Wellesley Editorial Committee. Chicago: The University of Chicago Press.

Tripp, Robert B. 1981. "Farmers and Traders: Some Economic Determinants of Nutritional Status in Northern Ghana." *Journal of Tropical Pediatrics* 27:15-22.

United Nations. 1987. *Fertility Behaviours in the Context of Development*. New York: United Nations, Department of International Economic and Social Affairs. (ST/ESA/SER;A/100).

U.S. Department of Labor, Employment Standards Administration, Women's Bureau. *Facts About Women Heads of Households and Heads of Famiilies*. Washington, D.C.

Valentine, Charles. 1968. *Culture and Poverty: Critique and Counterproposals*. Chicago: University of Chicago Press.

----------. 1970. "Blackston: Progress Report on a Community Study in Urban Afro-America. Mimeo. St. Louis: Washington University.

von Braun, Joachim and Rajul Pandya-Lorch. 1991. *Income Sources of Malnourished People in Rural Areas: Microlevel Information and Policy Implications*. Working Papers on Commercialization of Agriculture and Nutrition No. 5. Washington, D.C.: International Food Policy Research Institute.

von Braun, Joachim, Detlez Puetz and Patric Webb. 1989. "Irrigation Technology and Commercialization of Rice in the Gambia: Effects on Income and Nutrition" Research Report #75, Washington, D.C. International Food Policy Research Institute

von Braun, Joachin, Hartwig de Haen and Juergen B. Lanken. 1990. "Commeercialization of Agriculture under Population Pressure: Effects on Production, Consumption and Nutrition in Rwanda." Research Report #85. Washington, D.C. International Food Policy Research Institute.

von Braun, Joachim and Graciela Wiegand-Jahn. 1991. "Income Sources and Income Uses of the Malnourished Poor in Northwest Rwanda." Pp. 117-130 in *Income Sources of Malnourished People in Rural Areas: Microlevel Information and Policy Implications*, edited by Joachim von Braun and Rajul Pandya-Lorch. Working Papers on Commercialization of Agriculture and Nutrition No. 5. Washington, D.C.: International Food Policy Research Institute.

Vosti, Stephen A. and Julie Witcover. 1991. "Income Sources of the Rural Poor: The Case of the Zona da Mata, Minas Gerais, Brazil. Pp. 47-68 in *Income Sources of Malnourished People in Rural Areas: Microlevel Information and Policy Implications*, edited by Joachim von Braun and Rajul Pandya-Lorch. Working Papers on Commercialization of Agriculture and Nutrition No. 5. Washington, D.C.: International Food Policy Research Institute.

Vreede-de Stuers, Cora. 1967. "Indonesia." Pp. 361-384 in *Women in the Modern World*, edited by Raphael Patai. New York: Free Press.

Wolf, Diane. 1991. "Female Autonomy, the Family, and Industrialization in Java." Pp. 128-148 in *Gender, Family, and Economy: The Triple Overlap*, edited by Rae Lesser Blumberg. Newbury Park, CA: Sage.

Wood, Charles. 1989. "Women-headed Households and Child Mortality in Brazil, 1960-1980." Paper presented at the Joint Population Council/ICRW Seminar Series, Consequences of Female Headship and Female Maintenance, February 27-28, Washington, D.C.

World Bank. 1991. *Gender and Poverty in India*. Washington, D.C.

Young, Michael and Peter Willmott. 1957. *Family and Kinship in East London*. New York: The Free Press.

3

Not Enough to Go Around:
An Etic Model for the Scientific
Study of the Causes of Matrifocality

Anna Lou Dehavenon

Since 1950 population pressure, the mechanization of agriculture, and urbanization world-wide have produced profound changes in cities and the local systems with which they interact. Often these changes are associated with high rates of matrifocality, and "subsistence urbanization" (Breese 1966: 5), a condition in which many people in cities have access to only the barest necessities of life. The goal of this chapter is to develop a model for the scientific study of the causes of matrifocality in low-income groups.[1] It also analyzes the matrifocality and subsistence urbanization experienced by large numbers of families now living in New York City. The concluding discussion includes suggestions for ameliorating the material factors associated with these conditions.

A number of authors describe changes in domestic structure associated with urbanization (Aldous 1962; Cohen 1971; Lewis 1952; Mencher 1958; Ross 1961), different kinds of urban shelter (Marris 1960; Petonnet 1973; Rainwater 1970; Safa 1974; Young and Willmott 1957), and high frequencies of single, female-headed, or matrifocal families (Adams 1960; Clarke 1953, 1957; Comitas 1964; Gonzalez 1969; Kunstadter 1963; Marino 1969; D.B. Smith 1965; M.G. Smith 1962; R.T. Smith 1956). Because these authors do not employ the same logico-empirical operations to collect and analyze data, it is difficult to use their findings to test hypotheses on the causes of cross-cultural differences and similarities in domestic structure. The issues raised by the nonconformity of the data operations transcend the methodological, since they relate to the causal relationship between particular forms of family life and poverty, and to the formulation of public policy.

In spite of important anthropological contributions to the epistemology of family life, most contemporary public policy is based on outdated social theory which defines the nuclear family as the unique, minimal unit of social organization (LaBarre 1954; Murdock 1949; Parsons 1955). This perspective often portrays the single, female-headed family as "disorganized", "pathological", and the cause of poverty.

Donald Bender and Richard N. Adams discuss some of the definitional problems associated with the scientific study of domestic life. Bender suggests that affinal and consanguineal relationship, coresidence, and domestic function (often thought of as aspects of a single phenomenon labeled 'family') are in fact semi-dependent variables (Bender 1965:493). He furthermore proposes that even when the concept of 'household', as the residential group in which domestic functions are performed, is distinguished from the concept of 'family' as the kinship group, the conflation of coresidence and the performance of domestic functions poses a serious empirical problem. Bender concludes by emphasizing the need to look at all three phenomena separately.

Richard N. Adams emphasizes how the flexibility of social organization enables the evolution of diverse family forms as adaptations to specific socio-economic conditions (1960:31). The empirical model he proposes consists of the permutations among three familial dyads: one based on coitus, one of mother and child, and one of father and child. Adams suggests that while the first two dyads are based on biological activity, the third is not, and that while the relationship of infant nursing is both biological and economic, any further economic dependency among all three of the actors is defined socially, not biologically.

An Etic Model for the Scientific Study of Population Maintenance and Rates of Matrifocality in Low-Income Groups

Figure 3.1 is a closed boundary system model of population maintenance and rates of matrifocality in low-income groups.[2] It is based on three assumptions: 1) that all human groups reproduce within the constraints of particular socio-economic environments; 2) that the human reproductive process involves a population of adults with a particular mating pattern, a population of newborns, and residential units for their nourishment and enculturation; and 3) that faced with a local shortage of stable wage employment and housing, the parents of children exploit multiple, differentially proximate resource options to maintain these units.

The model defines the matrifocal family as one in which the father is nonresident more of the time than he is coresident during the years when his children grow up, and during which time the mother (and/or her kin) provide residential stability and perform local domestic functions more frequently than the father (or his kin). During his nonresidence, the father may perform particular domestic functions, but his departure from the family living unit limits these functions, while profoundly affecting local residential patterns, mating patterns, and adult sex ratios.

The model has three levels. These are: Level I, the population of newborns;

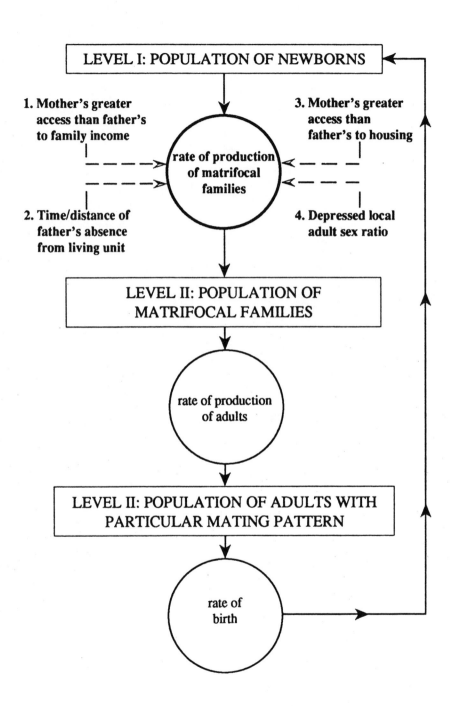

FIGURE 3.1. Systems Model of Population Maintenance and Rates of Matrifocality in Low–Income Groups.

Level II, the population of matrifocal families; and Level III, the population of adults with a particular mating pattern. The levels describe the state of the modeled system, and a given level is the accumulation resulting from the flows in and out of that level. Three flow rates affect the levels: the birth rate, the rate of production of matrifocal families, and the rate of production of adults. Four variables affect the rate of production of matrifocal families. These are the material factors identified with matrifocality in a number of demographic and ethnographic studies (Adams 1960; Clarke 1953, 1957; Comitas 1964; Gonzalez 1969; Kunstadter 1963; Marino 1969; D. B. Smith 1965; M.G. Smith 1962; R.T. Smith 1956). They include 1) the mother's greater access than the father's to family income, 2) the time and distance of the father's absence for cash employment from the family living unit, 3) the mother's greater access than the father's to housing, and 4) the locally reduced adult sex ratio. The model is etic because the data used to develop and test it are the output of logico-empirical operations in which the units of observation are meaningful and appropriate to the community of scientific observers (Harris 1964, 1968; Lett 1990). The units in these operations can be applied cross-culturally and quantified.[3]

The first application of the proposed model was in a comparative analysis of the data from a number of studies which document high rates of matrifocality (Cohn 1955; Gonzalez 1969; Kay 1963; Kerr 1958; Lynch 1969; Marshall 1965; Mencher 1962; Moynihan 1965; D.B. Smith 1965; Van Velsen 1969). The analysis showed that all these works (except Moynihan's) maintain Bender's distinction between family, household, and domestic function (Dehavenon 1971). They also find a correlation between matrifocality and both parents' exploiting multiple cash and non-cash income options which require the father to leave the household more often (and to go farther away) than the mother. When only the father migrates, as in the Liverpool example of Kerr, the Tahitian example of Kay, the American black example of Gonzalez, and the Nayar study of Mencher, the families they leave behind consist of two or three generations of matrilineal kin. While the Tongans studied by Van Velsen and the Camar studied by Cohn and Lynch have a preference for virilocality, the matrifocal units the fathers in these groups leave behind to go work in African mines or Indian urban centers are coresident with matri- or patrilineal kin. When--as in David Smith's British Caribbean example and Gloria Marshall's Yoruban study--both parents migrate for work, the families in which their children stay behind include two or three generations of matrilineal kin, in the first instance, and of patrilineal kin in the second. In all these examples, the local housing supply and cash employment are scarce, and the adult sex ratios are depressed.

Developing the Model in the Study of Matrifocality
in Research on a Low-Income New York City Group

Longitudinal research[4] on the causes of hunger and homelessness in New York City families with children provides micro data on the experiences of families living in the areas of the boroughs of Brooklyn, the Bronx and Manhattan with the highest rates of unemployment and public assistance participation. Primary data on 1,576 families who experienced food emergencies in 1985, and secondary data from a number of sources, are used to further develop the model proposed in this chapter. A food emergency is defined operationally in this research as existing when a family which has run out of food (or is in imminent danger of doing so) applies for and receives a small, nonperishable food supply from a private, community-based agency. Many of the families in this work are single, female-headed. Most are black or Hispanic.

Model Variable 1: The Mother's Greater Access than the Father's to Family Income

Background: The Effects of Unemployment and Poverty in New York City on Family Income in the 1980s. Between 1969 and 1977, the city lost more than 600,000 jobs. The 1981 federal budget eliminated 300,000 more and the job training and work incentives previously available to parents on public assistance. By 1990, the city's overall poverty rate was 25.2 percent, and more than three-quarters of the 1.8 million people living in poverty were black or Hispanic (Rosenberg 1992). In 1991, the labor force participation rates for all groups reached an 11-year low point, but the unemployment rates of minority men were higher than those of white men. However, what is significant for the model being developed here is that the unemployment rates of minority women were lower than those of minority men.

Public assistance, e.g., "welfare", is the only formal income available to families who do not have a primary wage earner. Nationally, the purchasing power of public assistance payments shrank 42 percent between 1969 and 1991. In New York City, the Consumer Price Index rose 278 percent during the same period, but the basic public assistance grant for food and all expenses other than shelter and medical costs for a median family of three increased only 61 percent--from $179 to $291 per month (Dehavenon 1992).[5]

In 1984, the median public assistance family received $7,464, or almost $1,200 less than the poverty level. Furthermore, a person working full-time at the minimum wage earned only $6,964 (Levitan and Shapiro 1986). As a result of this lower income--and because they rarely had employer-paid health insurance--the families of these workers were usually worse off than those on public assistance. Because of these trends, the family food emergencies documented in the research increased exponentially in the early 1980s as reported in the *New York Times* (Dehavenon 1982; Rule 1982). So did the number of homeless families.

Family Food Emergencies in New York City. The research sample was drawn from neighborhoods where 90 percent of the population described them-

Table 3.1 Formal Income Sources in Food Emergency Families in 1985

| Income Source | All families | |
	N	(%)
Public Assistance (PA) only	812	51.5
Supplemental Security Income (SSI) and PA	40	2.5
SSI (14 applying or re-applying PA)	39	2.5
SSI and Social Security (SS)	4	.3
SS (3 applying or re-applying PA)	15	1.0
SS and PA	10	.6
Employment (11 applying or re-applying PA)	61	4.0
Unemployment benefits, pension, disability, food stamps only, child support (10 applying or reapplying PA)	56	4.0
No income	88	5.6
No income: applying PA	180	11.4
No income: re-applying PA	271	17.2

Total:____

Observations N=1,576
*Total does not equal 100.0 because of rounding.

selves as Hispanic, or Non-Hispanic Black, in the 1980 U.S. census (Dehavenon 1986). In 1985, 33 percent to 48 percent of those who lived in these areas received public assistance, Supplemental Security Income (the federal program for the poor, elderly and disabled), or Medicaid (the federal health insurance program for the poor). The research revealed that the principal reasons for family food emergencies in the 1980s were unemployment, the inadequacy of public assistance payments (including having to spend food money on rent), and the city's policy of closing large numbers of public assistance cases for administrative reasons unrelated to family need (Dehavenon 1988, 1990).

Table 3.1 shows the formal income sources reported by 1,576 food emergency families in 1985 which was a typical year. It also shows that most of the families (84.6%) were interacting with the public assistance system as recipients, new applicants, or re-applicants whose cases were closed for administrative reasons; 5.6 percent had no income and were not applying for public assistance; only 4 percent reported work as the family's source of income.

It is significant for the model proposed here that the rules and practices which governed public assistance eligibility in 1984 resulted in unemployed or disabled fathers being included in only 12.5 percent of the city's cases in which there were children (Casey 1985).[6] With this percentage as a guide, the analysis of Table 3.1. shows that only 25.6 percent of the food emergency families could have legally included both a mother and a father. This percentage consists of 12.5 percent of those on, applying, or re-applying for public assistance (10.7% of the families in Table 3.1), as well as those whose income sources did not preclude the father's coresidence, e.g., employment (4%), supplemental security income (5.3%), and unemployment insurance benefits, social security, pension payment, or disability payment (5.6%). To summarize, public assistance (by far the most frequently reported formal source of income in Table 3.1) was much more available to families in which the mothers--but not the fathers--were coresident.

The food emergency families also received support from a number of informal sources. These included gifts or loans from husband/fathers, grandparents and other nonresident family members, friends, neighbors, landlords, grocers, and loan sharks. Often this help was received in the form of gifts or exchanges of food, money, food stamps, subway tokens, clothing, cooking facilities, and electric current. In-depth interviews with two principal informants reveal some of the other goods and services which low-income, New York City families exchange for a fee, or a service. These are shown in Table 3.2, as to their availability to men, women, and children.

Table 3.2 shows that men were more likely than women to sell goods and services in the street. It also shows that men's informal activities were more likely than women's to involve personal performances, mobile equipment, illegal sales and a high risk of arrest, incarceration, injury, and death from theft and the manufacture of drugs and alcohol. Women, more frequently than men, sell the goods and services associated with homemaking and personal care, e.g., clothing, items of adornment, cooking services or cooked food, child care, and hair-dressing. While both men and women engage in prostitution, they and children beg for food and money for food.

To summarize these findings in terms of the Model Variable 1, the women were somewhat less likely to be unemployed than the men. The women were, however, much more likely than the men to receive public assistance payments for themselves and their children. The men's informal income pursuits were more dangerous than the women's and much more likely to result in incarceration, injury or death which would remove them from the family living unit.

Model Variable 2: The Time and Distance of the Father's Absence from the Family Living Unit

The research on family food emergencies does not collect systematic, quanti-

Table 3.2 Availability of Informal Cash Income and Services to Men, Women and Children

	Women	Men	Children
SERVICES FOR $$			
Hustling or working "off the books" in:			
piece work (clothing factories)	X		
drug "factories"	X	X	
pimping		X	
pick up and delivery		X	
moving households with van		X	
using car as taxi		X	
janitoring		X	
painting		X	
Temporary or Spot Work			
day work loading trucks		X	
pack bags at supermarket	X		X
carry bags from supermarket		X	
collecting cans		X	
preaching		X	
musical performances		X	
dance performances		X	X
Personal Services			
cooking	X		
baby-sitting	X		X (14+)
hair dressing	X		
renting out living space	X		
prostitution	X	X	
Enter the Military		X	
GOODS FOR $$			
Hustling or illegal sale of:			
numbers	X	X	
stolen goods		X	
subway tokens		X	
bootlegged alcohol		X	
illegal drugs		X	X
blackmarket babies	X		
Sale of			
single cigarettes	X	X	
vegetables on sidewalk & from trucks		X	
ices, hotdogs, sodas, etc. from carts		X	
clothing on sidewalks and in small "flea markets"	X	X	
household goods, books, records on sidewalks, and in small "flea Markets"	X	X	
jewelry	X	X	
cosmetics	X	X	
cooked foods	X		
BEGGING	X	X	X

fied information on the whereabouts or activities of fathers not living with their families. It can be surmised, however, that the time and distance that separate men from the family unit, and the degree of their contacts with and economic contributions to them over time, also vary depending on whether or not they are employed, homeless, in prison, sick, or dead.[7]

Model Variable 3: The Mother's Greater Access than the Father's to Housing and Emergency Shelter

Background: New York City's Low-Income Housing Shortage.   Since the early 1970s, the city has experienced increasing shortages of low- and moder-ately-priced rental housing. These are the result of cutbacks in federal subsidies for the construction and maintenance of low-income housing, landlords' nonpay-ment of taxes, abandonment and arsoning of their buildings for the insurance, and the city's failure to rehabilitate significant numbers of the tens of thousands of living units it inherited as a result of landlord tax default. Other causes of the shortage include gentrification, and the effects of inflation on controlled rents and on public assistance shelter allowances. By 1985, 60 percent of the city's families on public assistance paid all (or more than) their allowance for rent. Five thousand homeless families lived in the city's emergency shelter system, and more than 100,000 others were doubled or tripled up in the apartments of family members and friends, because they could not afford their own. Table 3.3 shows the housing conditions reported by the food emergency families in 1984 and 1985.[8]

Table 3.3 shows that by 1985 one quarter of the food emergency families were not living in their own apartments: the 19 percent who lived doubled up were incipiently homeless, because they did not pay rent to the landlord and were therefore the ones who would have to leave if crowding or interpersonal conflict became too great; five percent of the families were absolutely homeless,

TABLE 3.3 Real and Incipient Homeless Families in Food Emergencies in 1984 and 1985

	1984 All families		1985 All families	
	N	(%)	N	(%)
Own apartment	1,160	77	1,188	75
Doubled up	265	18	300	19
Public place[1]	54	4	37	2
City shelter system	27	2	51	3
Total:	1,506	101[2]	1,576	99[2]

Observations N 1984 = 1,506; N 1985 = 1,576
   [1]Includes an abandoned building or the street
   [2]Totals do not equal 100.0 because of rounding.

because they lived in a public place, or in the city's emergency shelter system.
The allowance public assistance families receive for shelter is their only
formal income for rent. The level of this allowance has increased only 35
percent since 1975. A median public assistance family of three now receives
$287 a month, or less than half the amount needed to rent a one-bedroom
apartment (Dehavenon 1992). As was shown in the analysis of Table 3.1, only
12.5 percent of families on public assistance receive support for more than one
primary caretaker of the children. Since the sole caretaker is almost always the
mother, it is she who has access to money for rent. If homeless families are not
already on public assistance when they ask the city for emergency shelter, their
eligibility is assessed immediately. This is done in order for the city to obtain
for as many of these families as possible the 75 percent of the costs of
emergency shelter which the federal and state governments pay only for families
on public assistance. To summarize these findings in terms of Model Variable
3, mothers on public assistance have greater access than fathers to rent for an
apartment and to emergency shelter when the family is homeless.

Model Variable 4: Local Adult Sex Ratios

Background: Adult Sex Ratios and Their Social Consequences. Guttentag
and Secord (1983: 199-213) analyze the social consequences of certain demographic characteristics in order to show how human groups with low adult sex
ratios experience "family disruption, divorce, one-parent families headed by
women, illegitimacy, remaining single, and failure to marry." They conclude
1) that low income, inferior education, and prejudice accentuate already
depressed sex ratios and aggravate the social conditions which lower them even
further, and 2) that these conditions are not the direct result of historical circumstances, such as the existence of a single, female-headed family form as part of
a group's culture.

In most human groups, males have higher death rates than females at all ages.
However, the much higher mortality rates of black than white American males
at all ages leads to a greater decline in the black sex ratio, particularly at the
adult ages when children are conceived, born, and enculturated. Historically, the
sex ratio of American blacks was below 100 for a considerably longer period
than that of whites. The fact that infant mortality rates have decreased much
more for whites than for blacks is one of the reasons for this differential.
Because of the inferior maternal and other health care blacks receive, they also
suffer greater fetal loss and have lower sex ratios at birth (103.1 as compared
with 105.95 for whites in 1970). Similarly, this lack of access to quality health
care results in higher rates of mortality for black male infants, children and adolescents than for white males at the same ages. According to Guttentag and Secord, other reasons for the low black adult sex ratio include the disproportion-

cord, other reasons for the low black adult sex ratio include the disproportionate inclusion of black males in the prison and other institutional populations, the underenumeration of black males in the U.S. census, and their greater participation than white males in the armed forces overseas.

Urbanization also contributed to lower black sex ratios in cities. In response to the increased mechanization of southern agriculture after World War II, four million blacks moved to cities between 1950 and 1970. By 1978, three-quarters

TABLE 3.4 Comparison of Factors Which Affected Adult Sex Ratios in Black, Hispanic, and White Groups in the 1980s

	black male	black female	Hispanic male	Hispanic female	white male	white female
Part 1 Percentage of population in prison in NY State (1980)	49.4	2.2	17.9	.6	28.9	1.0
Part 2 Percentage of single homeless adults NY City (1985)	54.0	11.0	20.0	17.0	8.0	3.5
Part 3 Mortality per 10,000 from 10 chief causes of death: ages 15-44 NY City (1985)						
1) AIDS	9.4	1.8	8.0	1.2	6.1	.3
2) homicide	12.4	1.5	10.0	1.1	1.7	0.0
3) malignancy	3.4	3.2	2.2	1.6	3.4	3.3
4) heart disease	5.6	2.4	2.4	1.0	2.5	.8
5) drug dependency	4.7	1.5	3.3	.6	1.6	.5
6) cirrhosis	5.2	2.0	3.8	.6	1.5	.5
7) accidents	2.3	.4	1.9	.3	1.7	.3
8) influenza or/pneumonia	2.9	1.5	1.5	.3	.8	.3
9) suicide	1.3	.3	1.9	.4	1.3	.4
10) cerebro/vascular	1.1	1.0	.8	.3	.2	.3

Sources: U.S. Census 1980; Detailed Population Characteristics, New York State. Table 207. NY City Human Resources Administration 1985; Bureau of Management Information Systems: Survey of single homeless adults who remained in shelter system 10 days or more. Summary of Vital Statistics 1986; NY City Department of Health.

of all blacks lived in metropolitan areas, 55 percent in inner cities. The impact of this migration--which was predominantly of young adults--on black marriage pools was dramatic because of the larger gender difference among the young blacks than the young whites who moved to cities. The northeast (including New central region gained three black women for every two black men.

Concomitantly, the marital opportunities of blacks declined substantially, as the sex ratio for unmarried black males, ages 18-44, and unmarried black females, ages 16-42, decreased from 105 in 1950 to 73 in 1970. Guttentag and Secord conclude that the shortage of young, marriageable black males has been a chronic problem in New York City for at least a half century, and that in the 1970s there were two black females for every black male in the early 20s age cohort most eligible for marriage. The migration of blacks from rural to urban areas had accentuated the existing shortage of black men to produce a marriage squeeze the effects of which will be felt by black women for a long time, especially those who live in the larger northeastern and southern cities.

The Effects on Black and Hispanic Adult Sex Ratios in New York City in the 1980s. Table 3.4 compares data on some of these factors as they affected the adult sex ratios of whites, blacks and Hispanics at ages 15 to 44 in New York City and in the neighborhoods from which the family sample was drawn.

Table 3.4 shows that for ages 15 to 44, minority males were much more likely than white males, and the females in all three groups, to be in prison or home-less. Minority men were also more likely than white men (and the women in all three groups) to be dying from seven of the ten chief causes of death at ages 15 to 44, e.g., AIDS, homicide, drug dependency, cirrhosis, accidents, influenza and/or pneumonia, and cerebro/vascular disease. These findings support Gutten-tag and Secord's finding that the marital opportunities of black women in New York City are more substantially reduced than those of white women by the losses of black men from the available marriage pool. We next look at how these and other factors affected the adult sex ratio and domestic structure in the food emergency families. Almost all these families (90%) were black or Hispanic.

The Adult Sex Ratio and Domestic Structure in the Food Emergency Families. The food emergency families reported the age and gender of the family members who were living together at the time they were interviewed. These are shown in Table 3.5.

Table 3.5 shows that 3,929 (64.2%) of the coresident family members were children under age 18, and that the sex ratio for adults over age 18 was only 22.6 to 77.4. This dramatically skewed adult sex ratio demonstrates the effects of the factors identified by Guttentag and Secord, the public assistance system's bias against including fathers as the caretakers of the children (See the discussion of Table 3.1), the rise in homelessness in Table 3.3, and the higher rates of homelessness, imprisonment, illness, and death among minority men than among white men and the women in all three groups.

Table 3.5 Age and Gender in Food Emergency Households in 1985 as a Percentage of the Total

age	female	male	% of total
Less than 1	116	121	3.9
1 - 4	541	488	16.8
5 - 14	1,154	1,011	35.3
15 - 17	278	220	8.1
18 - 24	408	175	9.5
25 - 44	1,113	255	22.5
45 - 64	168	61	3.7
65 or more	12	6	.3
Totals:	3,790	2,337	100.0
Females:			61.9
Males			38.1

Observations N = 6,117 family members

Table 3.6 shows the frequencies of the 19 different domestic structures and three family types in which 2,188 adults were organized to nurture and encul-turate the children in the food emergency families. These structures are identi-fied in terms of the number, age, and gender of the coresident adults to provide the etic framework within which kinship is socially (or emically) defined.

Three-quarters of the families in Table 3.6 were Family Type 1, e.g., they included only one adult. For this Family Type, the single, female-headed family is the most frequently reported structure (68.7%). There is, however, considerable diversity among these one-adult families which would not have been revealed by focusing primarily on those which were matrifocal. Fathers, grandparents of both genders, and great-grandmothers also took responsibility as single adults for nurturing and enculturating the children.

One-sixth of the families were Family Type 2, e.g., they included two adults. A smaller number (2%) included three. Again, there was considerable diversity in the permutations in the age and gender of the adults in these two Family Types. When the contact persons were asked to identify their relationship to the children in the food emergency families, 75 percent responded "mother", and 17 percent responded "father." Others identified themselves as a grand-or great-grandparent, aunt, uncle, older sibling, or friend of the children for whom they sought food. The diversity in the three Family Types in Table 3.6 confirms the adaptiveness of domestic structure in response to the conditions in a particular environment, in this instance to extreme poverty.

To summarize in terms of Model Variable 4, the local adult sex ratio in these families was very depressed, and while other constellations of adults took pri-mary responsibility for maintaining some of the families, the most prevalent domestic structure was the one with a single, female head.

Discussion

This analysis reveals a significant association between domestic structure in the food emergency families and three of the four model variables in Figure 3.1. which affect the rate of production of matrifocal families in low-income groups. The principal findings for each variable are reviewed as the basis for articulating policy recommendations addressed to relevant decisionmakers at the federal, state and city levels of government.

Table 3.6 Domestic Structure in the Food Emergency Families with Children by Number, Gender and Generation of Adults

	All families N	(%)
Family Type 1: One Adult		
female of parental generation	989	62.5
female of parental generation, children above and below 18	100	6.2
male of parental generation	54	3.3
female of grandparental generation	29	1.7
male of parental generation, children above and below 18	5	.3
female of great-grandparental generation	2	1.2
Subtotal:	1,179	75.2
Family Type 2: Two Adults		
male and female of parental generation	248	15.6
female of parental, female of grandparental generation	76	4.7
females of parental generation	18	1.1
female and male of parental generation, children above/below 18	13	.8
female of grandparental, male of parental generation	6	.3
male of grandparental, female of parental generation	1	.06
male of great-grandparental, male of grandparental generation	1	.06
female of grant-grandparental, female of parental generation	1	.06
Subtotal:	364	22.68
Family Type 3: Three Adults		
female of grandparental, male and female of parental generations	17	1.0
female and male of great-grandparental, female of parental generation	10	.6
male of grandparental, male and female of parental generation	3	.2
female and male of grandparental, male of parental generation	2	.1
male and female of grandparental, female of parental generation	1	.06
Subtotal:	33	1.96
Total:	502	99.8[1]

Observations N = 1,576
[1]Total does not equal 100.0 because of rounding.

Model Variable 1. The Mother's Greater Access than the Father's to Family Income

The analysis shows that the unemployment rate of minority men was higher than that of minority women, that annual income for a full-time worker at the

66

minimum wage was lower than for public assistance, and that only a small proportion of families were able to include the father on their public assistance budget. It is therefore recommended that the federal government 1) increase the minimum wage to a level which supports a family, 2) provide men and women with the education, job preparation, and adequately paying, subsidized work they need to support a family, 3) include both unemployed parents on public assistance budgets by implementing the existing unemployed-parent program for all those who are eligible, and 4) require the individual states to provide a level of public assistance which meets family need by indexing payments to the Consumer Price Index, as is done with Social Security.

Model Variable 3. The Mother's Greater Access than the Father's to Housing

The analysis shows that because the primary income source of most the families was public assistance (which does not usually include fathers), mothers had greater access to (albeit inadequate) income for rent and to emergency shelter when they were homeless. It is therefore recommended that the federal government resume the construction of subsidized, low-income housing and that New York State increase the public assistance shelter allowance to levels which permit families to rent their own apartments. The city and state should also increase the construction of new subsidized, low-income housing as well as the renovation of more of the housing units the city seized through landlord tax default. The city should place homeless families in their own private quarters and include all the family members identified by the parent(s). This would enable mothers to maintain their personal support systems during pregnancy and avoid isolating parents in crisis from one another and from their children.

Model Variable 4. Depressed Local Adult Sex Ratios

The analysis shows that the adult sex ratio in the food emergency families was very depressed. The implementation of the above recommendations, which include the unemployed father on the family's public assistance budget and increase the minimum wage and subsized job and housing programs, would give him access to health care and the income he needs to help support the family. In general, these reforms would strengthen the father's capacity to live with the children when he and the mother want him to.

In conclusion, this chapter applies an etic model for the scientific study of the causes of matrifocality in research on a low-income New York City group. The analysis reveals associations between three of the model's variables and a high frequency of single, female-headed families in a group which knew rising hunger and homelessness in the 1980s and 1990s. Based on the findings, policy recommendations are formulated to ameliorate these conditions while increasing the capacity of family members to live together. Future applications of the model in studies of matrifocality in this and other populations can test its usefulness further.

Notes

1. I am indebted to my colleagues Margaret S. Boone and Aidan Southall for their valued comments on earlier drafts of this chapter. The research is funded by the Foundation for Child Development, J.P. Morgan and Co. Incorporated, the New York Community Trust, the Olive Bridge Fund, and the 1990 Josephine Shaw Lowell Award of the Community Service Society.

2. Forrester (1969) develops and demonstrates the use of a closed boundary systems model in a quantified computer simulation analysis of urban change.

3. For example, if the research data included continuous videotape recordings of the development of informants' life histories, demographic characteristics, nonverbal behaviors, and the social and physical environments in which these behaviors take place, we could observe and measure them intersubjectively without interacting with the informants' semantic categories.

4. This research was carried out (and produced an annual report) each year between 1979 and 1992. The agencies which participate are located in the New York City Community Planning Districts with the highest rates of unemployment, poverty, and public assistance participation. After agency staff supply a family with social services which include a nonperishable food supply to be eaten in the home, they ask the family contact person to respond to the questions on a two-page form for the study of the causes of hunger and homelessness. Staff members emphasize that the family's name will not be used and they can return to the agency for help in the future if they decide not to participate. In 1992, the agencies are the Citizen's Advice Bureau in the South Bronx; the Catholic Charities Family Centers in Bedford Stuyvesant, Bushwick, and North Brooklyn; the Entitlements Clinic of West Harlem; the Little Sisters of the Assumption Family Health Center; and St. Cecilia's Parish Services in East Harlem.

5. New York State's public assistance payment consists of two grants: one for shelter and one for basic needs, e.g., food, clothing, furniture, utilities, transportation, etc. The federal food stamp allotment is designed as a supplement to the food budget in the basic needs grant.

6. In 1984, the Aid for Dependent Children-Unemployed Parent cases in the federal public assistance program were 8 percent of all cases nationally, 5 percent of all cases in New York State, and 2 percent of all cases in New York City. In addition, 10.5 percent of the state's General Assistance cases were family cases, for a total of 12.5 percent in which a father, or second adult, could have been included in New York City.

7. This data, if available, could be used to analyze the degree of matrifocality over time by quantifying the amount of time fathers are, and are not, coresident with their families. The model could be used to measure matrifocality in both individual families diachronically and in populations diachronically and synchronically.

8. This decrease in the percentage of the research families with their own apartments continues. In 1991, only 49 percent had ever had one.

References

Adams, Richard N. 1960. "An Inquiry into the Nature of the Family," in Gertrude Dole and Robert Carneiro, eds., *Essays in the Science of Culture in Honor of Leslie A. White*, pp. 30-49. New York: Thomas Y. Crowell.

Aldous, Joan. 1962. "Urbanization, the Extended Family, and Kinship Ties in West Africa." *Social Forces* 41:6-11.

Bender, Donald R. 1967. "A Refinement of the Concept of Households: Families, Co-residence and Domestic Function." *American Anthropologist* 69:493-504.

Breese, Gerald. 1966. *Urbanization in Newly Developing Countries*. Englewood Cliffs: Prentice Hall.

Casey, Timothy. 1985. Personal Communication. Center on Social Welfare Policy and Law.

Clarke, Edith. 1953. "Land Tenure and the Family in Four Selected Communities in Jamaica." *Social and Economic Studies* 1:8-118.

____. 1957. *My Mother Who Fathered Me: A Study of the Family in Three Selected Communities*

68

in Jamaica. London: George Allen and Unwin.

Cohen, Myron L. 1971. "The Family in Transition in Taiwan." *Fogarty International Center Proceedings* 3: 99-104.

Cohn, Bernard S. 1955. "The Changing Status of a Depressed Caste," in M. Mariott, ed., *Village India: Studies in the Little Community. American Anthropological Memoirs* 83: 55-77.

Comitas, Lambros. 1964. "Occupational Multiplicity in Rural Jamaica." *Proceedings of the American Ethnological Society*. Pp. 41-50.

Dehavenon, Anna Lou. 1971. *Urbanization and Matrifocality: An Etic Simulation Model of the Evolution of the Matrifocal Family Structure*. Unpublished manuscript.

_____. 1982. *Hunger, Poverty and Disease in East Harlem: A Study of the Food Emergencies in 723 Households with Children in 1981*. New York: East Harlem Interfaith.

_____. 1986. *The Tyranny of Indifference and the Reinstitutionalization of Hunger, Homelessness ions of Food Emergencies in 1,576 Households with Children in Manhattan, Brooklyn and the Bronx in 1985*. New York: East Harlem Interfaith.

_____. 1988. "Administrative Closings of Public Assistance Cases: the Rise of Hunger and Homelessness in New York City." *New York University Review of Law and Social Change*. Vl. XVI (4): 741-746.

_____. 1990. "Charles Dickens Meets Franz Kafka: The Maladministration of New York City's Public Assistance Programs." *New York University Review of Law and Social Change*. Vol. XII. 231-254.

_____. 1992. "From the Nature of Cultural Things to the Causes of Hunger and Homelessness in New York City in the 1990s." Maxine L. Margolis and Margine F. Murphy, eds., *Science, Materialism and the Study of Culture* (in preparation).

Forrester, Jay W. 1969. *Urban Dynamics*. Cambridge, Mass: M.I.T. Press.

Gonzalez, Nancie L. Solien. 1969. *Black Carib Household Structure: A Study of Migration and Modernization*. Seattle: University of Washington Press.

Guttentag, Marcia and Paul F. Secord. 1983. *Too Many Women? the Sex Ratio Question*. Newbury Park: Sage Publications.

Harris, Marvin. 1964. *The Nature of Cultural Things*. New York: Random House.

_____. 1968. *The Rise of Anthropological Theory*. New York. Thomas Y. Crowell.

Kay, Paul. 1963. "Aspects of Social Structure in a Tahitian Urban Neighbourhood." *The Journal of the Polynesian Society* 72 (4): 325-71.

Kerr, Madeline. 1958. *The People of Ship Street*. London: Routledge and Kegan Paul.

Kunstadter, Peter. 1963. "A Survey of the Consanguineal or Matrifocal Family." *American Anthropologist* 65: 56-66.

La Barre, Weston. 1954. *The Human Animal*. Chicago: U. of Chicago Press.

Lett, James. 1990. "Emics and Etics: Notes on the Epistemology of Anthropology," Thomas N. Headland, Kenneth L. Pike and Marvin Harris, eds., *Emics and Etics The Insider/Outsider Debate*. Pp.127-142. Newbury Park: Sage Publications.

Levitan, Sar A. and Isaac Shapiro. 1986. "The Minimum Wage: A Sinking Floor." *The New York Times*. Op-Ed page. January 16.

Lewis, Oscar. 1952. "Urbanization Without Breakdown: A Case Study." *Scientific Monthly* 75: 31-41.

Lynch, Owen M. 1969. *The Politics of Untouchability: Social Structure and Social Change in a City of India*. New York: Columbia University Press.

Marino, Anthony. 1969. "Family, Fertility and Sex Ratios in the British Caribbean." Unpublished Manuscript. Cornell University.

Marris, Peter. 1960. "Slum Clearance and Family Life in Lagos." *Human Organization* 19: 123-28.

Marshall, Gloria. 1965. *Women, Trade and the Yoruba Family*. Ph.D. Thesis. Columbia University.

Mencher, Joan. 1958. *Child Rearing and Family Organization in a New York Barrio*. Ph.D. Thesis, Columbia University.

_____. 1962. "Changing Familial Roles among the South Malabar Nayars." *Southwestern Journal of Anthropology* 18 (3): 230-45.

Moynihan, Daniel P. 1965. *The Negro Family: A Case for National Action*. Washington, D.C: U.S. Government Printing Office.

Murdock, George. 1949. *Social Structure*. New York: Macmillan.

Parsons, Talcott. 1949. "The American Family: Its Relations to Personality and to the Social Structure," T. Parsons and R. F. Bales, eds., *Family, Socialization and Interaction Process*. Pp. 3-33. Illinois: Free Press of Glencoe.

Petonnet, Colette. 1973. *Those People: The Subculture of a Housing Project*. Westport: Greenwood Press.

Rainwater, Lee. 1970. *Behind Ghetto Walls: Black Family Life in a Federal Slum*. Chicago: Aldine.

Rosenberg, Terry J. 1992. *Poverty in New York City, 1991: A Research Bulletin*. New York: Community Service Society of New York.

Ross, Aileen. 1961. *The Hindu Family in Its Urban Setting*. Toronto: University of Toronto Press.

Rule, Sheila. 1982. "Many Families in East Harlem Seek Food Aid." *New York Times*. January 28: p. B1.

Safa, Helen I. 1974. *The Urban Poor of Puerto Rico: A Study in Development and Inequality*. New York: Holt, Rinehart and Winston.

Smith, David B. 1965. *Occupational Multiplicity and the Negro Family in the British Caribbean*. Ph.D. Thesis. Columbia University.

Smith, M.G. 1962. *West Indian Family Structure*. Seattle: University of Washington Press.

Smith, Raymond T. 1956. *The Negro Family in British Guiana: Family Structure and Social Status in Three Villages*. London: Routledge and Kegan Paul.

Van Velsen, J. 1961. "Continuity of Tonga Tribal Society," Aidan Southall, ed., *Social Change in Modern Africa*. Pp. 230-241. London: Oxford University Press.

Young, Michael, and Peter Willmott. 1957. *Family and Kinship in East London*. London: Routledge and Kegan Paul.

4

A Way Out of No Way: Female-Headed Households in Jamaica Reconsidered

Deborah D'Amico

. . .when you look at what black women do, you are looking at people who have to fashion a something else, a way out of no way . . . .We have to do whatever we have to do in order for there to be a new day (Johnson Reagon 1982:85).

Introduction

Female-headed households in Jamaica have been the subject of study, debate and controversy for some time. The perspectives used to examine the existence, frequency and determinants of this household form, however, have varied, and have made different contributions to the anthropological literature. The present vantage point allows us to assess past explanations and descriptions of such households, and to offer a more comprehensive understanding of the circumstances which create and perpetuate the conditions under which female-headed households are most likely to exist and to increase. This effort is motivated by a concern with the poverty associated with many of these households, and not with an attempt to explain the form *per se*.

What We Knew Then

I do not intend a comprehensive review of the literature on family in Jamaica and the Caribbean here; rather, I want to discuss some of the major tendencies which emerge from this literature in a critical way. The purpose is to ascertain what is useful in the current context.

Problems of Social Causation and Historical Derivation

As Edith Clarke stated almost thirty years ago, the Jamaican family cannot be explained in isolation. Thus, monographs describing studies of Jamaican families were usually introduced by a literature review which examined theses regarding New World African families in general. Historical explanations began with the Herskovits-Frazier debate, which counterposed the impact of African cultural "survivals" and of plantation slavery.

In a 1963 review article which discusses the literature on the Caribbean family, R.T. Smith notes that by the early 1950's, the study of contemporary social structure emerged as an alternative to cultural persistence as an explanatory device (R.T. Smith 1971: 453). For example, both Simey (1946) and Henriques (1953) connected the high incidence of female-headed households, or as Simey phrased it, "disintegrate" families, with the existing social and economic conditions of lower-class Jamaicans. What was left unclear, however, was the policy implication of this association.

In discussing family forms found among the poor in his introduction to Edith Clarke's work, M.G. Smith says the following:

> Several of the most intractable social problems that confront West Indians centre on these. . . . patterns of family life . . . .These familial conditions affect labour productivity, absenteeism, occupational aspirations, training and performance, attitudes to saving, birth control and farm development, and to programmes of individual and community self-help, housing, child care, education and the like (M.G. Smith 1966: vi, vii).

Smith also noted that Kerr, a psychologist, attributed to

> such disturbing familial contexts a modal personality type of the Jamaican lower class: characterized by deep-set defensive mechanisms and tendencies to shift blame or responsibility for any lapse or misfortune to other persons or to external circumstances . . . .(Smith 1966: vi).

These statements reveal the confusion in the literature surrounding the causal connection between class and family structure. A heavily moralistic tone contributed to a tendency to see Jamaican family patterns as in part the cause of the lack of economic success on the part of most Jamaicans. Simey, for example, referred to male-headed households as "Christian" (M.G. Smith 1966: ix).

Matrifocality, Male Marginality and the Scientific Correlates of Household Form

Synchronic studies utilizing census or survey data to compare family organization in different communities, in Jamaica as well as elsewhere in the English-speaking Caribbean, were done by R.T. Smith in Guyana (1965), Edith Clarke in Jamaica (1957), and M.G. Smith in Jamaica, Grenada, and Carriacou (1962). The latter also attempted a rural-urban comparison by studying family and "mating" patterns in different kinds of communities in both Jamaica and Grenada.

R.T. Smith (1956) attributed the prevalence of female-headed households to male marginality in the domestic setting; such marginality was explained by the wider social conditions of high unemployment and political powerlessness, on the part of males, obtaining in societies stratified by race and class. Male marginality, in turn, resulted in what Smith termed "matrifocal" households in which women were dominant figures.

M.G. Smith used his data to criticize this conclusion on two bases: first, it was "ethnocentric" in its definition of household and family and did not sufficiently consider "folk" categories for and evaluations of domestic and kin relations. Thus he accused R.T. Smith of ignoring the significance of "extra-residential mating", which he perceived as the predominant mating form among lower-class West Indians. The second basis on which M.G. Smith criticized R.T. Smith was a purely theoretical one; the former felt that explanations which were "intrinsic" to the family system itself were superior to those which found it necessary to refer to "extrinsic" factors, i.e., historically or socially outside of the immediate family structure, such as migration and urbanization. Thus, for M. G. Smith what was important was an explanation of family *sui generis*, which gave primacy to community perceptions and definitions of family and household. He made a careful distinction between internal (community) status systems/norms and external ones (national or implicitly international, since reference is made to colonial and post-colonial relationships) (M.G. Smith 1966:xviii, xix).

Clarke's data were said to validate M.G. Smith's assertion that explanations for family form should be rooted in social (as opposed to economic) structure, which should be investigated in relation to community organization. Her findings that female-headed households were more likely to occur in what M.G. Smith calls a "proletarian" community centered around its relationship to a sugar estate than in a peasant community with lower incomes is triumphantly cited as proof of the poverty of an "economic" explanation (xxviii).

An extensive re-analysis of the literature on family and households in Jamaica and the Caribbean would be instructive not only from the viewpoint of a sociology of knowledge, but as a history of change in what is all too often regarded as a static category--the female-headed household. It is to the credit of earlier investigators that their data still speak to us and that the voices we hear are not only those of the social scientists. Such an analysis is beyond the scope of the present paper, which aims to suggest the direction of our thinking and of our data and its implications for change.

What We Know Now

If we look at the historical development of Caribbean family studies in even a sketchy way, we can see a progression toward resolution of the above warring explanations and toward inclusion of previously opposed analyses within a more comprehensive framework. Recent work in this area builds on theoretical advances and new data generated in the social sciences in the 70's and 80's.

Oppositions between cultural and historical explanations, born in the debate between Herskovits and Frazier, as well as oppositions between national socio-economic factors (R.T. Smith, Henriques) and principles of family structure operating at the community and household level (M.G. Smith, Clarke) are subsumed by careful work and analysis which look at the interplay between concrete historical circumstances and cultural resistance, reformulation and response not only in the Caribbean, but elsewhere. (See, for example, the work of Mair [1974] on women in slavery in Jamaica, Gutman [1976] on the family among the enslaved in the U.S., Sudarkasa [1982] on the continuities shared by African and Afro-American families, and Mintz and Price [1976] on Anthropological approaches to the Afro-American past in the Caribbean.)

Likewise, the notion of social organization as fragmented into domains of causality, such as community/national, social/economic, male/female, public/private, family/society, etc. has been continually re-worked in Anthropology. From Steward's levels of socio-cultural integration, we have moved to analytic frameworks which encompass the global nature of the historical relationships among and within societies (see, for example, Wolf 1984). Similarly, work which focuses on women and/or the family has evolved from a perspective which dichotomized private and public arenas of social life to approaches which look at the nature of the relationships among family and the state, gender and the international division of labor, households and global political economy (see, for example, Nash, Safa et al. 1986, Rapp 1978, Fernandez Kelly 1984, etc.).

Current analyses of Jamaican families build on advances in theory and data generated in the 1970's and 80's, as well as on the questions raised, the patterns noted and the data collected by the pioneers cited above. A deeper understanding of socio-economic trends of the early twentieth century, sophisticated archaeological analyses of plantations, and a closer look at the implications of both slavery and proletarianization for women have generated important contributions to studies of changing family forms.

Such work points to the existence of particular kin arrangements among the enslaved in Jamaica. Both Mair and Higman note that the so-called matriarchal or matrifocal household, that is, one dominated by women, was characteristic of Creole domestic units which had ties to the masters, and not of the majority of slave households (Higman 1976: 161, 168); Mair states that the original Jamaican matriarch was brown and not black (1974:441). Both note the prevalence of "nuclear" households on plantations, and Mair cites evidence for the embeddedness of these households in larger extended kin groups (1974:384), as do Mintz and Price with regard to the post-Emancipation period (1976:39).

Although they do not focus specifically on households, Post (1978) and Beckford (1980) provide evidence for increasing pressures on families during and after the early part of this century. They document the reorganization of agri-culture in Jamaica as a result of the involvement of international monopoly capital. The consequent loss of access to land and the low wages offered to agri-cultural workers meant that families were increasingly hard-pressed. Migration of men abroad in the early part of the 20th Century and of women to towns fragmented the solidary kin groups previously based on family land. Increasingly, women found themselves responsible for the day-to-day survival of themselves and their children, and with lower wages than men and less help from extended families. Evidence from this period makes comprehensible the findings of Edith Clarke regarding a proletarian sugar workers' community, and shows the link between the incidence of female-headed households and the undermining of the peasant land base which accompanied the penetration of the Jamaican economy by U.S. multinationals.

Fit into this analysis, Clarke's finding that female-headed households were common in a community tied to a sugar plantation does not support the primacy of social organization over economic factors, except in the most simplistic way. Rather, this work suggests, as do the newer analyses of kinship among the enslaved, that political economy provides a set of circumstances which condition the ability to sustain permanent and extended kin ties in Jamaica.

Multinational corporate domination of the Jamaican economy and the concomitant political relationship to the U.S. which has characterized Jamaica in the postwar period form the basis of critical development and policy analyses done by "dependency" economists (Beckford, 1972 Beckford and Witter 1980, Girvan, 1973, 1976, etc.) These analyses provide the starting point for new concept-ualizations of women and their relationships to households. They provide a framework for linking color and class stratification in Jamaica to global political and economic trends. When utilized along with some of the contributions from Marxist feminist theory, a powerful synthesis is effected; it then becomes possible to explain households and gender as connected to processes which span the community, the nation and the world. Such explanations allow us to approach with analytic unity what have previously been seen as separate systems or research problems.

Using such a synthetic analysis of capitalist patriarchy, Mies argues that non-wage labor exploitation of both men and women in the Third World, such as informal or subsistence labor, shares with housework a history of exploitation in the process of capitalist accumulation (1986:33). The tendency for women in many Third World countries to be associated with non-wage and low-wage work results from this many-faceted relationship to a global development process which appears to be widening the chasms of race, class and gender. Recent work concerned with female-headed households in Jamaica and the Caribbean docu-ments the region-specific dynamics associated with this kind of development.

Gender Dynamics: The View from the Present

Previous explanations for the existence of female-headed households focused on their association with male unemployment in populations experiencing exploitation on the basis of class and/or race; however, this leaves us wondering why women in the same exploited groups *do* shoulder the responsibility for households. In fact, recent work which highlights the poverty associated with female-headed households has stressed that such poverty is more likely to occur in the absence of a male wage earner precisely because female earnings tend to be *lower* than those of men.

Beliefs about power relationships within the household, gender-appropriate movement and activity outside the household, and different or highly variable responsibilities for housework and child care which are assigned on the basis of gender color the responses of men and women to their particular economic situation and affect the ways in which raising children can be structured within particular circumstances. It is this ideology of gender which current work on women in Jamaica illuminates, revealing the heretofore hidden dimension of gender, along with its integral connection to race and class.

In her article in the WICP volume on family, Durant-Gonzalez draws on her own anthropological work in Jamaica, as well as on survey and field data from elsewhere in the Caribbean. She concludes that employment trends, single parenting, male sharing and the cultural expectation that women should bear and rear children all contribute to a situation in which the majority of Caribbean women bear a disproportionate responsibility for the care and upbringing of children (1982: 1, 3). Moreover, in the Caribbean context, bearing and rearing mean providing for (1982:4). This occurs despite the fact that over 70% of employed women are concentrated in low-paying jobs and that women are much more likely than men to be involved in informal sector activities. Although Durant-Gonzalez found that in Jamaica, women's involvement in marketing (higglering) and motherhood brought status and recognition, and that for Caribbean women an African ideal of motherhood combining the roles of mother and worker obtains (1982:16), she notes that the economic context in which this occurs in practice does not allow adequate provision for the daily needs of households which women are expected to meet. Thus, she concludes that the present-day Caribbean household head is "caught and moved around in a set of conflicting cultural, economic and social forces" (1982:21).

While kin and neighbor networks have been suggested as ways in which women can compensate for shouldering financial responsibilities despite inadequate access to income, such networks have undergone historical changes in their ability to assist members. There is no reason to assume that networks composed primarily of women and of poor men would have access to sufficient resources to compensate for the inequalities of class and race which network members are likely to have in common. Moreover, data from St. Kitts indicate important vari-ation in women's networks according to age; if this is true for elsewhere in the West Indies, women may be only building their networks, rather than experi-encing their full potential, during their early childbearing years (Gussler 1980: 4). Powell (1982) has provided a detailed discussion of network variables and a model for network analysis which will greatly facilitate precision in specifying the density of ties and the value of resources which flow through them. Until we have such specific information on networks utilized by Jamaican female household heads, we cannot afford to be sanguine about the ability of networks to compensate for the inequalities of race, class and gender which these women must bear.

Massiah's paper in the WICP family volume is concerned with the characteristics of women who head households, drawn from regional census data on the Caribbean and from pilot studies of smaller groups of women in particular countries. She concludes:

> . . .females account for about one-third of all household heads in the region. They tend to be older and to live alone to a greater extent than men [who head households] . . . They tend to be less educated than their male counterparts and to be less engaged in paid employment [including self employment] . . . .[and] the pattern of their occupational distribution is markedly different (1982:77). The general picture which emerges is one in which members of the [female-headed] household rely on a single female adult, the mother, to provide daily income (1982:80).

Female Wage and Informal Sector Labor Patterns and Effects on Households

If our concern with female-headed households is motivated by their poverty, rather than by an assumption that this family form is morally or culturally inappropriate, we need to explore the ways in which such households subsist in the economic context of contemporary Jamaica. Labor force statistics from 1985 document the disparity in employment between male and female household heads; the unemployment rate for female household heads was slightly under three times the rate for male household heads (21.7 % as against 7.7%). The unemployment rate for the total labor force was 25.6%; 66.2% of these unemployed were women. While adult women had an unemployment rate of 23.6% (as against 9.2% for men 25 years and older), for women under age 25 the rate was 65.7% (young men had an unemployment rate of 30.4 % during the same period). Moreover, 14.8% of persons counted as working were part-time workers, and 60% of these were women (1986:16). Accompanying these statistics in the latest report by the Statistical Institute of Jamaica was the sobering comment:

> Because of the family responsibilities of household heads, their unemployment situation is also a key indicator from a social welfare viewpoint. When the fact that approximately 18% of unemployed women are household heads is taken into account, the problem of female unemployment becomes even more critical (Statistical Institute of Jamaica 1986:16.7).

The accompanying report suggested that the decline in employment for women over age 25 was possibly a result of contraction in public administration and other service work (1986:16). These factors are in turn related to government decisions to reduce spending in order to meet IMF loan conditions.

During 1985, the inflation rate was 25.7%, while the Consumer Price Index rose 26.8% between 1984 and 1985. Average prices for food and clothing rose "significantly". During 1985, the Jamaican dollar depreciated in value relative to the U.S. dollar from J$4.95 to a low of J$6.40 in October of that year. This devaluation and the rise in prices can also be linked to the influence of the IMF.

The work of Bolles is significant in that it looks at employed working-class urban women, and pays particular attention to the effects on households of factors especially significant in Jamaica and the developing world, notably the implications of conditions imposed by IMF loans and the current international division of labor. She documents the strain which these economic conditions create for the networks which women develop to supplement inadequate wages, and the effects on the way in which households are formed:

> At other times, a woman would have a child for a man, in order to expand her financial network to support her household. Even if the relationship ended, a child could hopefully hold a man financially, if not physically, to the household with child support. But today, with the high rate of unemployment for the population, more men are jobless and with weaker ties even to the informal sector. Therefore, having a baby means creating another drain on the women's scarce resources, which she as primary supporter cannot afford. In addition, the man can no longer fulfill the meagre obligations which he had been able to in the past (1979:23).

In a paper which presents case studies of women in different kinds of households and how they have weathered the Manley and Seaga years, Bolles ties household conditions firmly to factors of global economy and to specific national policy. Such work is invaluable for policymakers who care to heed it, and for women's organizations seeking documentation acceptable to the powerful to demonstrate their case for or against specific programs. In an analysis of economic crisis and female-headed households, Bolles shows how women utilize household membership and participation in both wage work and the informal economy to compensate for their disadvantaged position vis-a-vis wage labor employment (1986).

My own work in Jamaica examines the relationships of women to their households, to participation in the informal sector, and to the kind of planned economic development often proposed as a path to industrialization in the developing world (D'Amico-Samuels, 1986). In the context of a developing tourist industry, women without property in the immediate resort area had access to seasonal, scarce and low-paying wage work, or to informal sector activities, primarily vending craft items, fruit, and soft drinks. Since such selling was technically illegal in most of the resort area, it was a seasonal, precarious and sometimes dangerous way to earn a living. Many women did it because they were either the most important source of support for households or because they were important contributors to households with other low-income earners.

Among the seventy vendors whom I interviewed in a particular craft market, female-headed households (in which one woman lived with her dependent children) and female-headed extended households (in which the oldest family member was an unmarried or widowed woman designated by the vendor as household head, living with one or more of her children, their children, and sometimes their spouses) constituted fully half of all women vendor's households and one-third of the total number of households among vendors of both sexes.

Although their market shops provided the *most* significant income source for the majority of both men and women, there were important gender differences in the relationship of household support to market income. While only 20.4% of women vendors said they could rely on another of their *own* sources of income, more than twice this percentage (44.4%) of men indicated some form of self-support other than the market. Moreover, despite the fact that income from the market might be a woman's most important and only self-generated earnings, this income was more than three times as likely as a male vendor's to fluctuate seasonally.

Data on assistance in the market shops both document the advantage of women's heavier involvement in matrifocal kin networks, and at the same time support the claim that men's shops are more prosperous than women's. Seven of the eighteen shops owned by men had paid employees, while women were more likely to rely on the unpaid assistance of kin, primarily daughters.

Women's greater reliance on matrifocal kin ties, however, can be limiting as well as supportive. As Harrison has pointed out with reference to the informal sector in Kingston, men's access to a wider variety of ties through male peer groups may be a factor in their more lucrative involvement in the informal sector (1983). It should also be remembered that women are very heavily obligated to both older and younger kin, and that what this means for women and their households at different stages of the life cycle remains to be more precisely explored. Moreover, reliance on consanguineal ties or extra-familial networks does not alter the unequal relations of men and women within these groups, nor should it mask the fact that, with regard to household and child maintenance, women family and network members seem to bear the greatest responsibility.

The obligations of women to children and to kin take on greater significance in view of their comparatively limited incomes. Limits on women's income in the market which I studied included the tendency for women to sell cheaper, more redundant items and to cater to the tourist population only. Straw goods and flour sack clothing were the main items in thirty-nine of the forty-nine female-owned shops. An immediate and practical reason for selling this partic-ular combination of goods was offered by the women vendors: "Straw moves faster and costs less." This combination is most advantageous to a woman with countless daily expenses; it enables her to earn a more guaranteed, though smaller, amount of money frequently. Stocking mainly straw and flour sack gives a woman with a limited income more flexibility in building up stock and lower replacement costs. Especially interesting in this regard is the fact that the shops owned by two women partners all fell into the straw and flour sack combination, while none of those in which women were partners with men did so.

The predominant craft combination sold by men included wood carvings and black and brown coral jewelry; only eight of the market shops stocked these as their main items. While the higher price of such items did not automatically guarantee higher incomes for the vendors selling them, the extreme redundance of the straw and flour sack combination militated against lower prices being balanced by a greater quantity of sales for any one woman. Moreover, while only nine of the forty-nine shops owned by women could be described as cater-ing to both the tourist and the local population, fully half of the men's shops were involved in businesses which could be described in this way.

In the market in which I conducted interviews, women clearly specified that their household responsibilities often precluded investing in more expensive items for sale, or in equipment which could generate additional income, such as a sewing machine or a blender. This factor lay behind the differences in shop prosperity between males and females. Income figures for male and female vendors in the market verified the disparities described above. Men's average figures (J$178.50) were greater than women's (J$135.50) by fully $50 weekly.

Although my figures do not allow comparison on the basis of kind of household along the dimensions of gender inequality outlined above, they do illuminate the way in which women fare less well than men in the informal sector. Such disparity has been noted for other parts of the world (Nelson, 1979), and for Kingston in Jamaica (Harrison, 1983). Moreover, my data demonstrate that the reasons for this inequality lie in part in the disproportionate share of responsibility for households which women bear.

Involvement in informal sector activities is widespread among women in the

Caribbean and Latin America; Schmink notes that the majority of work in the informal sector is done by women in these areas (1985:2). Women participate in this sector in order to generate income when wage labor is unavailable or to supplement income if wages are inadequate, especially in the context of austerity programs which reduce the real income of workers. For women, informal labor may also offer a way of combining work with child care and domestic chores.

The tendency for capitalist development projects to exacerbate, rather than ameliorate, inequalities of class, gender and color has been well documented. In the case of Jamaican women who rely on marketing for income, the arena of work they have carved out since the days of slavery is presently being eroded by the "modernization" of marketing. As Massiah states for the region as a whole:

> . . . although women are still found in large numbers in the informal sector, few of them retain prominence in the local food distribution chain. Instead, they are to be found as petty traders lining the streets of the major towns, subject. . .to the vicissitudes of the international monetary economy. At the same time, the decline of the extended family has brought to the forefront the problem of combining income earning and home maintenance activities. For women who head households this represents a crucial consideration (1982:98).

How the Other Gender Lives, or the Not-So-Marginal Male

Every interpretation of female-headed households makes reference to the relationship between this household form and male unemployment (see Blumberg, 1978 for example). What is often obscured, however, are the ways in which male unemployment impacts on households. Men's marginality to the wage labor market should not be interpreted to mean that they are marginal to women or to households. Rather, the ways in which they participate and do not participate, as well as their own interpretations of their roles, are crucial to an understanding of female-headed households. Recent work highlights this relationship from both male and female points of view.

According to Ennew and Young, the importance of cash as a marker of masculine status begins early for Jamaican males, and with very serious consequences for the street boys whom they studied:

> The importance of immediate cash income . . .becomes an early and stultifying influence on the child's view of himself and his life. They may start with higglering or vending, but, if the rewards are too small, they may turn to gambling or stealing . . . .Juvenile offenders who come before family court are mostly boys. Money is the most central and most accessible means they have of making sense of the world (1981:49, 54).

Whitehead's work among Jamaican men indicates that men associate sexual relationships with financial support, saying that women take a man's money at the same time as they take his strength (sperm), and that both children and money serve as symbols of virility (1978: 19-21).

This association of sex with financial support helps explain the rationale for non-support which Jackson encountered in her study of Family Court cases in Jamaica. Jackson reports that non-support of children by fathers was the major concern of Jamaican women seeking help from Family Court, accounting for 70% of the 444 cases which she surveyed. She states that:

> The most frequent reason given by women with respect to the problem of non- support is that after the union breaks down, support for the child or children becomes unreliable or non-existent. This problem holds even with legal unions. According to the women, men tried to link sex with support, and as one expresses it "no sex, no support" (1982:40).

While paternity and money are both related to social status among men and dominance over women, men are conscious of the threat which too many children pose to the provider role (Whitehead 1976, 1978:24). Hence, a man who cannot support his household lives in fear of being cuckolded, as a woman is justified in seeking support (and sex) elsewhere.

Interesting insight into class and gender is gleaned when one considers this association from different points of view. As Whitehead reports, middle and upper-class Jamaican men are more able to fulfill expectations of support from wives and lovers, so their lack of sexual fidelity is condoned. Poor men, however, suffer insecurity about their relationships, since their own beliefs justify infidelity on the part of women with whom they are involved. In this scenario, both poor and better-off women are expected to accept the infidelity of the financially able man, while they remain faithful to him. Poor women involved with poor men may have cultural approval to seek support and sex elsewhere, but they also have to bear responsibility for the children of the men who disappoint them. Children are a likely possibility in such cases as both men and women see them as crucial to binding a relationship.

The traditional West African counterpart to the woman who is both worker and mother was a man who, together with his kin group, made available the means through which women could take on greater financial responsibility for the raising of children than did men (Marshall, 1964: 189, 191, 201). Such male backing for female economic ventures might include land belonging to the patrilineal kin group which a woman could farm, seed capital with which to begin trading, produce grown by the husband which a woman could sell or some combination of these. During slavery the joint working of provision grounds, and after Emancipation the growth of peasant agriculture and of large kinship groups tied to land may have provided the means for men in Jamaica to aspire to this role. However, the undermining of the peasant land base, the increase in migration of both sexes, and the chronic unemployment which have been the results of multinational domination and proletarianization of the Jamaican economy have greatly reduced the male material and emotional support which previously underwrote both traditional and New World African roles. Nor do the standards of capitalist patriarchy offer a respectable place for an unemployed, impoverished male. Men who feel they cannot fulfill either of these provider roles create another male identity, centered around male peer groups and extra-domestic social settings (Whitehead, 1977, 1978; Wilson 1973).

As Whitehead states, women appear to be powerful domestic figures by default, rather than by design. This doesn't mean that individual women don't say they value their independence and wouldn't rather be a household head receiving support from a man than be married to one (see, for example, Massiah 1982: 86). Nor does it mean that men always choose to leave women in such circumstances or to withdraw their support from them. Rather, both men and women make choices within such an impoverished context that default is a better word than choice. Investigation of the connected and often conflicting meanings which color and class factors attach to kinship and sexual relations is an effort which promises complex insight into the interrelation of race, status and gender (see, for example R.T. Smith, 1978 and Brackette Williams 1984).

Discussion

During my fieldwork in Jamaica, the lines of connection among women who head households, the children being raised in them, the men whose circumstances affect them, and the larger political economy in which all these individuals play a part were integral to understanding the poverty associated with female-headed households. Such households have become the arenas most likely to reproduce the inequalities of class, color and gender on which the dangerous polarities of today's world rest. The women who hold such households together, who must find a way out of no way, challenge these inequalities daily. At this point in time, we need analysis which can inform their struggle as well as suggest ways in which we can participate in efforts to alter the political and economic conditions under which such households exist. It is my view that propounding theses that emphasize gender or race or class in a way which masks the indivisibility of these in women's actual lives, or that ignores the international context of households of any type, does not accomplish these aims.

Taken together, the input of the work of the last decade or so has refined our knowledge of the interrelationships among gender, race, class, colonialism, the international division of labor, etc. This work has emerged in the context of the UN Decade for Women, greatly enlarging the chorus of voices to which we must listen if we are to understand the significance of female-headed households, in Jamaica or anywhere else.

Emerging from the trends toward theoretical synthesis cited above are foci on phenomena which seem to capture many complex forces in their explanatory net.

For example, women and development, as a subject for study, forces one to tackle the issues which affect women at the household and community level with tools gleaned from a comparative, historical and cross-cultural literature. Because women's situations are implicitly or explicitly considered against an international backdrop, an analytic search for the commonalities and differences among women of different classes, races, and nations is evident in much of the literature on women and development, as well as among women working in organizations directed toward change.

Perhaps this has contributed to an eagerness to seize on apparent similarity, particularly on the part of women from more privileged races, classes and/or nations. Witness the feminization of poverty thesis, based largely on the rise in the number of female-headed households in the U.S. and on the vulnerability of women, white and black, to impoverishment with the loss of male income through divorce or desertion. Burnham (1982) has identified the major fallacies in this perspective, pointing out that the feminization of poverty analysis obscures class and race differences among women and consequently, among the households of which they are part, regardless of similarities in form. Moreover, such an analysis downplays the extent of poverty among black men. Burnham reminds us that the "emiseration of black women has not been accompanied by a rise to affluence of black men", as has been the case among the white middle class, in which the post-divorce rise in living standards among men has occurred as a consequence of the impoverishment of women and children (1982:17). She cautions that:

> Strategies which seek to unite women across the class spectrum while remaining oblivious to both the peculiarities of the conditions faced by minority and poor women and to the oppression suffered by minority and other working class men have always doomed the women's movement to the perpetual hegemony of white middle class women. The 'feminization of poverty' analysis and strategy promises to be a repeat performance (23-24).

Such criticism should make us wary of trendy topics which attract attention and funding.

Because the female-headed household is the arena in which many women and their kinfolk do battle with the overwhelming and combined impact of color, class and gender exploitation, it has a reality which should concern anyone with a commitment to changing the circumstances which give rise to these forms of exploitation. At the same time, however, we should be clear analytically and politically about what the female-headed household represents. Confusion regarding the race and class differences in frequency and poverty of these households, and/or the historical and cultural circumstances which affect their viability and acceptability easily lends itself to misguided policy, and echoes some of the errors of the early literature on family cited above. For example, it was by abstracting the female-headed household as a form that the erroneous interpretation of gender which labeled black women matriarchs was developed.

When the race and class context of households are part of the analysis, it becomes clear that:

> . . .women are called matriarchs when the power they exercise relative to the men of their own group is in some respect greater than that defined as appropriate by the dominant culture. Given this standard, women need not be the equals of men, much less their superiors, in order to qualify as matriarchs (Lebsock, 1982:272).

We should not have to, in Audre Lorde's words, reinvent the pencil every time we want to send a message. Boserup's work on women and development, the subsequent study of the relationship of gender to economic change, and the critique of Western feminist thinking on this issue by Third World women should instruct us with its history. The movement was from exclusion of women by analysts and planners, to a focus on gender often abstracted from the class, national and cultural realities in which women live. Currently, work by groups such as Dawn point the way toward incorporating analyses of gender within a global framework which encompasses all of these concerns:

> We reject the belief that it is possible to obtain sustainable improvements in women's economic and social position under conditions of growing relative inequality, if not absolute poverty, for both women and men. Equality for women is impossible within the existing economic, cultural and political processes that reserve resources, power, and control for small sections of people. But neither is development possible without greater equity for and participation by women (DAWN 1985: 14).

If we apply such a perspective to the topic of female-headed households in Jamaica, how will our focus, analysis and input into policy be altered? We will focus not on female-headed households per se, but on the dynamics of race, class and gender which together insure that many of these households are poor, and on strategies which acknowledge the contemporary crisis of world capitalism, in which the structural conditions giving rise to the poverty of these households are rooted (Davis 1986: 36, 39).

Any analysis which makes visible the global dimensions of race, class and gender exploitation also prevents us from escaping the choice of our own role in describing such exploitation and the history which associates research with policy. For the Caribbean, women scholars and activists have provided a set of guidelines for planning, doing and disseminating the results of research which addresses women's issues in a regional context of race, class and dependent development (Research and Methodology Work Group 1986). As researchers, we can begin to alter the destructive uses to which social science analyses of female-headed households have been party, by insuring that our work contributes, in its process and product, to the empowerment of poor women and those with whom they share their lives.

References

Beckford, George. 1972. *Persistent Poverty*. New York: Oxford University Press.

Beckford, George and Witter, Michael. 1980. *Small Garden, Bitter Weed*. Morant Bay, Jamaica: Morant Publishing House.

Blumberg, Rae Lesser. 1978. "The Political Economy of the Mother-Child Family," in *Family and Kinship in Middle America and the Caribbean*, V. Marks and A. Romer, eds. Leiden, Netherlands: Publication of the University of the Netherlands Antilles and the Department of Caribbean Studies of the Royal Institute of Linguistics and Anthropology: 526-576.

Bolles, A. Lynn. 1986. "Economic Crisis and Female-Headed Households in Urban Jamaica." In *Women and Change in Latin America*, ed. by June Nash, Helen Safa and contributors. Massachusetts: Bergin and Garvey.

_____. 1985. "Jamaican Women's Strategies and Resources: Surviving Manley and Seaga." Paper presented at 84th Annual Meeting of the American Anthropological Association, Washington D.C.

_____. 1981. *The Impact of Working Class Women's Employment on Household Organization* in *Kingston, Jamaica*. Unpublished Ph. D. dissertation, Rutgers University.

_____. 1979. Kitchens Hit by Priorities: Employed Working Class Jamaican Women Confront the IMF. Paper presented at the Latin American Studies Association Meeting, April 1979.

Boserup, Ester. 1970. *Women's Role in Economic Development*. London: George Allen and Unwin.

Burnham, Linda. 1985. "Has Poverty Been Feminized in Black America?" *Black Scholar* March/April: 14-24.

Clarke, Edith. 1959. *My Mother Who Fathered Me: A Study of the Family in Three Selected Communities in Jamaica*. London: George Allen and Unwin.

D'Amico-Samuels, Deborah. 1986. *You Can't Get Me Out of the Race: Women and Economic Development in Negril, Jamaica, West Indies*. Unpublished Ph. D. dissertation, Graduate Center of City University of New York.

Davis, Angela and Davis, Fania. 1986. "The Black Family and the Crisis of Capitalism." *Black Scholar* 17, 5: 33-40.

DAWN (Development Alternatives with Women for a New Era). 1985. *Development, Crises, and Alternative Vision: Third World Women's Perspectives*. Norway: A.S Verbum.

Durant-Gonzalez, Victoria. 1982. "The Realm of Female Familial Responsibility." In *Women and the Family* (Women in the Caribbean Project, Volume 2): 1-27. Barbados: Institute of Social and Economic Research (ISER), University of the West Indies (UWI) at Cave Hill.

Ennew, Judith and Young, Pansy. 1981. *Child Labour in Jamaica: A General Review*. London: Anti-Slavery Society.

Fernandez-Kelly, Maria Patricia. 1984. *For We Are Sold, I and My People: Women and Industry in Mexico's Frontier*. Albany: State University of New York Press.

Frazier, E. Franklin. 1966. *The Negro Family in the United States*. Chicago: University of Chicago Press.

Girvan, Norman. 1973. "The Development of Dependency Economics in the Caribbean and Latin America." *Social and Economic Studies* 22 (1): Special Issue on Dependency and Underdevelopment in the Caribbean.

_____. 1976. *Corporate Imperialism: Conflict and Expropriation*. New York: Monthly Review Press.

Gutman, Herbert. 1976. *The Black Family in Slavery and Freedom 1750-1925*. New York: Pantheon.

Gussler, Judith D. 1980. "Adaptive Strategies and Social Networks of Women in St. Kitts." In *A World of Women: Anthropological Studies of Women in Societies of the World*, Erika Bourguignon, ed. New York: Praeger.

Harrison, Faye. 1983. "Toward a Perspective on Women in the Jamaican Urban Informal Economy." Paper presented at conference entitled Common Differences: Third World Women's Perspectives, University of Ilinois at Champaign-Urbana.

Henriques, Fernando. 1953. *Family and Colour in Jamaica*. London: Eyre and Spottiswood.

Herskovits, M.J. 1941. *The Myth of the Negro Past*. Boston: Beacon.

Higman, B.W. 1976. *Slave Population and Economy in Jamaica 1807-1834*. Cambridge: Cambridge University Press.

Jackson, Jean. 1982. "Stresses Affecting Women and their Families." In *Women and the Family:* 28-61. Barbados: ISER, University of the West Indies at Cave Hill.

Johnson-Reagon, Bernice. 1982. "My Black Mothers and Sisters or On Beginning a Cultural Autobiography," *Feminist Studies* 8,1.

Lebsock, Suzanne. "Free Black Women and the Question of Matriarchy: Petersburg, Virginia 1784-1820," *Feminist Studies* 8,2.

Lorde, Audre. 1984. *Sister Outsider*. Trumansburg, N.Y.: The Crossing Press.

Mair, Lucille Mathurin. 1974. *An Historical Study of Women in Jamaica: 1655-1844*.
Unpublished PhD. dissertation, University of the West Indies at Mona, Jamaica.

Marshall, Gloria (Niara Sudarkasa). 1964. *Women, Trade and the Yoruba Family*. Unpublished PhD. dissertation, Columbia University.

Massiah, Jocelyn. 1982. Women Who Head Households. In *Women and the Family*: 62-130.
Barbados: ISER, University of the West Indies at Cave Hill.

Mies, Maria. 1986. What is Feminism? In *Patriarchy and Accumulation on a World Scale: Women in the International Division of Labor*. London: Zed Books.

Mintz, Sidney W. and Price, Richard. 1976. *An Anthropological Approach to the Afro-American Past: A Caribbean Perspective*. Philadelphia: Institute for the Study of Human Issues.

Nash, June, Safa, Helen eds. 1986. *Women and Change in Latin America*. Massachusetts: Bergin and Garvey.

Nelson, Nicci. 1979. "How Women and Men Get By: The Sexual Division of Labor in the Informal Sector of a Nairobi Squatter Settlement." In *Casual Work and Poverty in Third World Cities*. R. Bromley ande C. Gerry, eds. Chichester: John Wiley and Sons.

Post, Ken. 1978. *Arise Ye Starvelings: The Jamaica Labor Rebellion of 1938 and its Aftermath*.
The Hague: Institute of Social Studies, Martinus Nijhoff.

Powell, Dorian. 1982. "Network Analysis: A Suggested Model for the Study of Women and the Family in the Caribbean." In *Women and the Family*: 131-162. Barbados: ISER, University of the West Indies at Cave Hill.

Rapp, Rayna. 1978. Family and Class in Contemporary America: Notes toward an Understanding of Ideology. *Science and Society* 42: 2778-300.

Research and Methodology Work Group. 1986 Policy Statement. Mt. St. Benedict, Trinidad: University of the West Indies Women's Studies Program Inaugural Seminar.

Schmink, Marianne. 1984. "The Working Group Approach to Women and Urban Services." N.Y.: paper prepared for *Ekistics* special issue on women and available from Population Council/USAID.

Simey, T.S. 1946. *Welfare and Planning in the West Indies*. Oxford: University of Oxford Press.

Smith, M.G. 1966. "Introduction." In *My Mother Who Fathered Me* by Edith Clarke (sixth impression, 1979). London: George Allen and Unwin.

_____. 1962. *West Indian Family Structure*. Seattle: University of Washington Press.

Smith, R.T. 1978. "The Family and the Modern World System: Some Observations from the Caribbean." *Journal of Family History* 3: 337-360.

_____. 1971. "Culture and Social Structure in the Caribbean: Some Recent Work on Family and Kinship." In *Peoples and Cultures of the Caribbean*. M. Horowitz, ed. New York: Natural History Press.

_____. 1956. *The Negro Family in British Guiana*. London: Routledge and Kegan Paul.

88

Statistical Institute of Jamaica. 1986 *Economic and Social Survey of Jamaica 1985*. Kingston, Jamaica: Planning Institute of Jamaica.

Sudarkasa, Niara. 1982. "African and Afro-American Family Structure." In *Anthropology for the Eighties*, Johnnetta B. Cole, ed. New York: Free Press.

Whitehead,Tony. 1978. "Men, Money and Mating: Symbols of Masculine Strength in a Jamaica Sugartown." Paper presented at 77th Annual Meeting of the American Anthropological Association, Los Angeles, California.

_____. 1977. Men, Family and Family Planning. Paper presented at the 76th Annual Meeting of the American Anthropological Association, Houston, Texas.

_____. 1976. *Men, Family and Family Planning: Male Role Perception and Performance in a Jamaica Sugartown*. Unpublished Ph. D. dissertation: University of Pittsburgh.

Williams, Brackette. 1984. "Hegemony and Ideological Resistance in the Cultural Production of Ethnicity in Guyana." Paper presented at 83rd Annual Meeting of the American Anthropological Association, Invited Session on Culture and Historical Materialism, Denver, Colorado.

Wilson, Peter. 1973. *Crab Antics: The Social Anthropology of the English Speaking Caribbean*. New Haven: Yale University Press.

Wolf, Eric R. 1984. *Europe and the People without History*. Berkeley: University of California Press.

Women and Development Studies Group, University of the West Indies 1986 *Policy Statement, Report of the Research and Methodology Working Group to the Inaugural Seminar of the University of the West Indies Women's Studies Programme*. Trinidad: ISER, Uuniversity of the West Indies at St. Augustine.

5

Caught in the Shift:
The Impact of Industrialization on
Female-Headed Households
in Curaçao, Netherlands Antilles

Eva Abraham

Introduction

The establishment of a Shell refinery at Curaçao, in 1918, was followed by a period of prosperity. Full employment for men coupled with social benefits for wives and legitimate or recognized children of workers on the one hand, and the relative economic marginalization of women on the other, led to an increase in the percentage of marriages, while the percentage of children born to unmarried mothers[2] decreased. After 1952, however, this trend started to reverse.

In the sixties employment for women appeared to stimulate the restriction of births through the use of contraception. Formal employment also proved to be a great stimulus for women's activities in the informal economy. After 1980, with general economic decline and soaring unemployment for women and men, a large number of female-headed households has emigrated to the Netherlands. This article sketches changes in the position of women, and dwells in particular on the impact of economic developments on marriage rates and percentages of children born to unmarried mothers.

Before Industrialization

Because of poor soil and irregular rainfall, plantations never flourished and were often rather a status symbol than a source of income. Until the 1920's the island's economy was based on large-scale international trade and shipping, operated by a small group of elite white families. Within these elite groups there was a highly patriarchal family system. Women were subordinated to their husbands and fathers and their primary biological and social roles were those of wife and mother of legitimate heirs. In the black population, however, many households had a female head, who often was the chief provider for herself and her children. Men in various roles (father, husband, son, brother, lover) might make material contributions to one or more housholds (Abraham-Van der Mark 1973:155). In the beginning of the century, however, because of the constraints of poverty, many men were forced to emigrate, often leaving women behind to fend for themselves.

Before industrialization came to the island, women performed many of the agricultural tasks, engaged in crafts such as weaving straw hats for export, and sold agricultural products, fish, homemade foodstuffs, and handicrafts. Apart from their important economic roles, they played a leading role in rites of passage, in various voluntary organizations and as healers and specialists in *brua*, which includes both black and white magic.

The prestige and authority of women as mothers and as focal role bearers in the kinship network is celebrated in a great variety of old songs, proverbs, sayings and expressions in *Papiamentu*, the local language of the Dutch Leeward Islands. Similar indications of men's position are lacking. Women held the family together during slavery and afterwards. The emotional bond between mother and child was and still is strong, intense and permanent. There is a saying that a child without a mother is food for the *warawara* (a bird of prey). Adult men used to lament their miserable existence after their mother's death in such songs as: "Ai, Dios, my mother has died; ai, Dios, I have no longer a mother in this world, a stray dog is better off than I am" or "If my mother were still alive, I would not roam about drinking rum and having nowhere to go" and "Who will wash my clothes? Who will do the ironing? I'm a desperate and destitute man: I have lost my mother."

The sexual alliances between men and women, on the other hand, were often not enduring and marriage was the exception rather than the rule. During slavery the focus of the family was a woman with her children, as slaves were not allowed to marry. Next to the slaves there were the free "people of color" who formed a considerable part of the population. Although they were not excluded from marriage, they did not take the institution for granted either. Father Latour, describing the baptismal register of Dr. Antonio Navarro that covers the period from February 1758 to April 1759 writes that of the 1189 people baptised by Navarro only 53 were born within wedlock. He concludes that it was characteristic of the 18th century that only 5% of all children were born to legally married parents.

The government seems to have been indifferent. Requests made by the militant priest (later bishop) Niewindt to allow slaves to marry, and not part couples by selling them separately, were neglected. Niewindt writes (1828): "The prohibition to marry was thus maintained and the majority of the population forced to live in a state of immorality". Although in the decades preceding Emancipation priests were occasionally allowed to marry slaves, such marriages had no legal value. In the *History of the Mission of Curaçao* written by "Some Dominican Priests" it is emphasized that after Emancipation, the Roman Catholic Church continuously tried to put pressure on officials, whom they reproached for "allowing many concubinages to continue through their absolute lack of interest".

In 1864, one year after Emancipation, children born to unmarried mothers in the total population were estimated to be over 81%. This percentage declined slowly, to 80% in 1875, 69% in 1884 and 62% in 1894.

In order to promote legal marriage the Roman Catholic Church introduced and maintained a number of cruel, punitive measures against the offspring of those "living in sin". Children born outside marriage had to be baptised separately from those whose parents were married: before dawn or after sunset, and not on Sundays; the usual candles had to be omitted, as well as the ringing of church bells. Moreover, these children were allowed to have a godmother but no godfather. These rules were maintained until the 1950's.

Industrialization: The Shell Refinery

After the establishment of the Shell refinery in 1918, dramatic changes occurred. The immigration of thousands of laborers and an increasing number of births caused rapid population growth. Moreover, the great variety of national and ethnic groups among the newcomers resulted in a complex system of social stratification. The majority of the immigrants were intended to be nonpermanent residents, to be disposed of whenever it suited the management. They were both socially and physically segregated (Van Soest 1976: 242-249). Gradually, however, the number of local men employed by Shell became considerably larger, and by the late 1940's, as the percentage of local workers continued to increase, Shell launched a series of measures offering material rewards to legally married couples. Indeed, this seems to support June Nash's observation that to service and maintain a male work force:

> The family is implicitly recognized as a cheap solution, as revealed by industrial managers' attempts to foster the nuclear family by subsidizing reproductive costs and direct payments to workers for family dependents. (1976:8)

Legal wives and children of employees were given medical care and, after 1950, when their husband/father died they received a pension. Moreover, married couples were given the opportunity to buy houses on attractive terms. Later more benefits were added. On top of that management addressed each laborer who was known to live in concubinage, pointing out that it is a man's moral duty to support his woman and children and make sure that they will have some income after his death. Other companies launched similar measures and some of them considered children of unmarried couples who had been recognized by their father as legitimate. According to a former personnel manager of Shell, many workers responded by getting married. Unfortunately data on their numbers and on those of recognized children are not available.

Interviews, however, revealed that there were various cases similar to that of Lucila Rogelia, who had only the three eldest of her nine children officially recognized by their father. She explained:

When the three eldest were born my man worked for X and we got free medical treatment for the children. After he lost that job recognizing the other children did not make sense, it did not make any difference. (Abraham-Van der Mark 1973)

Indeed, in the years that followed industrialization legal marriage became more prevalent, the percentage of female-headed families decreased, and the rate of children born to unmarried mothers went down from 52% in 1920 to 23.9% in 1952. Compared to various Caribbean societies where the percentage of children born outside marriage has always exceeded that of those born within marriage (such as Antigua, Barbados, Haiti, Jamaica, Surinam) this percentage is quite low.

Three tables show the impact of the Shell refinery on marriage and births to unmarried mothers. Table 5.1 shows an increase in the rate of marriage; from 3.6 per 1000 in 1915 to 9.4 in 1935.

Table 5.2, depicting the course of the number of births differentiated according to those within and those outside marriage over the years 1911 to 1968, shows a decline in the percentage of births to unmarried mothers, a decline that became clear only after 1924. This continued until 1952, when the percentage of 23.9 was reached, that is lower than those of all preceding and following years. It can hardly be considered as pure coincidence that this low percentage was reached in 1952, 5 years after Shell introduced free medical care for laborers' wives and children born within marriage, and 2 years after the establishment of the pension fund for widows and orphans born within marriage or recognized, at which time all those known to live in concubinage were addressed and encouraged to change their way of life and get married.

If the number of people employed is taken as an indication of the expansion of the Shell refinery (table 5.3) it appears that 1952 is the peak year with 11,014 employees and workers. One year later this number has already decreased, a development that accelerated after 1957. At the same time the number of illegitimate births started to increase.

Between 1957 and 1966 the number of laborers employed by Shell decreased from 4896 to 3314, a difference of 1582. The impact of these layoffs was drastic as the labor force of Curaçao, that is, the percentage of the population that in active on the labor market, is relatively small. This is partly explained by the age distribution of the population, which is characterized by a high percentage of children under 16 as well as the relatively young age (55) at which people retire.

The kinship network traditionally functions in such a way that, as a rule, everyone who has an income provides, wholly or partially, for various others, children as well as adult relatives. Incomes are pooled within as well as distributed over various households, as members may have dependents do not live with them. This implies that one dismissal hits many people.

The increase of marriage and decrease of births to unmarried mothers between the twenties and fifties must, at least partly, be explained by the social benefits offered by Shell and other companies. However, it appears to be also a result of the total exclusion of women from the industrialization process. The oil refinery with its highly mechanized production techniques provided no employment for lower-class women. Although some females were hired as secretaries, typists, and analysts, the production department proved to be a totally male enterprise. Women were neither employed by the British Phosphate Company on the island nor by the various shipping and construction companies. The activity of companies in the latter sector increased as a result of the general economic prosperity due to the Shell refinery.

TABLE 5.1 Marriages in the Afro-Caribbean Population of Curaçao, 1870-1944

Year	Population	Marriages	Number per 1,000
1870	28,380	177	6.2
1875	35,127	192	5.5
1880	36,492	182	5.0
1885	36,000?	170	4.7
1890	40,000?	183	4.6
1895	42,000?	229	5.5
1900	44,000?	225	5.1
1905	45,656	179	3.9
1910	46,817	180	3.8
1915	50,605	183	3.6
1920	57,171	246	4.3
1925	57,030	414	7.3
1930	64,014	503	7.9
1935	69,199	653	9.4
1940	80,112	651	8.1
1944	96,188	645	6.7

Source: History of the Mission in Curaçao, p. 4.

Industrialization also brought with it the end of agriculture and crafts in which women had played an important role. Moreover, the traditional female terrain of small trade was taken over by males of new ethnic groups that had settled on the island or foreigners who regularly visited the island to provide the market with new supplies. Thus, women were left with only a few economic tasks, and

TABLE 5.2 Children Born to Unmarried Mothers, 1911-1967

Year	Total	Illegitimate	Percentage
1911	976	-	-
1912	863	477	55.3
1913	857	422	49.2
1914	979	502	51.3
1915	701	367	52.4
1916	997	310	51.1
1917	1080	566	52.4
1918	1109	537	48.3
1919	1025	504	49.2
1920	881	454	51.4
1921	856	-	-
1922	1010	458	45.3
1923	1258	602	47.9
1924	844	394	46.6
1925	1302	556	42.7
1926	1139	499	43.8
1927	1197	477	39.8
1928	1566	635	40.5
1929	1609	657	40.8
1930	1801	694	38.5
1931	1514	547	36.1
1932	1575	584	37.1
1933	1578	568	36.0
1934	1819	648	35.6
1935	1623	570	35.1
1936	1875	594	31.7
1937	1789	613	34.3
1938	1822	546	30.0
1945	2653	720	27.3
1946	2834	782	27.6
1947	2979	780	26.2
1948	2970	753	25.3
1949	3185	779	24.4
1950	3479	838	24.1
1951	3531	873	24.7
1952	3662	875	23.9
1953	3821	943	24.7
1954	3803	932	24.5
1955	3850	1093	28.5
1956	3874	973	25.1
1957	4277	1152	26.9
1958	4280	1142	26.9
1959	4317	1162	26.9
1960	4410	1232	27.9
1961	4324	1182	27.3

(continues)

Table 5.2 *(Continued)*

1962	4378	1249	28.5
1963	4246	1254	29.5
1964	4078	1178	28.9
1965	3883	1201	30.9
1966	3390	1139	33.6
1967	3376	1178	34.9

Sources:
1. Before 1930 Colonial Reports (Kolonie Verslagen)
2. 1931-1950 Report on the Netherlands Antilles; Vol.II, Annual Statistical Report
3. 1951-1960 Statistical Yearbook of the Antilles, Department of Economics and Welfare
4. 1961-1991 Central Bureau of Statistics

Table 5.3 Number of Workers Employed by Shell, According to Nationality

Year	Foreigners		Europeans		Antillians		Other		Total
	N	%	N	%	N	%	N	%	N
1948	4733	46	792	8	3677	36	1100		10,302
1949	4358	46	750	8	3371	35	1041	11	9,520
1950	4701	47	791	8	3478	35	1067	10	10,037
1951	4774	46	839	8	3703	36	1089	10	10,405
1952	4806	44	878	8	4208	38	1122	10	11,014
1953	4578	43	928	9	3945	37	1165	11	11,616
1954	3920	39	905	9	4109	41	1117	11	10,051
1955	3546	36	948	10	4252	43	1099	11	9,845
1956	3363	33	1013	10	4777	47	1008	10	10,161
1957	3200	32	983	10	4896	48	985	10	10,064
1958	2932	30	949	10	4775	50	923	10	9,579
1959	1841	24	782	10	4415	56	800	10	7,838
1960	1232	18	655	9	4329	63	673	10	6,889
1961	752	12	544	9	4275	70	564	9	6,135
1962	595	10	483	8	4282	73	520	9	5,882
1963	425	8	396	7	4037	76	451	9	5,309
1964	298	6	313	7	3752	79	397	8	4,760
1965	154	3	244	6	3528	83	339	8	4,265
1966	129	3	220	6	3314	84	299	7	3,962
1967	--		--		--		--		--
1968	--		--		--				3,880

Source: Shell Curacao, Personnel Management

became a reserve labor force to be used or cast aside in accord with economic needs. More and more articles that used to be homemade and sold by women were replaced by machine-made substitutes. The worker and his family in their capacity as consumers were first discovered by foreign peddlers and then other merchants, who invented the most seductive systems of installment purchase from which they reaped enormous profits.

While the earnings of more than 1.000 Shell laborers and employees, as well as many others who participated in the system of production, caused a rise in the general standard of living, there was also a concomitant increase in the cost of living. On the other hand, however, women's access to subsistence opportunities decreased, which, together with full employment for men, caused an increase in the gap in earnings between men and women. Ideally, women were now to be confined to marriage and children. For those without formal training or education -- that is, the large majority -- possibilities to earn money became limited to domestic work, selling sweets and cakes, and the trade in legal and illegal lottery tickets.

For the least-valued female occupations, sleep-in maids and prostitutes, women were brought in from outside the island: black domestics from the British islands, brown prostitutes from Cuba, Santo Domingo, and Colombia. Prostitution was set up as a highly profitable government-sponsored enterprise, providing a number of men of different socio-economic strata an attractive extra income. The advantage of importing domestics and prostitutes was that when their services were no longer needed, these women had no right whatever to stay on the island and could be disposed of without any problem. Even today foreign domestics who become pregnant are immediately repatriated.

Marginalization of Women and Increase in Legal Marriage

Blumberg and Garcia (1976) have formulated four "conditions" for the emergence and prevalence of female-headed households which are ultimately related to the mode of production. Empirically, these conditions focus on: 1) the demand for female labor in the society's major productive activities; 2) the compatibility of women's economic activities with simultaneous child-care responsibilities; 3) the compensation received by women for their participation in production both at an absolute level and in proportion to the compensation of the men of their class; and 4) the level and availability of alternate sources of income aside from women's own economic compensation, such as welfare, children's earnings, and so forth.

I shall now consider to what extent these conditons obtain in Curaçao. As is shown in this chapter, the demand for female labor in this society's major productive activities is quite low. Generally speaking, the close-knit social network of relatives among Curaçao's black population provides facilities for childcare, thus freeing some women for economic activities. Writing on Barbados, Sutton wrote (1977:306): "A job or career for a woman is never spoken of as an alternative to marriage or maternity. Although it is realized that a woman's responsibilities might necessitate her withdrawal from work for short periods, the 'dual career' conflict experienced by women in industrial societies is not marked. This reflects not only different expectations and assumptions about a woman's economic and social roles but also the presence of a family and kinship system that acts as a support for women of all ages." This also holds true for Curaçao.

After the establishment of the oil refinery, women's access to subsistence opportunities has continuously declined, and their financial resources are considerably lower than those of men of the same class, when they do obtain employment. My interviews with 375 families in Curaçao (Abraham-van der Mark 1973) revealed a direct relationship between female-headed households and poverty. Although most female heads of households in my sample received some financial contribution from a man, nearly all of them had a very hard time making ends meet. Moreover, male support may be withdrawn, especially if the man is not a legal husband. I quote my informant E.S.: "After the birth of the fifth child, it really became too much for him; he left and I have not seen him since."

For many female-headed households in the 1960's and 1970's the old-age pension of a living-in maternal grandmother was the only income that could be counted on, since the earnings of most women were irregular and unpredictable. All incomes in this category were considerably lower than in the male-headed households. Thus, as women's position becomes marginal, their dependence on men's earnings increases. In many cases marriage enabled a woman to obtain a standard of living that she would seldom have acquired if she had been forced to fend for herself. But in order to maintain this standard of living, a woman is dependent on the stability of marriage. Thus, the imbalance in the economic potential between husband and wife may be an explanation of Curaçao's low divorce rate (that is, until the eighties). As Blumberg suggests, when a woman's own economic possibilities are poor and the likelihood of her finding another man with a stable job is not very great, a woman married to an employed man will try to preserve the marriage.

In the late fifties, as a result of automation and other causes, the prosperity brought by Shell suddenly came to an end. There were large-scale layoffs and a rapidly increasing structural unemployment developed. This has had far-reaching effects for women, whether they were married or not. With or without the presence of a husband, it is taken for granted that earnings of children living in the household are controlled by their mothers. A woman's position becomes more and more stable and autonomous as her children start working. Adult sons who have left their mother's house often feel a lasting obligation to give her financial support, which sometimes may lead to tensions between mothers and daughters-in-law as they compete for a man's earnings. In the early 1990's, because of increased unemployment all of this has become more problematic.

In the late 1960's cutbacks at the oil refinery caused severe insecurity and frustration among workers as well as among those who had been laid off. As Shell put out to contract more and more maintenance and repair work, people who had lost their jobs at the refinery were now performing the same tasks for various companies who had been given the contracts by Shell, but at much lower wages. Escalating labor conflicts and the failure to reach an agreement on a collective labor contract resulted in a general strike that was accompanied by severe riots in May 1969, during which a good part of the island's capital was burned down.

Women did not actively participate in this strike, which was an outcome of conflicts in an economic sector that exclusively employed males. The impact of these riots has been considerable, such as a new evaluation of being black or colored as opposed to being white, a stronger position for the unions, and a number of social welfare measures. However, these welfare measures apply only to members of the labor unions, which increases the marginalization of the unemployed and those irregularly employed; this is particularly true for women.

Texas Instruments

Because of a rapidly deteriorating economic situation in the late sixties, a development program, drawn up by the Stanford Research Institute, was recommended for Curaçao in which electronic assembling industries were encouraged to settle on the island. These electronic assembling plants were able to take advantage of a special U.S. regulation that limits the import tariffs on products assembled abroad by American companies to an assessment based on the increased value (Kok 1974:46). A campaign was started to attract this type of industry, and the availability of a large reservoir of cheap female labor was strongly emphasized as one of the attractions. Thus, Curaçao presents a good illustration of how certain types of industry prefer males and other type prefer females (see Ramos 1970: 155-156), and at the same time shows that the preference for one sex over the other is not necessarily related to certain stages of the development process.

Four companies were seriously interested; but when they discovered the existence of unions and a minimum wage structure, one of these industries withdrew at the last moment to settle in Jamaica. Of the three corporations that did come to Curaçao, Texas Instruments, Schlumberger, and Rockwell, the latter moved out of Mexico when the ILO rule prohibiting the employment of women in night shifts became operative in that country. Rockwell and Schlumberger closed their establishments in Curaçao after only a few years.

Texas Instruments settled in Curaçao in 1968 and exported all of its products. To encourage it to come to Curaçao, it was given several advantages (Kok 1974:57) such as: a ten years' tax holiday; permission to leave Curaçao at will; buildings to be constructed for the company by the Curaçao government and let at a minimal rent. Although Texas Instruments is definitely an industrial company, it was classified in the lowest minimum-wage category, which is usually accorded only to companies providing services. This implied that in its first year the company paid its workers monthly wages of A.F. (Antillean florin) 175 ($91.62), the same salary as that of a full-time domestic worker. Gradually wages were raised to A.F. 320 ($167.54) in 1976. Texas Instruments provided employment for 1,600 women, who were hired for the assembly of semi-conductors.

This highly monotonous assembly-line work demands a great deal of accuracy. The women worked in three shifts: 8 A.M. to 4 P.M., 4 P.M. to 12 A.M., and 12 A.M. to 8 A.M. Wages were the same for the three shifts, and a major disadvantage was that assignment to a shift was permanent, so that women in the night shift had to remain in it for years without any hope for change. Although the work was dull, extremely fatiguing on the eyes, and poorly paid, it was highly valued, both because of the regular income and the many social contacts at work. Headaches and eye infections were not seen as a policy issue of the company but as the personal problems of the women concerned.

The importance of the company to the Curaçao economy was minimal (Kok 1974:57). Its contribution to the national production was quite small. It employed only unskilled workers receiving minimal wages, and it offered little stable employment.

The management of Texas Instruments resisted union organization but finally gave in (Verton 1977:90). However, when forced to accede to union demands for higher wages, the management first laid off some workers and then reduced the work force permanently. In 1976, only eight years after its arrival but with the end to its tax holiday imminent, the company closed its doors and left the island.

The six hundred women still employed at that time, nearly all single women who were the sole or main provider for their children and in many cases for other relatives as well, were discharged without any compensation. The union that represented them participated in the negotiations that were aimed at keeping the plant on the island, or at least getting compensation for the workers who were fired. However, it was completely powerless because the right to leave Curaçao at will was one of the conditions that the company had set upon its arrival and that had been accepted by the government. Reasons given for the departure were the general slackness in the American electronics industry because of Japanese competition, and more particularly the fact that in 1975 France, one of the company's foremost clients, raised the tariffs for semi-manufactured articles produced in other countries of the European Economic Community (to which Curaçao belongs as an associate member).

Despite the disadvantage of the firm to the local economy, other governments approached Texas Instruments asking for the relocation of the factory in their countries on conditions that were even more favorable than those which had been met in Curaçao. Amongst these was the Haitian government, which guaranteed female workers for wages that were only 20% of those paid in Curaçao, as well as the prohibition of unions. The Curaçao plant, however, was not relocated but simply shut down.

A small survey undertaken by Cuales in 1977 gives a glimpse of the impact of employment by Texas Instruments on the women involved. First, data from the local Foundation for Family Planning showed an increased use of contraceptives by the employed women (Cuales 1977:44-45). Moreover, regular employment provided an impetus for these women to search for still other means of increasing their incomes (Cuales 1977:53-61). A few women tried to earn extra money by sewing, washing and ironing, in addition to their fulltime jobs at Texas Instruments. But in particular the traditional female domain of petty trade was given new life when these women met a large reservoir of potential clients at work: legal and illegal lottery tickets, foodstuffs of all kinds, clothing, jewelry, and craft products were sold within the factory. Sometimes the sellers even acted as agents for female relatives or friends. An astonishingly large variety of items was sold on credit, with accounts to be settled on payday. Many rotating credit associations were organized as well.

In short, entrepreneurship flourished. This did not, however, affect women's work on the assembly line, as the Curaçao plant of Texas Instruments proved to be the second in productivity (output per worker) among the company's plants, a plant in West Germany being the first. After the Curaçao plant was closed down, women decreased their commercial activities or gave them up altogether, because they lost the numerous social contacts with potential buyers as well as the money to invest in merchandise.

Interviews with a number of women who had worked at the company showed that their pattern of consumption, especially for expensive items, had changed (Cuales 1977:61). They had purchased refrigerators, stoves, furniture and cars. This may seem incredible considering the low wages, but in all cases these commodities had been bought under a very easy system of installment purchase. However, as a consequence of this installment buying, many women had large debts when they lost their jobs.

After Texas Instruments

Of the women who were discharged in 1976, only a few have found other employment. Some became street sweepers; but the majority, at least 50 percent of those employed by the electronic industry, have emigrated to the

Netherlands where they benefit from the material security of the welfare state (verbal communication with Mr. Martina, Office of the Delegate Minister of the Netherlands Antilles, The Hague 1981).

The majority of the forty-three women who were interviewed in Curaçao by Cuales felt resentment about their sudden dismissal, but said that they would not hesitate to go back to Texas Instruments or any other firm if that were possible.

> If Texas or whatever American company comes here tomorrow, I'll be the first one to start working for them. I'd rather start today than tomorrow and I do not want to work for eight years as I did for Texas but for twenty years or more (Cuales 1977:60).

In the seventies female participation in politics, which has always existed, increased. Female ministers are no longer exceptional, and the present (1991) prime minister, Maria Liberia, is a distinguished senior politician who has already served twice before in the same position.

The government has passed and enforced certain laws which are aimed at the diminishing of inequality between the sexes. Moreover, women appear to have acquired a new militancy. They started working in jobs that before were exclusively male, such as police, custom officers, and guards, in addition to street sweepers. The number of women working in tourism and in shops and boutiques that sell clothing and articles of luxury to tourists increased in the seventies. Curaçao, as well as St. Maarten and Aruba, boast of being unique in employing women as croupiers in their casinos. It appears, however, particularly in casinos, that exploitation of women occurs (see Kagie 1981). Then there have always been two ways of social mobility open to a limited number of women. One is through the patronage system of a political party. Political activity and loyalty may be rewarded by a job, even if one is not qualified for the particular work. However, this may be risky, because today's winner is tomorrow's loser. The other way is selling illegal lottery tickets (Jacobs 1987). A few women have acquired a small fortune in this way. They provide something for which many people on the island have a great passion and for which the demand seems to increase as the economy gets worse. In January 1988 the illegal but firmly established lottery called "number" became legalized. Now those selling the lottery tickets are liable for income tax.

The 1980's have still to be described. It is, however, undeniable that they are characterized by economic decline. Unemployment soared (from 20% in 1980 to 29% in 1989) after the departure in 1984 of the two big oil refineries, Shell and Lago, and their many subsidiaries, from Curaçao and Aruba. However, when Shell closed its doors a Venezuelan corporation called PEDESEVA took over the refinery and has kept it functioning, although on a much smaller scale and with considerably fewer workers who receive few social benefits. In Aruba tourism compensates for some of the jobs that were lost when the Lago refinery closed down. In Curaçao the large sums of tax money paid by foreign off-shore companies, which provided an important percentage of the national income in the seventies and early eighties, fell largely away because of legal changes that are curtailing such businesses. (See Kagie 1982 for information on the off-shore businesses in Curaçao). The devaluation of the *bolivar* in 1983 made Curaçao less attractive for Venezuelan shoppers and as a consequence many shops were closed. Considerable amounts of Dutch development money are coming in annually, but the way they are spent is often criticized and unskilled women are not among those that benefit from these funds. The ideology behind development policy aims at women's integration into the existing development process, which is predicated upon prevailing structures of inequitable distribution of resources between women and men. Recently the government of the Netherlands Antilles introduced a law offering highly attractive tax privileges to wealthy retired Europeans. Some of the conditions these people have to meet are investing a certain amount of money in a house and employing a full-time domestic servant at the minimum wage of A.F. 355 per month (approximately $170). This provides some women with a job.

Today (1991) women make up 40% of the labor force and are increasingly participating at the middle and even higher levels of both the public and the private sector. Many of them have been able to attain positions of influence and responsibility. Yet statistics of labor force participation indicate that socio-economic conditions continue to restrict women's participation and limit their mobility. (For women in the labor market in Aruba see J.R. Nicolaas 1990). Men are disproportionately represented in administrative decision-making jobs while women fill the service and clerical jobs. With few exceptions women tend to receive lower salaries than men with comparable qualifications doing similar work. The more educated women remain concentrated in the fields of education, nursing and social work which are the lowest paid.

Moreover, the number of uneducated, unskilled women at the bottom of the social hierarchy has increased considerably. The macro-economic development of the 1980's has had a deleterious effect on them and they are becoming more and more marginal. In 1989 the unemployment rate for women was 37.8% compared to 26.3% for men. In 1991 a new definition of "unemployed" has been introduced, restricting the term to those who have applied for work in the previous month. This results, of course, in lower unemployment rates that mistakenly suggest economic improvement.

Half of all unemployed women are 15 to 25 years old and face a bleak future. In this category the unemployment rate is 58.8%, compared to 51.8% for men of the same age. In 1990, of the female heads of households, only 24% were formally employed, compared to 58% of the male heads. Statistics indicate that the relatively slight economic decline after 1988 hit women harder, as between 1988 and 1990 formally employed female heads of households decreased 4.4%

compared to a 0.6% decrease in formally employed male heads. A small survey carried out by Van't Hoofd and Westerlaken (1989) shows that the majority of these women cannot make ends meet and depend on support of relatives to survive. Moreover, many of them live continuously in debt. One of the women they interviewed stated that if she had more money she would buy a mattress and paint her room: "I have washed the walls, but I have no money for paint. And I have always wished to give a birthday party for my daughter. I have never been able to do that" (1989: 110).

Considerably more women than men of all age groups are looking for employment, yet many, especially the older women among them, have given up being registered as "unemployed and in search of work". In general, many people prefer looking for work through their social network instead of using the services of the Department of Labor (de Jong Van Dijke, Koopman, 1980).

As for family life, the proportion of female-headed households increased in the 1970's and remained stable in the 1980's (30% of all households) due to the fact that many of these women felt that they had no options in Curaçao and migrated to the Netherlands. They usually arrive with high expectations but many of them are forced to become dependent on a new pater familias, the state. Welfare provisions in this country are much better that in the Antilles but because of cuts and new policies the Dutch welfare system is being restricted. Good educational facilities for children in the Netherlands are often mentioned as another advantage of settling in this country, but it appears that a large proportion of Antillian male adolescents get involved in petty and not so petty criminal activities. According to the media this has now become a major problem. However, data giving evidence that the proportion of young Antillians with a criminal record is larger than that of native Dutch of the same age group are not available.

The Curaçao divorce rate has gone up and the marriage rate has decreased. The prognosis is that the number of people who will not get married during their lifetimes is increasing (Van Leusden H., 1985), and the percentage of children born to unmarried mothers that has grown steadily since 1952 (when it was 23.9%) is, in recent years, rising more rapidly. In 1989 it was 54%.

The relationship between the decreasing marriage rate and the increasing percentage of children born to unmarried mothers on the one hand and economic factors on the other has yet to be studied, as findings that applied to the situation in the late sixties do not hold in the nineties. The family network, for example, has changed, and while people depend on it more than ever, it appears to be less able to cope with adversity and poverty. This may be explained by the growth of poverty as well as by certain government policies (such as particular housing projects and welfare provisions) that appear to stimulate a process of individualization.

TABLE 5.4 Percentages of Children Born to Unmarried Mothers

Year	Percentage
1969	33.6
1970-74	34.0
1975	35.8
1976	37.8
1977	38.2
1978	42.2
1979	42.7
1980	45.4
1981	46.8
1982	47.9
1983	49.1
1984	48.5
1985	52.7

Source: NIDI, Fertility trends in Aruba and Curaçao, Hans van Leusden, working paper no. 58.

One other change is that, unlike in the sixties, living together as an alternative to legal marriage is no longer associated exclusively with the lower socio-economic strata. Van Dijke and Terpstra (1987) state that the pro-portion of those living together has increased in all income groups. The mothering role continues to be highly valued.

These changes need to be analyzed and, moreover, a theoretical framework has to be developed that is capable of explaining women's and men's independence and dependence in Caribbean society. Such a framework has to include the study of men. To answer the question "Where did all the men go?" it is necessary to get an understanding of the prevailing gender ideology, the roles of women and men, and the changes in the relationships between the sexes (see Anderson, Barrow, Dann).

Curaçao provides an example of the marginalization of women under capitalism: from slavery up through industrialization we see that women's position is not necessarily based upon family demands, for the family structure itself may be determined by the marginal role of women in a particular economic system (see Saffioti 1978). The position of women in the lower socio-economic strata has gone from relative autonomy to increasing dependency.

To summarize, women have lost their autonomy. Though they have always depended on their social networks because of increasing poverty, since the 1960's these networks have been stretched continuously until today many of them have broken down. Unskilled women with young children have no options on the labor market. Of those who have migrated to the Netherlands, many have become dependent on the welfare society.

105

Notes

1. With special thanks to Kenk ten Napel, Central Bureau of Statistics, Curaçao, Netherlands Antilles. Statistics have, unless stated differently, been taken from the Central Bureau of Statistics.
2. I am grateful to Barbara Katz Rothman for pointing out to me that the terms illegitimacy and illegitimate children are negative and stigmatizing. Therefore I will refer to births of children of unmarried mothers.

References

Abraham-Van der Mark, Eva E. 1973. *Yu'i Mama, Enkele facetten van gezinsstructuur op Curaçao*. Assen:Van Gorcum.
--------. 1983. "The impact of Industrialization on Women: a Caribbean Case." In *Women, Men and the International Division of Labor*, Eds. June Nash and Maria Patricia Fernandez-Kelly. Albany: State University of New York Press.
Anderson, Patricia. 1986. "Conclusion: WICP" in *Social and Economic Studies*, vol. 35, no. 2.
Barrow, Christine. 1986. "Male Images of Women in Barbados", in *Social and Economic Studies*, vol. 35, no.3.
Blumberg, Rae Lesser with Maria Garcia Pilar. 1976. "The Political Economy of the Mother-Child Family: A Cross-Societal View." In *Beyond the Nuclear Family*. ed. L. Lenero-Otero. London: Sage.
Cuales, Sonia M. 1977. Verslag van een leeronderzoek naar de positie van de Curacaose vrouw die bij Texas Instruments heeft gewerkt in de periode van 1968-1976. Unpublished report, Leyden.
Dann, Graham 1987. *The Barbadian Male: Sexual attitudes and practice*, Macmillan.
De Geschiedenis van de Missie op Curaçao (History of the Mission), door enkele Paters Dominicanen. Curaçao, 1945.
Jacobs, M. 1987. *De illegale nummerverkoop op Curaçao: 'bendementu di number'*. Unpublished manuscript, University of Amsterdam, Anthropological-Sociological Institute.
Jong, M. de, Dijk, T. van, Koopman, G. 1981. *Senor(a) ta traha?* Curaçao: University of the Netherlands Antilles.
Kagie, R. 1981. "Traditie, Hanen, en Roulette." In *N.R.C,/Handelsblad*, May 12th.
Kagie, R. 1982. *De laatste Kolonie, de Nederlandse Antillen: Afhankelikheid, belastingprofijt en geheime winsten*. Bussum: Het Wereldvenster.
Kok, Michiel 1974. *De Economische Struktuur van de Nederlandse Antillen*. Curaçao: St. Augustinus.
Latour, M.D. 1951. *Pro-Kathedral St.Anna, 1752-1952*. Curaçao.
Van Dijke, Anke and Terpstra, Linda 1987. *De positie van jonge, ongehuwde vrouwen met kinderen, uit de lagere sociaal ekonomische strata op Curaçao*. CARAV, Leyden.
Nash, June. 1976. "A Critique of Social Science Roles in Latin America" In *Sex and Class in Latin America*, eds. J. Nash and H. Safa, Pp.1-21. New York: Praeger.
Nationale Advies Raad voor Ontwikkelingssamenwerking.1978. *Advies Nederlandse Antillen*. The Hague: Ministerie van buitenlandse Zaken.
Nicolaas, J.R. 1990, in Rose Marie Allen, Paul van Gelder, Mike Jacobs, Ieteke Witteveen (eds.), *Op de bres voor eigenheid, afhankelijkheid en dominantie in de Antillen*. Working group on the Caribbean, University of Amsterdam.
Ramos, Joseph R. 1970. *Labor and Development in Latin America*. New York: Columbia University Press.
Saffioti, Heleieth 1978. *Women in Class Society*. New York: Monthly Review Press.

106

Sutton, Constance and Markiesky-Barrow, Susan 1977. "Social Inequality and Sexual Status in Barbados." In *Sexual Stratification: A Cross-Cultural View*, ed. A. Schegel, pp.292-326. New York: Columbia University Press.

Van 't Hoofd, Danielle and Westerlaken, Jolanda 1989. *Arm om arm, ongehuwde moeders met onderstand op Curaçao*. International development Information Network, Tilburg.

Van Leusden, Hans 1985. "Fertility trends in Aruba and Curaçao between 1900-1974." Working paper no. 58. Voorburg, NIDI.XX.

Van Soest, Jaap. 1976. *Olie als Water. De Curacaose economie in de eerste helft van de twintigste eeuw*. Curaçao: Centraal Historisch Archief.

Verton, Peter. 1977. *Politieke dynamiek en dekolonisatie, de Nederlandse Antillen tussen autonomie en onafhankelijkheid*. Alphen aan de Rijn: Samson.

6

Some Conceptual Issues:
Female Single-Parent Families
in the United States

Anne Okongwu

The sharp and steady increase in female-headed households in the decade between 1970 and 1980 stimulated a resurgence of interest by social scientists and policy makers in female single-parent families. This shift in the composition and organization of the American family, combined with the escalation in poverty among women and children, was of particular concern because although this dual phenomenon of female headship and poverty transcended racial, class and regional boundaries, it was disproportionately distributed among the Black and White population. It was in this context that the term "feminization of poverty" emerged, a term designed to capture and stress the declining economic position of women, which Stallard, Ehrenreich and Sklar described as follows:

Two out of three poor adults are women and one out of five children is poor. Women head half of all poor families: 50 percent of white children; 68 percent of black and Latin children...100,000 additional women with children fell below the poverty line each year from 1969 to 1978. In 1979 the number surged to 150,000 and was matched in 1980. Households headed by women - now 15 percent of all households - are the fastest growing type in the country. (Stallard, Ehrenreich and Sklar, 1983: 6-7)

Although this focus on the escalation in poverty among women and children proved useful in alerting the general public to the vulnerability of female-headed households, the concept "feminization of poverty", by giving primary attention to gender, masks important differences in the vulnerability of women of different races and classes to poverty. Thus it acts to obscure the critical importance of the interaction of race and class relations in the United States in conditioning the degree to which families of all types, and female-headed families in particular, are at risk of falling into poverty. (See Burnham 1985, and Baca Zinn 1989 for a fuller discussion of this issue.)

Moreover, despite the recognition that the number of white female-headed households outpaced black female-headed households in growth during this period and that more of these families were becoming poor, little attention was given until the mid-1980s to differences in the poverty experiences of black and white female-headed households. In particular, the differences in the ways in which the change to single-parent status affects the onset and duration of poverty among black and white female-headed households were hardly discussed. (See Bane 1986 for a discussion of these differences.) Failure to attend to these important issues can lead to the false conception that female-headed families are roughly a homogeneous group, with similar experiences and problems which can be addressed through uniform public policies.

The statistics generated during this period demonstrate that the growth in female-headed households extended across racial and class boundaries. For example, between 1970 and 1982 white and black female-headed households increased from 7.8 percent to 15 percent and from 30.6 percent to 46.5 percent respectively (Cummings 1983). However, primary social research and public policy attention continues to be given to black welfare dependent families. Given the higher proportion of female-headed families among the black population, and their disproportionate representation among the nation's poor, this focus of inquiry, while important, does not allow for exploration into the similarities and differences in the needs and experiences of black and white single-parent families of differing socioeconomic positions, nor does it deepen our understanding of the ways in which the historical interaction of race, class and gender relations acts to shape the contours of contemporary family life among female single-parent families.

This chapter explores the ways in which race, class and gender relations are experienced in the daily lives of contemporary female single-parents in the United States. This ethnographic study employed in-depth open-ended question-naires, and careful analysis of the kinship/friendship network system of each of the families, to explore the similarities and differences in the ways in which nineteen mothers generated income to support their families while simultaneously organizing child care, child rearing and domestic activities. The study also gives attention to the degree and types of contributions of the children's fathers, and the ways in which they were integrated into the organization of these activities.

The data which serve as the basis for the discussion were gathered from nineteen black and white female single-parents of differing socioeconomic positions between 1980 and 1983. The women were divided into three categories based on their occupational status: 1) Professional mother working full-time (4 black and 4 white); 2) mother working full time while involved in career-ladder situations (4 black and 3 white); and 3) mothers receiving public assistance (2 black and 2 white). The discussion begins by articulating some of the limitations inherent in the concept "female-headed family" and the ways these limitations were addressed in this study. This is followed by a description of Philadelphia (the context of the study) and a discussion of some of the major findings of the research along with their implications.

The Concept "Female Single Parent": Some Limitations

The study demonstrates that there is a wide range of variation among female single-parent families. As a result the terms "female single-parent family" and "female single-parent household" may obscure more than they clarify. These concepts, in and of themselves, do not reveal the gender or number of adults actually involved in the processes of providing economic support to the household, nor do they indicate how child care, child rearing, and domestic activities are carried out. Further, these terms do not provide a sufficient basis for determining the socioeconomic position of the family. The data suggest that the most important distinguishing characteristic of female-headed single parent families is that the mother has the ultimate responsibility for insuring economic support for the family and for determining the organization of child-related and domestic activities.

For example, one black professional mother who participated in the study lived with her son in a rented house. However, since becoming a single parent, she has always arranged to live close to her parents and her brother's family. Each morning, before she obtained a car, she rode to work with her parents, dropping her son off at school on the way. After school her son attended a structured after school program. If she was delayed at work, or if there was a school holiday or early dismissal, her son went to the home of his uncle, who live four doors away from their house, to stay with his aunt who was a housewife and his cousins. In addition, her parents are close and regular participants in child care and child-rearing activities. They also provide economic support when needed. The child's father has remarried and lives in another state with his new family. It was agreed that he would not send regular child support, but would send financial help when able. In addition, he speaks with his son on the phone, and the child spends some part of long holidays with his father's family every year. In this female-headed household, four other adults are regularly involved in child care and child-rearing activities. This support has been essential for the mother's occupational mobility and the economic stability of the household. This example and many others in the study give some indication of the wide range of variability in the organizational patterns of female-headed households and the numbers of adults involved in assisting the mother to carry out child care, child-rearing, and economic activities.

Close examination of these families, as well as a recently completed study of sixty female headed families in New York City (Okongwu 1992) suggests that the central difference between this family type and the legally designated two-parent family is that in the two-parent family, the mother has a legal and moral claim on her husband's income on a regular basis, even if this claim is not realized. Her access to this income becomes tenuous if the husband leaves the household. Even if the husband continues to contribute to the household, there is no guarantee that this support will be reliable. As a result, his contribution is voluntary, *de facto*, no matter what civil statutes apply. This is demonstrated by the nationally high rates of non-payment of child support. As a result the mother, as a single parent, must depend upon her own income-generating activities (Burnham 1985; Hansen, written personal communication).

A clear understanding of these points has important policy implications, given the growing numbers of female-headed households and their concentration at the lower levels of the economic scale (see Epstein 1979; Johnson 1980). This positive correlation between female single-parents and poverty has led some researchers to follow the direction of Moynihan's 1965 report which focused on family structure as the most important variable responsible for poverty and poverty-related problems among female-headed families (Moynihan 1965; Kilson 1981; Murray 1984). However, it is important to keep in mind, as we address the problems confronting female-supported households, that gender and family structure in and of themselves do not necessarily cause poverty. Instead, we argue that poverty results from the interaction of the historical development of structures of inequality in operation within a given society. These become intensified through articulation with systems of inequality, exploitation, and incorporation generated by expanding international capitalist development. Thus, in our examination of female single-parent families in the United States we stress the importance of the interaction of structures of inequality, i.e. race, class and gender, rather than family structure in and of itself as the primary factors which condition the standard of living and quality of life of women and children.

The impact of these sets of social relations is reflected in the disparity between the wages of men and women, and black and white workers, as well as the uneven distribution of poverty among single-parent families. For example, Johnson, comparing male and female-headed single-parent families, states:

> The proportion of families below the poverty line that were maintained by a mother was nearly three times that of families maintained by a father only (42 and 55 percent respectively) (Johnson 1980: 22).

Further, although there is a higher rate of poverty among female single-parent families than among single-parent and two-parent families headed by men, the distribution among white and black female single-parent families is also uneven. A report issued in 1980 (the initiation point of this study) stated that the rate of black female single-parent families living in poverty was significantly higher than that of white female-headed single-parent families: 58% and 38% respectively (Community Nutrition Institute *Weekly Report*, September 1980). The disparity in income between black and white female-headed single-parent families is further demonstrated when their median incomes are compared. In 1980 the median income for black female-headed households was $7,425, while for white families it was $11,905 (McGhee 1984). This is related to the fact that although until recently black women had a higher rate of labor force participation than white women, they were concentrated in lower levels of the occupational scale and consequently had lower incomes (Wallace 1980).

The ability of families with two potential wage earners to have higher incomes, and the ability of males (particularly white males) to realize higher incomes mitigates against the effects of class, race and gender in determining the higher standard of living of two-parent families. However, the fundamental problem i.e. social inequality based on sex, race and class, is not eradicated. These sets of social relations are also manifested in disparities in income between black and white two-parent families. For example, in 1982 the median income of two-parent black families was $13,598; during this same period the median income for two-parent white families was $24,593 (Vaughn-Cooke 1984).

Census statistics demonstrate that this pattern of income disparity has remained constant. In 1986 the median income of two-parent black families, although higher in 1982, was significantly lower than that of comparable white families. For black two-parent families the median income was $26,586, while for white two-parent families it was $33,800. During this same period the median income for white female-headed households was $15,716 and for black female-headed households was $9,300 (Bureau of the Census Current Population Reports, Series P-23, No. 146, 1986). Further, in reference to discussions of family structure and poverty it is important to note that in 1986, 44 percent of families living in poverty in the United States were two-parent families (Bureau of the Census 1986). These statistics demonstrate that the problem of poverty is not restricted to any particular family form. Moreover, the focus in the literature on poor female single-parent families runs the risk of centering the discussion of poverty among women and children on only a segment of this population. Thus the term "feminization of poverty," like "female single-parent family," masks the important class dimensions that determine the standard of living, not only among women and children, but also among the men who are connected to these families.

This problem is partially addressed in this study through including black and white mothers of differing socioeconomic positions in the sample. The families were not treated as isolated units, but as units embedded in a complex kinship and friendship network system. Special attention was given to variations in the composition and content of material resources, services, and information exchanged through the social network systems of the mothers. An attempt was made to explore the degree to which the standard of living, lifestyles and future life chances of these families were conditioned by race and class variables. Careful attention was given to the ways in which these social relations were mediated through the family's kinship/network system in a context of shifting government socioeconomic and political policies.

The term "income generation" was selected in order to allow for the examination of both the informal and formal ways in which income was generated to support the standard of living of the family. A distinction was made between the concepts "life-style" and "standard of living" in order to separate the subjective and objective dimensions of choices made by the mothers in relationship to family living. In the context of this study, "life-style" was defined as the choices made within the constraints imposed by the human and material resources available to the family. In contrast, "standard of living" was viewed as the resources utilized, given the full range of resources available within a given social context. Thus differences in the standard of living of families in the American context are seen as being linked to social mechanisms governed by race, class and gender relations. These result in differential access to the society's goods, services, information and other resources.

Female-Headed Single-Parent Families in a Dynamic Context

The context for the study was Philadelphia, Pennsylvania, a traditional eastern city in the United States. The choice of Philadelphia between November 1980 and December 1983 proved to be a particularly appropriate context for a study of this type. The period was characterized by radical changes in political, economic and social policy brought about by the election of Ronald Reagan as President of the United States. This resulted in drastic cuts in social programs on the Federal, State and City levels. At that time Philadelphia was the fourth largest city in the United States, with a population of 1,688,210 (U.S. Census Report, 1980). However, its population was declining in response to the changing opportunity structure in the city brought about the national transformation in the economic structure from an industrial to service economy. Philadelphia, an old traditionally industrial city, was particularly affected by these changes.

In January 1981, the unemployment rates were high and continued to rise during the data collection period. In 1980 the unemployment rate was 7.8 percent in Pennsylvania and 7.5 percent in Philadelphia. By the first quarter of 1983, these rates peaked at 11.2 percent for the country and 20.6 percent for the nation's black population (Vaughn-Cooke 1984). During this period Pennsylvania had one of the highest unemployment rates in the country (14.3 percent), while the unemployment rate in Philadelphia during this period was 10.8 percent. In addition, Philadelphia had the unwelcome distinction of having the highest rate of black unemployment among the nation's ten largest cities (Perry 1981). This is particularly significant when it is taken into consideration that roughly 40 percent of the city's population is black.

The female unemployment rate in Philadelphia was also high. In 1983, the unemployment rate for the total female population was 13 percent. Among the black and white female populations the rates were 17.7 and 10 percent respectively (Office of Employment Security, 1981). These rates were reflective of the steady closing of factories, supermarket chains, and small businesses. For example, it has been estimated that between 1970 and 1980, 140,000 manufacturing jobs were lost in Philadelphia (Hershberg 1981).

Philadelphia also reflected the national rise in female single-parent households. Between 1970 and 1982 there had been a national rise of both black and white female-headed households. For white families the percentage had increased from 7.8 to 15 percent, and for black families, from 30.6 to 46.5 percent (Cummings 1983). In 1980, 17 percent of white families and 52 percent of black families in Philadelphia were female-headed (Cazenave 1983).

The extended examination of these nineteen female-headed families demonstrates the importance of studying families within an international, national, and local context. On the national level, the process of capitalist development in the United States has created particular forms of urban development (Gordon 1978). These combine to structure the dynamic context in which people organize and experience their families. Philadelphia today is a post-industrial city in the process of restructuring its economic base. Between roughly 1930, when the city began the process of transformation, to 1980, there were major changes in the city's productive base, and the composition of its population (Hershberg 1981). The period is characterized by an initially slow, but steadily escalating decline in the manufacturing sector. Industries moved to industrial parks outside the city, and then to other parts of the country and the world in an effort to reduce the production costs. The black population rose to 40 percent, and in addition there was a flow of Asians and Hispanics into the city. The decline in the manufacturing sector resulted in a serious decline in employment for semi-skilled and unskilled workers, precisely the occupational sector that a high proportion of the new migrants to the city were best able to fill.

The natal families of these nineteen mothers had been differentially incorporated into this process. The historical interaction of race, class and gender had given rise to differential opportunity structures, which in turn resulted in their differential incorporation into the social structure. Thus the specific ways in which these families experienced the transformations in the economic, social and political climate differed. This point can be best illustrated through some actual examples drawn from natal family histories of a few of the mothers.

1. Katie, a 26-year-old white mother with a four-year-old daughter, is working full-time in a career-ladder situation (salary $16,000 per year). Her maternal grandmother had migrated with a sister from an upstate Pennsylvania community to work in a factory at age fourteen. She met her husband, also a factory worker, in Philadelphia, married and had three children. One of her daughters, Katie's mother, after completing a few years of high school, also married a factory worker, Katie's father. Although he had not completed high school at the time of marriage, he later completed high school and was trained as a draftsman. Katie's mother never worked outside of the home. The family lived in a house they were purchasing in a predominately white working-class neighborhood in Philadelphia. Katie is the oldest of their six children. She began working part-time at a residential home for retarded children while still in high school. About a year after she graduated, her aunt, a clerk, helped her to get a job as a "wire girl" in the private investment company where she worked. At twenty-one, while still working, and unmarried, she became pregnant and chose to have her child. After the birth of her daughter she applied for public assistance, which provided the major source of financial support for her household. Members of her father's family, her mother, brothers and maternal grandmother helped with some babysitting and other services, such as shopping, washing of clothes for the baby, and small amounts of money ($5-$10 at a time). During that period, Katie also applied for student financial aid to attend college part-time. Two years after the birth of her child she stopped school and returned to her job in the same investment house. However, she was dependent on government subsidized day care for her daughter in order to work.

2. Sarah, a black mother in the career-ladder category, belongs to a family that migrated from the south in the mid-1940s. Her father found a job in a factory, and later married her mother whom he met after she came to Philadelphia from his home state. Later he joined the military, and after returning home they had two children. He again found a job in another factory, and they bought a house in black working-class neighborhood. During the time the children were growing up their mother always worked part-time as a domestic worker. While the children were in high school she completed practical nurse training. Sarah went to college after completing high school and worked part-time during her second year. She completed two years of college before the birth of her son. While pregnant, she applied for public assistance in order to have access to medical care, since

she received no health coverage from her part-time job, and was no longer covered under her father's health-care plan. She remained on public assistance for about two years after the birth of her son. Her parents and her son's father provided some financial assistance, although the child's father was not working full-time when the baby was born. They also helped with the purchase of major items for the baby and the apartment and helped with child care. Sarah returned to full-time employment at the Philadelphia Board of Education at a salary of $9,396 per year when her son was two years old. Her son's father paid for child care and continued to help with major clothing purchases for his son. When she decided to return to school, her parents helped with school costs, and her mother picked up her child from nursery school daily. She also gave the child dinner and put him to bed on the nights Sarah went to class. Shortly before completing her B.A. degree, Sarah was laid off from her job because of budget cuts. While she was unemployed, she was dependent on unemployment compensation and related government subsidies, buttressed by financial help from her parents and son's father, who at that time was still not fully employed.

3. Natasha, a white mother in the full-time professional category earning $25,000 from her primary job, was the daughter of a first-generation Russian immigrant. While growing up she lived in New York, first in the Bronx, and later in an affluent Westchester community. Her father was a college graduate, and after the birth of his two daughters he completed law school at night while working full-time. He later became a prominent tax lawyer. Natasha married after completing three years of college. While married, she had three children and completed her B.A. degree. After separating from her husband (a psychologist), she was able to complete her Ph.D. Her mother, who was a widow at the time of the separation, was still living in New York. She was concerned about providing continuity of care for her three young grandchildren while her daughter worked full-time and recognized the importance of Natasha continuing school and completing her Ph.D. for job security and occupational mobility. She addressed these concerns by paying for a full-time live-in housekeeper to care for the children while her daughter worked and completed her degree. Natasha explained that this enabled her to put in the additional time at her job that helped her to achieve occupational mobility, and to complete her degree, knowing that her children were being well cared for. At the time of this study, she was able to depend on regular child support and support in child-related areas from her ex-husband, as well as financial support from her mother and sister in times of financial crisis.

These few examples are reflective of the wide variation in natal family histories among the mothers who participated in this study. Attention to these variations provides some understanding of the ways in which these families became incorporated into the occupational structure of Philadelphia during the 1940s and early 1950s. To some extent, we are able to gain insights into the ways in which race, class and gender shaped the choices these families were able to make in the areas of employment, housing and education for themselves and their children. Further, they demonstrate important differences in the ways in which families organized themselves in the process of carrying out family life. For example, we are able to see how the class location of the natal families shaped the educational choices of the fathers in these natal families, and the ways in which these choices conditioned their integration into the occupational structure.

Also reflected in even this small sample is the historical difference in work patterns among black and white married women. Among the black families in this study, almost all the mothers of the participants worked outside their homes at least part-time at some point while their children were growing up. Among the white families, regardless of the class location of the family, only a few (3) of the mothers of the participants worked outside their homes. This pattern reflects the historical pattern of economic survival among black families in the United States. The lower wages of black males in relation to their white counterparts at each level of the occupational scale has resulted, until very recently, in black married women having a much higher labor force participation rate than their white counterparts (Mullings 1986; Wallace 1980).

The particular resources held by these natal families are reflected in the resources they were able to share with their daughters when they became single parents. In most cases, these intergenerational exchanges importantly conditioned the strategies that the mothers, as single parents, were able to employ to realize occupational mobility, economic stability during times of financial crisis, and the organization of child care arrangements. Moreover, these case studies underscore the necessity of examining female single-parent families within the context of the social network system in which they are embedded.

Current Options and Strategies

There were also important differences among these nineteen families in:

1. Placement in the occupational structure and employment histories;
2. Income-generating strategies;
3. Range and types of government subsidies utilized;
4. Composition of their kinship/friendship network systems; and
5. Content of exchanges transmitted through their kinship/network systems.

The data strongly suggested that these variables importantly conditioned the actual standard of living of these families, and their degree of vulnerability to the radical shifts in the economic, political, and social policies during this period. The following instances are representative of some of the ways that these mothers were affected by these policies:

1. Several of the mothers became unemployed or experienced the serious anxiety of expecting to be laid off from their jobs.
2. One mother, a sales representative for a large national food company, experienced a reduction in income and possibility for promotion due to the high unemployment rates and the closing of stores in the low-income area where she represented the company. In this instance, additional pay and promotion were dependent on meeting and exceeding set area quotas in sales.
3. In cases where mothers lost their jobs, they had serious difficulty finding other comparable employment.
4. Cuts in the work incentive program connected to Aid to Dependent Families, and changes in the requirements for government subsidized child care for pre-school children created serious problems for one mother returning to full employment after several years of welfare dependence. In this instance, these cuts almost resulted in her leaving her job. These cuts also affected several mothers who were attending school full-time in preparation for full-time entry into the work force.
5. Reductions in food-stamp allotments were directly felt by two mothers, one receiving unemployment compensation, the other primarily dependent on public assistance.

A review of the sample families' experiences during this period shows important differences in the effect of these shifts on their households. The mothers who were least affected were 1) a high-grade federal government employee, and 2) two mothers who worked in the private sector providing services to financially secure populations. In this group of eight women, seven of them were embedded in financially secure kinship/friendship network systems. The other eleven mothers were affected to varying degrees. The mothers who were most seriously affected were those who were most dependent on government subsidies for the essentials of life, and who were embedded in kinship/friendship network systems that were unable to provide financial assistance or a range of required services. In this heterogeneous group of female single parents, the data clearly demonstrated that family structure was not the sole determinant of how or of the degree to which these families were affected during this period of economic stress.

Some Limitations of the Use of Income Education and Occupation as the Determinants of Class Location

Key to the previous discussion was the importance of including the variables of race, class and gender in discussions of contemporary families. In this regard, the study of these female single-parent families provided some valuable insights into the limitations of using occupation, income and education as the sole determinant of class status. The use of only these indices in the American context, in addition to ignoring the historical dimension of class location, also focuses on current individually held attributes, and thereby separates individuals from the families to which they belong and the sets of social relations through which their class positions are actualized. For example, a focus on only these variables does not allow for the inclusion of intergenerational transfers of wealth or assessment of the range and types of material resources, services and information that families actually have access to and the means through which they gain access to social resources. This limits our understanding of the range and degree of social resources actually available to individuals and families, and the ways in which these determine their standard of living and life chances. These points will be further illuminated by the discussion that follows.

The nineteen families in this study showed a wide range of variation within and between occupational categories. The criteria used to make comparisons were:

1. Residential area;
2. Household furnishings and appliances
3. Household help;
4. Range of choice available in diet, clothing, services and educational opportunities for themselves and their children;
5. Organization of household activities; and
6. Organization and amount of money spent on social activities and experiences for themselves and their children.

In many instances there appeared to be sharp incongruencies between the family standard of living and the stated income from the mother's primary income-generating source (job or public assistance). Some examples were

1. A white professional mother (Ph.D., job income $25,000, 3 children) realized a much higher standard of living than a black professional mother (M.A. plus 30 credits, job income $35,000, 1 child);
2. A black mother, completing a B.A. degree (income source public assistance, 1 child) realized a significantly lower standard of living than a white mother (also completing a B.A. degree with 1 child);

3. A white mother (career-ladder situation, B.A. degree, job income $13,000, 1 child) had a higher standard of living than a black professional mother (completing a B.A. degree, job income $26,000, 2 children).

In this study these differences were more frequently demonstrated along racial lines. However, given the limited number of families studied and the selection process, these same variations could have occurred within the same racial grouping. The critical point being stressed here is that the range of variables used to explain these variations had to be expanded beyond education, income and occupation in order to more accurately locate these families in the class structure. In this regard, three other factors were included: 1) natal family and resources (including opportunities and experiences) shared with the mother during various stages in life; 2) training and employment history; and 3) composition of the kinship/friendship network systems and content of the material resources, services and information that pass through them.

In addressing this problem it was necessary to look beyond the stated income generated from the primary generating source, to the *process* of income generation. This approach allowed for the examination of income from this and other sources, including formal and informal work-related fringe benefits. These were then integrated with resources, services and information transmitted through the mothers' social network systems, and those emanating from the state. This proved useful in determining the range and types of material resources, services and information that the families actually had access to and the means through which they gained access.

In all nineteen cases, the families were embedded in a complex network system of kin and friends. A varied range of resources, services and information passed through their network systems. These flows importantly conditioned the mother's personal income-generating strategies (occupational choices, work histories, etc.) and the level and types of subsidies which the family applied for and received from the state. All of these combined to determine the standard of living realized by the family and the content and organization of child care, child rearing and domestic activities.

Careful examination of the families' social network systems suggested that there were fundamentally two types: 1) Heterogeneous network systems (those composed of people of differing socioeconomic positions, skills and life experiences); and 2) Homogeneous network systems (those composed of people with similar socioeconomic positions and life experiences). Heterogeneous network systems tend to provide a wider range of resources and information. These may act to expand the range of resources, services and information to which the members have access. In contrast, homogeneous network systems may act to enable members to make more effective use of resources to which they have access, but do not expand the total pool.

TABLE 6.1.a. Professional White Mother, Director of the Learning Center of a Private University, Ph.D., Recent Stated Income $25,000, Three Children

Resource	Integration	Source
1. Full-time, live-in housekeeper for 1st few years after separation from her husband	Allowed her to keep her job and engage in career mobility activities while insuring quality domestic/organization and child care	Kinship/Friendship Network System (mother)
2. Orthodontic braces for each of her three children	Saved cost, important because work-related fringe benefits excluded dental care	Kinship/Friendship Network System (friend who is a dentist)
3. Flexibility in time and location of job related task	Allowed her to earn additional income through various types of part-time work	Informal job-related fringe benefit
4. Referrals for services that she provided	Allowed her to earn extra income	Kinship/Friendship Network (friends); Job-related fringe benefits
5. Tuition and room and board for her daughter's college education	Saved over $8,000 per year for 4 years	Job-related fringe benefits
6. Regular child-support payments and financial help with car repairs	Extra source of income	Kinship/Friendship Network System (ex-husband)

TABLE 6.1.b. Professional Black Mother, Director of Public Relations for Philadelphia Branch of Federal Agency, B.A.+ Graduate Work, Stated Income $30,000, One Child

Resource	Integration	Source
1. Financial safety-net insuring her current standard of living in case of temporary unemployment (never used this option)	Allowed her to pursue a career mobility strategy of accepting jobs based on long-term career goals and higher salary rather than job security; thus she was able to double her income over a six-year period	Kinship/Friendship Network (parents)
2. Child care services	Allowed her to work late if necessary	Kinship/Friendship Network System (Sister-in-law, parents)
3. Information crucial to her excellent job performance and future career mobility	Job performance and career mobility	Informal work-related benefit and Kinship/Friendship Network System (Friends)
4. Referrals for her services	A little extra income	Kinship/Friendship Network System (Friends)
5. Emotional support and help with child care over the summer; help with child rearing activities via phone and visits	Allowed her to take additional work leading to career mobility over summer; Enabled her to expand the range of experiences for her son	Kinship/Friendship Network (son's father, remarried with three other children and unable to provide regular financial assistance)

TABLE 6.1.c. Professional Black Mother, Federal Employee, Completing B.A. Degree, Stated Income $26,000, Two Children

Resource	Integration	Source
1. Child care	Allowed for job-related travel	Kinship/Friendship Network (mother)
2. Tuition for two job-related courses per semester	Allowed her to return to school to complete B.A.; helpful in future career mobility	Job-related fringe benefits
3. Loans	Enabled her to make house repairs and to deal with emergencies and to make ends meet; crucial to her financial stability because her family and friends could not give financial assistance	Work (Credit Union Fringe Benefit)
4. Free legal advice	Helped reduce divorce costs	Kinship/Friendship Network (Friend)
5. Limited financial help and help with child rearing activities via phone and visits	Reduced financial strain	Kinship/Friendship Network (Children's father lived out of state)

TABLE 6.1.d. White Mother, Working Full-Time Career Ladder Situation, Wire Person in Private Investment Firm, 1 Year College, Stated Income $16,000, One Child

Resource	Integration	Source
1. Information and informal training	Allowed for career mobility through regular job changes and better preparation for upward movement	Informal job-related benefit; Kinship/Friendship Network (Aunt and friends)
2. Very limited financial assistance: $5-10 at a time and baby clothes	Important help immediately after the birth of her child	Kinship/Friendship Network (Mother, grandmother, and friends)
3. Subsidized full-time child care	Enabled her to return to work when child was two-years old	Federal and private agency funds
4. Stock option plan discount on purchase of stocks	Expanded income and allowed some savings	Job-related fringe benefits
5. Two weeks pay as annual bonus	Expands actual income	Job-related fringe benefits
6. Full coverage family health plan	Crucial because she has limited cash and can't get financial help from family	Job-related fringe benefits
7. Loans ($100-200)	Help for financial emergencies	Kinship/Friendship Network (Friends)

TABLE 6.1.e. White Mother, Working Full-Time Career Ladder Situation, Director of a Non-Profit Organization, B.A., Stated Income $13,000, One Child

Resource	Integration	Source
1. Child care and help in child rearing	Necessary for her work-related travel and weekend work; allowed for career mobility	Kinship/Friendship Network System (Mother-friends) Child's father (he is unable to give regular financial help)
2. Clothes for her daughter (has rarely had to buy clothing other than shoes)	Allows her to redeploy her finances	Kinship/Friendship Network (Friends)
3. Used car	Necessary for her work; she was unable to buy a car when her old one gave out	Kinship/Friendship Network (Friends)
4. Free legal, medical, low-cost dental care	Was critical for the first few years. She worked after the birth of her daughter because she had limited health coverage and no other benefits	Informal job-related benefits and Kinship/Friendship Network (Friends)
5. Loans ($500-1,000), no interest and extended period for repayment	Helps with house related and other emergencies--because she has no savings	Kinship/Friendship Network (Friends)
6. Information on low-interest home improvement loans, services, and free or low-cost child related activities	Enabled her to repair and make improvements on her house and expand the range of activities and experiences for her child	Kinship/Friendship Network (Friends)

TABLE 6.1.f. White Mother Receiving Public Assistance, Completing B.A. Degree, One Child

Resource	Integration	Source
1. Housing	Parents purchasing house she lives in; her rent is the mortgage payments; this provides good housing and permits her collective lifestyle (joint meals and shared child care)	Kinship/Friendship Network System (Parents)
2. Extensive house renovations, savings on materials	Allowed her to make major improvements on her house and studio for her pottery making, which provides some limited income and which she exchanges for services with friends	Kinship/Friendship Network System (Friends, some of whom are in the construction business)
3. Student loans	Allowed her to return to school for a B.A.	Government student loans
4. Health care and food stamps	Health care and help with food costs	Government subsidy
5. Share car ownership	Enables her to go to school and make use of city resources for herself and son	Kinship/Friendship (Friend, single parent-they share car ownership and maintenance)
6. Child care and child rearing help	Enables her to study and attend night classes	Kinship/Friendship (Friends, child's father provides reported regular child support)
7. Subsidized full-time child care	Allows her to go to school	Government subsidy Network

The observed variations among these nineteen families appeared to be reflective of differences in the range, types and integration of resources emanating from personal income-generating strategies, kinship/friendship (natal family included) systems, and from the state. Tables 6.1.a-f illustrate the way some of the resources from these three spheres were integrated in the lives of six female single-parent families.

This abbreviated list of the types of resources transmitted through the Kinship/Friendship network system, and their integration with job-related benefits and state subsidies, demonstrates the importance of looking beyond stated income, education and occupation to determine the class location of contemporary families.

A review of the data gathered from the nineteen families showed important differences within and between racial groups and occupational categories. However, a similar pattern emerged in each of the three categories. In varying degrees the transfers made through the social network systems of most of the black mothers tended to *maintain* the standard of living of the family. In contrast, the exchanges made through the white families' social network systems acted in most cases to *expand* the family's standard of living. This critical difference suggests the need for more and larger comparative studies of the context of material resources, services and information exchanged through the social network systems of black and white families in the United States.

This will help to clarify the nature of the supposedly expanding black middle class, and give further insights into some of the factors that affect differential rates of educational success and career mobility of the black and white population in the American context. The data collected for this study demonstrated the importance of these sectors in determining the standard of living of black and white professional mothers earning roughly the same incomes from their primary employment sources. In this instance, although the eight mothers would be categorized as middle class, given their incomes, education and occupations, there was a fundamental difference in the standard of living and range of options available to the white and black mothers. These differences importantly conditioned the kinds of child care and child-rearing experiences they were able to provide for their children.

Among the mothers engaged in career mobility activities, as a group, there were also important differences shown between the black and white mothers in degree and rate of career mobility. The mothers in this category had lower incomes than the mothers in the professional category. The White mothers also tended to belong to poorer natal families than the White mothers in the professional category. An interesting difference shown in this group was the range of variation in the kinds of material resources, services, and information that the white mothers received from friends in their social network system. These proved to be critical in determining their career mobility strategies, and their rates of career mobility, and also acted to help them realize higher standards of living than the black mothers in this category.

Among the mothers in the public assistance category, the studies group was too small to make any general statements; however, the same pattern emerged in the four families examined. The white mothers belonged to more economically stable natal families and had higher standards of living than the black mothers. These four women's experiences demonstrated the importance of the flows exchanged through the kinship/friendship network system in helping the mothers to prepare themselves for more stable and financially rewarding careers. Without the help they received from their families and friends they would not have been able to provide their children with the standard of living and types of child-rearing experiences they felt were necessary while receiving public assistance. Further, it would have been impossible for the poorest mother of the group to make the transition from welfare dependence to full-time employment. For the other three women who had different work and educational histories, these exchanges enabled them to use the period of welfare dependence for better occupational placement. As one participant (who had received braces) stated upon reading this study, "Braces are not babysitting!"

Her point may be extended to suggest that it is not that the poor share more, but rather, they have different "bundles of resources" to share. Often those are more visible and more closely related to the essentials of life, i.e. food, clothing, babysitting for small amounts of money, whereas those in higher socioeconomic positions make exchanges that are equally important but less visible, such as professional services, investment opportunities and other income-expanding information.

Conclusion

This discussion, based on data generated through an ethnographic study of nineteen black and white female-headed families, demonstrates the complex ways in which race, class and gender relations within the American context act to differentially shape the family experience of female-headed households of different classes and races. By focusing on these households as units embedded in complex kinship and friendship network systems and by examining the strategies used by the mothers over time to generate income to support their families while also ensuring child care and child-rearing experiences for their children, it became possible to see the ways in which transfers through their network system integrated with state subsidies and a range of income-generating strategies determine the actual standard of living of these families as well as the economic stability and occupational mobility of the mothers.

What becomes apparent through the use of this framework in the study of female single-parent families, is the wide range of variation in standard of living, life style, and range of choices available within and between occupational status categories and racial groups in the female single-parent population. Thus the relationship between female-headed households and poverty cannot be attributed solely to family structure.

The class experience of these families suggest that at its most fundamental level, differential class location is a reflection of differential access to the social product, i.e. goods, services and information available within a given society. The examination of the resources utilized by these families revealed several avenues through which individuals gain access to social resources: 1) individual income-generating strategies (wages and related benefits and/or ownership of productive property); 2) from the State, through various types of state and government subsidies; and 3) exchanges made through their kinship/friendship network system currently and in the past.

The means through which and the degree to which these families gained access to social resources differed. These current differences can be usefully understood as contemporary expressions of different personal and group histories, shaped by the nature of race, class and gender relations in the United States. Further, they underscore the importance of looking beyond family structure to the impact of structures of inequality to explain the significant correlation between female-headed households and poverty, and the unequal distribution of poverty among the female single-parent population. This focus of inquiry will prove useful to policymakers concerned with developing public policies and programs designed to meet the specific need of the highly heterogeneous population of female-headed families in the United States.

References

Baca Zinn, Maxine and Stanley Eitzer. 1989. *Diversity in American Families*. New York: Harper & Row Publishers.

Bane, Mary Jo. 1986. "Household Composition and Poverty" in Sheldon Danzigen and Daniel Weinberg, eds., *Figuring Poverty*. Pp. 209-23. Cambridge: Harvard University Press.

Burnham, Linda. 1980. "Has Poverty Been Feminized in Black America?" *The Black Scholar*, March/April, pp. 14-24.

Cazenave, Noel. 1983. "Black Families at the Crossroads? Retrospect and Prospects," in Cheron Sutton, ed. *State of Black Philadelphia*. Pp. 7-28. Philadelphia: Urban League of Philadelphia.

Community Nutrition Institute. 1980. "Single Parent Families Nearly Double Since 1970." *Weekly Report* 10: 36-7.

Cummings, Judith. 1983. "Disintegration of Black Families Threatens Gains of Decades." *New York Times*, Nov 20: 1,56.

Epstein, Marsha. 1979. "Children Living in One-Parent Families." *Family Economics Review*. Winter, pp. 21-23.

Francis-Okongwu, Anne. 1986. *Different Realities: A Comparative Study of Nineteen Black and*

White Female Single Parents. Dissertation. Ann Arbor: University Microfilms International.

_____. 1992. "Female-Headed Families in New York City: A Comparative Study of Black and White Low and Marginally Middle Income Families." In Progress.

Gordon, David M. 1978. "Capitalist Development and the History of American Cities" in William Tabb and Larry Sawers, eds., *Marxism and the Metropolis*. Pp. 20-61. New York: Oxford University Press.

Hershberg, Theodore. 1981. "Blacks in Philadelphia: 1850-1980: Immigrants, Opportunities and Racism," in Claude Lewis, ed., *The State of Black Philadelphia*. Pp. 4-29. Philadelphia: Urban League of Philadelphia.

Johnson, Beverly L. 1980. "Single-Parent Families." *Family Economics Review*. Summer/Fall, Pp. 22-27.

Kilson, Martin. 1981. "Black Social Classes and Intergenerational Poverty." *The Public Interest*, Summer, pp. 58-78.

McGhee, James D. 1984. "A Profile of the Black Single Female-Headed Household," in James Williams, ed., *The State of Black America 1984*. Pp. 43-67. New York: National Urban League

Moynihan, Daniel P. 1965. *The Negro Family: A Case for National Action*. Washington, DC: Office of Policy Planning and Research, U.S. Dept. of Labor.

Mullings, Leith. 1986. "Uneven Development: Class, Race, and Gender in the United States before 1900," in Eleanor Leacock and Helen Safa, eds., *Women's Work: Development and the Division of Labor by Gender*. Pp. 41-57. Massachusetts, Bergin & Garvey Publishers, Inc.

Murray, Charles. 1984. *Losing Ground*. New York: Basic Books.

Pennsylvania: Total Civilian Labor Force, Unemployment and Employment 1970-1980. 1981. Philadelphia: Research and Statistics, Office of Employment Security, Department of Labor and Industry.

Perry, Carolle. 1981. "Black Unemployment in Philadelphia," in Claude Lewis, ed., *The State of Black Philadelphia*. Pp. 40-46. Philadelphia: Urban League of Philadelphia.

Rawlings, Steve. 1980. *Families Maintained by Female Householders 1970-79*. U.S. Bureau of Census, Current Population Reports. U.S. Government Printing Office, Washington, DC.

Stack, Carol B. 1975. *All Our Kin: Strategies for Survival in a Black Community*. New York: Harper & Row.

Stallard, Karin, Barbara Ehrenreich, and Holly Sklar. 1983. *Poverty in the American Dream: Women and Children First*. Boston: South End Press.

Taeuber, Cynthia and Victor Valdisera. 1986. *Women in the American Economy*. U.S. Bureau of Census, Current Population Reports, Series P-23. No. 146. U.S. Government Printing Office, Washington, DC.

U.S. Bureau of Census, Current Populations Reports, Consumer Income Series, P-60, No. 160. *Poverty in the United States: 1986*. U.S. Government Printing Office, Washington, DC.

Vaughn-Cooke, Denys. 1984. "The Economic State of Black America, Is There A Recovery?" in *The State of Black America*. Pp. 1-23. New York: National Urban League.

Wallace, Phyllis. 1980. *Black Women in the Labor Force*. Cambridge: The M.I.T. Press.

Woody, Bette. 1989. *Black Women in the New Services Economy: Help or Hinderance in Economic Self-Sufficiency?* Working paper No. 196, Wellesley College, Center for Research on Women.

7

Similarities and Differences: Female-Headed Households in Brazil and Colombia

Mary Garcia Castro

Introduction

According to longitudinal analyses of contemporary census data (Buvinic et al. 1978), the husband-wife household pattern is on the decline while the proportion of female-headed households is on the rise, primarily in Third World countries and among the poor. In the 1970's, the literature on female-headed households assumed that they were primarily found among the "poorest of the poor".[1]

This article focuses on the growth of female-headed households and its association with poverty and gender ideology in two different Latin American countries Brazil and Colombia. Both countries share a combination of development and poverty, typical of the Latin American region. For the last two decades social and demographic changes have been stressed by scholars, such as fertility decline, an increase in the number of separated and divorced women, an increase in women's participation in the labor force, and large numbers of female-headed households.

In Colombia, about 25 percent of urban households were headed by women in 1990 (Profamilia 1991), while in Brazil the most recent available data (for 1988) refer to 15 percent households as headed by women (data from special tables of the PNAD/IBGE--National Household Survey, Brazilian Bureau of Census). According to various studies, in Colombia and in Brazil, women who are heads of households are indeed the "poorest of the poor". In Colombia, in 1986, about 30.4 percent of urban households were classified as below the poverty level and female-headed households comprised 16 percent of the total of that group (data from National Planning Department 1991). In Brazil in 1988 33% of households had family incomes below the poverty level. Of these about

23 % were headed by women (PNAD/IBGE).

Brazil and Colombia present a similar picture in relation to female participation in the labor force. In both countries, the informal sector accounts for about 30 to 40 percent of the urban labor force. Women and migrants, especially the youngest and the oldest ones, are over-represented in some typical occupations of that sector, such as domestic service, home-based paid work, street selling and the like. In both countries female heads of households' rates of participation in the labor force are high. Above 40 percent of female heads of households are gainful workers, and the majority of them are engaged in informal sector activities in the urban areas. The growth of female-headed households in the last decade was not as impressive in Colombia as it was in Brazil. For instance, in the period between 1976 and 1986, female-headed households in Colombia increased by 46 percent (Vallejo and Sierra Garcia 1991: 103), whereas in Brazil between 1970 and 1980 they increased by 85 percent (Garcia Castro 1989:115).

In Brazil, female headship and poverty ran side by side in the last two decades (1970-1990). But urban poverty in Colombia did not get worse in what was considered the crisis period between 1981 and 1986, as in other Latin American countries. According to Vallejo and Garcia (1991: 41) this was due to several peculiar factors in Colombian dynamics, such as: international emigration and fertility decline (demographic factors); the entrance of women and children into the labor market ("household employment strategies"--see Vallejo and Sierra Garcia 1991:42), and a goverment policy of encouraging minimum wage growth.

Brazil continues to present one of the worst income distribution structures in the world, according to a report from the World Bank for the 1980s, with data for 41 countries (Saboia 1991). The poorest 50 percent of the population shared 17.5 percent of the national income in 1960, 14.2 percent in 1970, and just 13 percent in 1985 (cited in Werneck Vianna 1991: 124).

In Colombia, despite the high representation of female-headed households among the poor, the femininization of poverty thesis is not considered as important as it is in the United States (Scott 1984, among others) and in other developed countries to explain the growth of the poor, since the growth of female-headed households among the poor is not so impressive. Data from the four most important Colombian cities--Bogota, Cali, Medellin and Barranquilla-- show that the proportion of female-headed households among the poor is quite similar to that found among non-poor households in 1976: 16.49 percent and 14.72 percent. In 1986, there were relatively even more female-headed households among non-poor households (23.08 percent) than among the poor households (22.03 percent), if family income is considered (Vallejo and Sierra Garcia 1991: 102). Female heads of households in Colombia turned out to be more visible in the urban context, and especially in the so-called middle and upper income strata. Compared to 1976, in 1986 there were 27 percent more female heads of households among the poorest 10 percent of the population, while among the richest 10 percent there were 90 percent more in 1986 than in 1976. The growth of female heads of households in Colombia is associated with improvement in women's educational status and marriage instability (Vallejo and Sierra Garcia 1991: 103). In Brazil (1988), while 23 percent of all poor households were headed by women, among non poor households, female-headed ones represented just 5 percent. The non-poor households include those earning between the minimum wage and three times the minimum wage. (Data taken from PNAD/IBGE).

While in Colombia separated and divorced female heads of households are considered to be in the worst economic situation, in Brazil widowed and aged female heads are worse off than women who are separated or divorced.

Two different studies conducted in Brazil and Colombia dealing with female-headed households were chosen for analysis. Each study employed different methods and generated different but related types of data. For this reason, this paper is not primarily a comparative analysis. Rather it deals analytically with the interaction between gender, economy and family, and how these are associated with female-headed households.

For the case of Brazil, emphasis is given to the growth of female-headed households. In this part, the article analyzes the assumption that the increase in female-headed households in developing countries is a universal and recent phenomenon. This discussion is based on my dissertation research (see Garcia 1989).

After the discussion of female-headed households in Brazil based on census material, I switch to the Colombian case, the discussion of which is based on reserach I carried out for the International Labor Office (ILO) in 1981 (see Garcia Castro 1987). Through a qualitative case study in a poor neighborhood in Bogota, information was gathered from in-depth interviews with 18 poor women over a period of six months in 1981, and through a survey of 98 women in other households (some female-headed and others male-headed).[2]

The topics covered by the survey as well as the intensive study included: women in paid and non-paid work; fertility and family planning; the use of government services; the system of mutual support among neighbors and between migrants and their family in the place of origin; the use of their (the main female's) free time; their ideological framework; and their sexual life. The basic research question of this part of the essay is: What do poor wives and poor female heads of household have in common in terms of ideology and objective constraints, and what differentiates these women?

Before the presentation of the two Latin American countries brief remarks on the concept of head of household are presented.

The Concept of Head of Household

The expression "head of household" is an ideological one. It assumes that there is an internal hierarchy in the family, that someone is the most important person in the family and that the others will depend on this person. According to Latin American census data, in houses where there are men there are no female heads of household, or they are not allowed to be presented as such to the interviewers. During the qualitative research I carried out in Bogota, when asked, poor wives used to say: "He is the head of the family". When they were single mothers, separated, abandoned, or widowed, they almost excused themselves with remarks like: "I am the head because he went away" or "The head does not live here." But I also found that there may not necessarily be a head in all family arrangements. Expressions such as "He is responsible for the house and the food", and "I am responsible for children, for cooking, and so on", were also common in the field research. Anyhow men were considered 'natural' heads of the households.

In the Brazilian census interviewer's manual, the instructions specify that the head of the household should be the person recognized as such by all members of the household. This is a common recommendation in the majority of the censuses that use the expression "head of the household" (United Nations 1984). This recommendation, however, is unrealistic because there is no provision for polling the household members, and under the conditions of such a massive undertaking as the census, this is not likely to happen.

In the census orientation, there is an implicit assumption that the family is an institution based on consensus: all members will agree on the selection of someone as the head. But, according to qualitative data gathered in Bogota, some few exceptions are found, and also conflicts between wives and husbands in identifying the head of the household.

In Brazil, in the 1970 census, the head of household was recommended as the best informant. In 1970 there were no cases of female heads in households with a couple. In the qualitative study in Bogota, 3 out of 45 wives declared they were the head of the household. In the 1980 Brazilian census the procedure changed, and women were accepted as heads even with husbands present. This change followed recommendations from an international seminar organized by feminists in 1978 (see Aguiar 1985), and research conducted by technicians of the Brazilian Bureau of Census (IBGE) (Garcia Castro et al. 1979).

The "head" concept has been especially misleading in the representation of women's work in the household, and in 1984 the United Nations (at the Nairobi Conference) recommended its replacement by other non-ideological expressions. The expression "female heads of household" commonly refers to women who do not live with a husband or male companion. It also refers to women who are not involved in a co-resident stable or enduring relationship. But it also assumes a hierarchy and assymetry in social relations.

Ambiguities related to the census concept of head of the household are not only problematic because they lead to pitfalls in measuring complex social processes in census-taking or to specific problems in the Brazilian census conceptual framework and data collection practices. The household head concept is also influenced by subjective representations of reality, and it is loaded with gendered ideological vestiges. In the end, a paradox emerges from the census definition of head of household, that is, the person responsible for the household. While reliance on the respondent to name the head without guidance from a more specific definition results in the underestimation of women's responsibilities, it also leads to a fair approximation of the common sense representation of reality. As mentioned, few wives declared they were the head of the household in poor neighborhoods in Bogota, even when they were the principal or the sole breadwinner of the family.

The Brazilian Case: The Growth of Female-Headed Households

Introduction

In a first section of the analysis of the Brazilian case that follows, the growth of this particular household pattern in the period 1950-1980 is examined, and sub-groups among female- and male-headed households based on census sources are identified. Then, with the support of historical material the notion that the female-headed household is a contemporary (1950-1980) phenomenon is questioned. Using the Brazilian data, the thesis that the increase of female-headed households is an outgrowth of "development with poverty" (Buvinic et al. 1978, among others), common to the pattern of industrialization in Third World countries, is then probed. It will be shown that an association between the economy at a given point in time and family dynamics may not hold in every situation in all developing countries, and that a number of cultural and historical factors must also be considered.

In the case of Brazil an alternative historical structural rationale is suggested as a means to understanding female-headed households. I argue that limits to cultural and emotional expressions in husband/wife relationships, as well as in child/parent relations, are imposed upon the poor in class-based economies and particularly upon the most vulnerable groups, such as women and old persons, in cases where women are heads of household, and that limits have been imposed upon these groups at all times and in all places. The acceptance of alternative family patterns is both culturally and economically based.

The current proportion of female-headed households in Brazil results from a combination of many diverse factors. These households have always existed among the poor in Brazil. Historical evidence, such as commentaries in travelers' accounts and parochial data on illegitimate children, suggests that single-mother and mother-children families were the rule, not the exception, among the poor up to the nineteenth century (Azevedo 1966, Candido 1951).

The point here is not to appeal to history to find enduring patterns which may lead to culturally deterministic assumptions. Rather, historical evidence of female headship is presented to identify those factors that can be used to account for the persistence and rise of female-headed households among the poor. These questions are approached from a dialectical perspective that regards past and present as being intertwined in our minds. However, the proximate causes--the social meanings--are in the economic formations of the here and now, understanding that economic and cultural expressions are related. Explanations for the proliferation of female-headed households in the colonial period (interclass relations under slavery) are no longer valid to explain this phenomenon today. Thus, there is no sense in defending these earlier causes as objective stimuli to more recent rates of female headship. Other processes have to be identified. For instance, as Safa (1985) and others have noted, proletarianization and correlated processes, such as migration and female labor force participation, have affected and stimulated the growth of female-headed households in the last three decades. This holds true in Brazil as well as in Colombia. Norms in male/female relations, and gendered social ideology that support women's subordination, make a woman "without a man" more vulnerable, especially if she is older. These factors will not be discussed in this section, since in the Brazilian case only secondary data are used, but they are evident in the qualitative case developed in Bogota.

This is not to say that historical patterns which reinforce the growth of female-headed households do not exist. These must be put together with analyses of the organization of production, of the organization of the reproduction of a gendered culture, and of population dynamics such as sex ratios, nuptial patterns and changes in age composition. A dialectical perspective which distinguishes origins, patterns of persistence, and proximate causes and effects will certainly yield a less simplistic understanding of female-headed households.

Contemporary Representations of Female-Headed Households in Brazil

The proportion of female-headed households in Brazil in the 1970s, when compared to other countries in the Americas, is not so outstanding. While in Brazil, 16 percent of all households in 1980 were headed by a woman, in the United States the proportion was 17.5 percent, and in Puerto Rico 18.30 percent. In Colombia (1984) about 20 percent of households were headed by women. This proportion goes up in the English-speaking Caribbean countries. For example, in Jamaica, in 1970, about 34 percent of households were headed by women[3] (see Table 7.1).

But international comparisons are misleading, because the census term "head of household" does not always cover the same scheme of domestic arrangements. In the English-speaking Caribbean countries, for example, the most common type of female-headed household is that in which the woman has never been married, but has been in a union of some kind during the period of data collection or before; and the census instruction leaves the household headship to be settled "by the person who claims the position", allowing the identification of female households in couple-based unions (Massiah 1980). In Brazil, however, in multi-person households headed by a woman, those headed by widowed (and to a lesser extent, divorced or separated) women predominate. But census instructions lead to underestimation of female heads in couple-based households.

Buvinic et al. (1978) have made an attempt to get better figures for the comparative study of census materials. They replace the *de jure* female head, identified through the census definition of head of household, with an indicator of "potential female heads of household". This is obtained from information on present marital status and on motherhood for the case of single women. Thus widowed, divorced, separated women as well as single mothers, are considered "potential female heads". Since marital status is a less ambiguous concept in the census, it allows for more accurate international comparisons, although it is recognized that "widowed, divorced or separated women and single mothers do not automatically become *de jure* heads of household" (Youssef and Hettler 1984:232).

If indeed widows, separated, divorced and single mothers had been counted as heads of household in Brazil, in 1970, 17 (rather than 13) percent of the households would have been recognized as headed by women. This proportion would be higher than those registered in several other Latin American countries, e.g., Ecuador and Paraguay--countries that exhibit the highest levels of poverty in South America (see Table 7.1).

Although the concept of female heads of household refers to women in differ-ent marital situations, only some are identified through the census. In the next paragraphs some of these additional female-headed situations enumerated in the census are examined. In particular, I wish to explore the following: first, one-person households; second, female heads according to marital status; and, third, female heads with a co-resident spouse.

The separation of female heads in one-person households from those in multi-person households makes sense, since women who live by themselves might have economic needs different from female heads of household who are mothers of small children.

The proportion of those who live by themselves was higher among female heads than among male heads. About 17.39 percent of Brazilian female heads in 1980 lived in one-person households, while among male heads the proportion was only 3.65 percent. Widows and older women predominated among these

138

Table 7.1 Proportion of Census-Defined and Potential Female Headed Households in Selected Countries. North, South, and Central Americas, and the Caribbean. 1970-1980

Region, Country and Category	Year of Reference	Proportion of Female-Headed Households (Census)	Proportion of Potential Female-Headed Households[a]
North America			
U.S.A.[b]	1976		
Non Hispanic			
White		14.1	-
Black		44.3	-
Mexican		19.9	-
Puerto Rican		38.6	-
U.S.A.[c]	1979[c]	17.5	-
CENTRAL AMERICA			
Costa Rica[d]	1973	-	14.0
Rural[e]		12.4	
El Salvador[d]	1974	-	29.0
Rural[e]	1971	16.3	
Guatemala[d]	1973	-	20.0
Rural[e]		11.4	
Honduras[d]	1974	-	26.0
Rural[e]			18.7
Panama[d]	1970	-	40.0
Rural[e]		14.8	
Nicaragua[d]	1971	-	17.0
Mexico [e]	1970	-	14.0
CARIBBEAN			
Puerto Rico[f]	1980	18.3	-
	1970	15.7	15.0[d]
Jamaica[g]	1970	33.8	-
Barbados[g]	1970	42.9	-
Cuba[d]	1970		15.0
Bahamas[g]	1970		19.0
Belize[g]	1970	24.8[d]	24.0
Trinidad and Tobago[f]	1970	27.0	
Guyana[g]	1970	22.4	
St. Lucia[g]	1970	40.9	

(continues)

Table 7.1 (continued)

SOUTH AMERICA

Colombia[h]	1975	-	25.0
4 cities[h]		15.0	-
Argentina[d]		-	13.0
Bolivia[d]		-	18.0
Chile[d]		-	32.0
Equador[d]		-	14.0
Paraguai[d]		-	11.0
Peru[d]		-	11.0
Venezuela[d]		-	11.0
Brazil[d]	1970		17.0
	1970[i]	13.0	-
	1980[i]	15.9	17.1

(a) See footnote 3.
(b) Data from US 1976 Survey of Income and Education in Tienda and Angel, 1982;
(c) Data from US Bureau of the Census, cit in Kamerman, 1984
(d) Data from US National Censuses, cit in Buvinic et al, 1978
(e) Data from US Bureau of the Census, Women in Development Data Base, 1980, cit. in Youssef and Hettler, 1982;
(f) Data from US Census in Puerto Rico;
(g) Data from 1970 Population Census of the Commonwealth Caribbean cit. in Massiah, 1982:
(h) Data from Urban Survey "Empleo y Probeza", Universidad de Los Andes, cit in Rey de Marulanda, 1982;
(i) Data from IBGE 1978 and 1983a (population censuses).

"women-alone" households.

The lower proportion of men living alone who are heads of household is consistent with another distinct situation experienced by male heads of household, the presence of a spouse. The proportion of male-headed households with a spouse, besides being higher than the number of female heads with a spouse, is stable in the four census periods considered: about 89.50 percent in 1950, 91.20 percent in 1960, 94.32 percent in 1970, and 92.01 percent in 1980. The Brazilian census information on presence of a male companion in female-headed households might be the result of census underestimation. In the three censuses with information on this question (1950, 1960 and 1980), the proportion of female heads with spouse was insignificant, e.g. about 2 percent in 1980.

Growth of Female-Headed Households in the 1950-1980 Period

Studies of female heads of household in Brazil have relied on different methods and data sources: published census materials (Barroso 1978); survey data of particular cities (Merrick and Schmink 1983); anthropological data

(Figueiredo 1983); and historical records (Kuznesof 1980a, 1980b). The interpretations are often diverse, but there is little dissent that the number of female heads has increased.

The growth of female-headed households in Brazil was 19 percent in 1950-60, 67 percent in 1960-1970, and 85 percent in 1970-1980. The increase in female heads was most impressive in the 1970 to 1980 period. This decade included the period of the so called "Brazilian miracle". It was characterized by periods of relative impoverishment of the working class but also by periods of relative recuperation of the worker's standard of living--more or less from 1976 on. If there is a linear association between poverty and growth of female-headed households, as some have suggested in other developing countries (Buvinic et al. 1978), there should have been a sharper rise of female-headed households in the period 1960-1970 than in the succeeding decade. In the 1960s, income distribution was more uneven and unemployment was on the rise. Yet, it is precisely in the more "affluent" 1970 to 1980 period that the increase in female heads of household is more noticeable. Among other unexpected findings in the data is the comparatively low growth of female-headed households in the 1950-1960 period. As pointed out, co-residential arrangements (*familias conviventes*) were only enumerated from the 1960 census on. Taking into account the high representation of female-headed households among these *familias conviventes*--about 20 percent in 1970--it was logical to expect a higher proportion of female-headed households in the 1960s. But the growth of female-headed households between 1950-1960 is moderate (19 percent), suggesting it would be insignificant if the same census enumeration procedure was followed in both censuses.

A comparison of the three decades suggests that there is a relationship between female-headed households and proletarianization, as suggested by Safa (1985), as well as a link between female-headed households and industrialization/ urbanization, as Kuznesof (1986, 1980a, 1980b) contended.

In comparison with the 1950-1960 period, the decade from 1960-1970 witnessed an outstanding growth of different processes correlated with proletarianization. Some examples of these were: male and female internal migration to the most industrialized region (the Southwest); the proportion of urban workers in the secondary sector; and the expansion of properly capitalist relations such as that between employer/employee in the urban and rural areas (Garcia Castro et al. 1979, Faria 1980, among others).

This analysis indicates that the Brazilian industrialization model, inaugurated in the 1960s, affected household dynamics. The contrast of the growth rates of female heads of households between the 1950-1960 period, when female heads increased by 19 percent, and the 1960-1970 period, when they grew 67 percent, was sharper than it was between 1960-70 and 1970-80, when female-headed households grew 85 percent. Changes in the representation of female-headed households between 1950 and 1980 are readily observable when one looks at the difference between urban and rural place of residence (see Table 7.2).

The differences between the proportion of urban and rural households headed by women in the last 3 censuses indicate that in Brazil this type of household is most visible in urban areas (see Table 7.2). For instance, the most urbanized area of the country, the Metropolitan Region of Sao Paulo, shows an outstanding growth of this household pattern: in 1980 there were 2.26 times more female-headed households than in 1970.

The differences between female-headed households in rural and urban areas are relative, since a high proportion of female heads in the urban areas are rural migrants. Census data do not enable us to investigate whether migrant female heads held such status before the migration or not.

Studies on migration in Brazil indicate that women generally predominate in the movement toward metropolitan regions, and that their rates of migration are very close to those of men in the older groups. For instance, there were approximately 104.6 men per 100 women among migrants who were 50 years or older in the metropolitan regions of Sao Paulo in 1970 (data in Garcia Castro et al. 1979: 39). The patterns of nuptiality of recent migrants (those with up to two years of residence in the metropolitan regions), whose age was standardized, were investigated in another study (Garcia Castro et al. 1979). This research indicated that 44.37 percent of recent migrant women (15 years or older) in the Metropolitan Region of Sao Paulo in 1970 were single and about 8 percent were widows or separated (data in Garcia Castro et al. 1979:50).

Female headship in the rural and in the urban areas is not a discrete phenomenon. In the rural areas there are more economic and cultural constraints upon a woman who is the sole supporter of the household. Some of these women migrate when they are widowed or abandoned. These cases have been studied by Schmink (1986) for Hispanic Latin America, and by Chaney (1980) for the English-speaking Caribbean. Other women migrate because as single mothers they are more likely to be socially stigmatized in rural areas (Garcia Castro 1979).

Another common explanation for the female headship phenomenon in the rural areas is male migration (Chaney 1980, Buvinic et al. 1978, Youssef and Hettler 1984, among others). This holds true for Colombia (DNP 1991a) as well as for Brazil. Male migration contributes to female headship in two ways: first, women are "left behind". Considering the extended practice of consensual or common-law unions in the rural areas in Latin America, it is probable that many migrant men enumerated in the census as single have left a wife in the place of origin. In 1970, the proportions of single male migrants 15 years or older, in the metropolitan regions of Salvador and Sao Paulo, were 31.61 and 30.08 percent respectively (data in Garcia Castro et al., 1979: 50).

Second, the expansion of some types of social relations of production peculiar to capitalism are also more favorable to the development of the female-headed

Table 7.2 Percentages of Urban and Rural Households, by Sex of the Head: Brazilian States of Sao Paulo and Bahia 1960-1980

Region and Resi- dence	Period and Household, by Sex of the Head					
	1960		1970		1980	
	MHH	FHH	MHH	FHH	MHH	FHH
A. BRAZIL						
Urban	45.39	61.41	56.94	71.00	68.51	81.35
Rural	54.61	38.59	43.06	29.00	31.49	18.65
B. BAHIA						
Urban	33.16	50.72	39.03	53.95	47.85	63.25
Rural	66.84	49.28	60.97	46.05	52.15	36.75
C. SAO PAULO						
Urban	63.55	83.50	81.28	92.26	88.80	95.78
Rural	36.45	16.50	18.72	7.74	11.20	4.22

MHH - male-headed households
FHH - female-headed households

Sources: original data in IBGE, 1963, 1978 and 1983a (population figures in censuses)

household in rural areas of Third World countries. When women are hired and paid on an individual basis, a male's domestic authority may be challenged. This thesis has been argued by Stolcke (1982) for the case of the temporary rural workers in the state of Sao Paulo, known as *boias frias*--a rural semi-proletarian who lives in town and goes to work, hired by a labor contractor for farmers. According to Stolcke (1982) one of the effects of proletarianization of women as *boias frias* (temporary rural workers) was the undermining of household stability, which was based in part on women's dependency on men's income. The abandonment of *boias frias* women by their mates, and the increase of alcoholism among men, is also illustrated by Stolcke's case study (1982). Similar patterns were detected by Smith (1978), for Blacks in the English-speaking Caribbean, and by Safa (1965 and 1971) who studied Puerto Ricans and Blacks in the United States. All of these studies question the assumption that it is the challenge to men's natural breadwinner role that stimulates male desertion.

Objective conditions, however, should not be obscured by cultural factors. Poor women always worked, but in the case of the rural subsistence economy in Brazil, they worked as "family members". A more capitalist relation provides the woman with independent means that facilitates her resistance to oppressive forms of the domestic sexual division of labor and authority, but, on the other hand, those relations are more likely to mean exploitation.

References to History in the Brazilian Case

Although the data for the last thirty years suggest a steady growth in female-headed households, female headship is not a new phenomenon in Brazil. On the contrary, if historical studies are consulted, the origins of this household pattern can be traced to colonial times, with evidence that the *de facto* female-headed household, and chiefly mother-children dyad, prevailed widely during colonial times up to the nineteenth century, to an extent that was perhaps greater than it is today.

This evidence suggests that different social meanings can be attached to the same form, the female-headed household. These social meanings are determined by the prevailing political, economic and cultural arrangements in each period. Historical evidence also precludes the reduction of the causes of a complex institution, such as family, to specific economic conjunctures.

Historical studies, such as those of Freyre (1968) and Oliveira Vianna (cit. in Kuznesof 1986) addressed the ruling class patriarchal family in the setting of Brazilian national culture. Kuznesof (1986) was the first to develop a structural analysis specifically on poor female-headed households, pointing out its relation to the process of proletarianization, which followed changes in modes of production in the period between 1765 and 1836, in the city of Sao Paulo.

In spite of the almost total lack of directly germane work on female-headed households, there is a broad body of pertinent literature on the Brazilian family, and its importance for the Brazilian national identity (Azevedo, 1966). As pointed out by Wagley (1963 cit. in Mayers 1970:78): "While in other Latin American cultures, familism has been an important aspect of social life, in Brazil there has been almost a cult of the family."

In colonial times, female-headed households among slaves and free labor were influenced by the predominant ruling class family type, i.e. the nuclear and the extended legal family. By this, I mean the patriarchal family, conceived not only as a specific domestic institution, but also as a power structure. I relate this form more to the Weberian type of domination than to the contemporary feminist usage of the term (see note 2). There are, however, some commonalities between the two conceptions, such as the subordination of women to the authority of the male head of the household. Thus, from a historical viewpoint the suggestion emerges that the specificity of the female-headed household is better understood if family, in its totality, is socially analyzed.

In the literature on the colonial family there are repeated references to indicators of what I call here "gendered cultural traits" or "gender ideology". Among such traits are the double standard of sexual morality; sexual division of roles; and sexual relations between masters (men) and slaves (women). Willem's (1953) description of the structure of the Brazilian family from colonial times up to the 1950s emphasizes that one legacy of the colonial times is the gulf separating socially sanctioned sexual activity of men from those of women: women are expected to remain in absolute chastity before marriage and absolute fidelity after—"a non-virgin is nearly always unmarriageable" (cit. in Mayers 1970:95). Candido (1951:304) also mentions that in the 1950s, if a woman who "lost her virginity" could not count on family economic resources, she would have just three alternatives: "prostitution, celibacy or a marital arrangement".

When a man has a child "it is the subject of much bragging" (Candido 1951). However, after a separation, the father's refusal to provide support to the children is then considered legitimate behavior. Many of these gendered cultural traits persist to this day.

Mayers (1970), in his study on the Brazilian family in the 1960s, noted that the expectation in Brazilian society for males is epitomized in the old but still popular saying: "A man may not be able to sleep with all the women in the world, but he should try" (cit. in Mayers 1970:95).

Candido (1951) notes that the characteristics typical of the patriarchal family in the colonial period were altered in the process of industrialization/ urbanization. In particular, he calls attention to the decrease of authority of the *pater familias*, challenges to the sexual division of labor at home by women's participation in the labor force, the elimination of capital punishment for members of the household who did not obey the patriarch or head of the household authority, a progressive "disintegration of the collective consciousness of kinship in favor of a restricted domestic organization of the conjugal structure"; loss of the political hegemony of the patriarchal (upper-class) family, replaced by the state and local authority (see Romero on the defeat of family oligarchies in the elections of 1945, 1946, and 1947, cit. in Candido 1951:305); and partial control of biological reproduction by women due to the accessibility of birth control methods.

While one should avoid generalizations about the family and focus on changes in the internal organization of the family, as well as in its social importance, one must note a peculiar persistence of gendered cultural traits in Brazil that reinforce the mother-children and the female-headed household pattern. Among these is the persistence of the *macho* type, described by Candido as follows:

The representation of the man as sexually strong and forward—the *macho* of slang—expresses a whole complex of historically conditioned sexual relations. It presupposes the traditional domestic status of the procreating patriarch, the *de facto* polygyny favored by slavery, and the secondary position of women (1951:295).

In the course of history, the female-headed household seems to be related more to androcentric features of Brazilian society, within the spheres of production and reproduction, than to expressions of female autonomy or resistance to that ethos. This is particularly true when we are speaking of the poor. On the other hand, cases of female headship by choice among the poor cannot be disre-garded, though this is more likely to occur when the woman has survival resources at her disposal.

Mother-Children Families in Colonial Brazil

The first decades of colonization were characterized by "an accentuated sexual promiscuity" (Candido 1951:292). The majority of the Portuguese colonists came alone, without their families, or as single men, and the imbalance between the sexes was high, with a scarcity of white women. The sexual relations between conquerors and Indian women, and afterward with Black slave women, gave rise to high rates of illegitimate children, and of unions not legitimized by the Church and the Crown. These unions were of diverse degrees of stability and various co-residential arrangements, such as the *mancebia*, when a young woman lived by herself or with her kin, and was supported by a lover. In concubinage, the woman was usually supported by a married man from the upper class. Not until the eighteenth century did the Portuguese government annul the law forbidding unions between whites and blacks, and between whites and Indians (Azevedo 1966).

There is relatively abundant documentation of illegitimate children in chronicles of visitors, parochial registrations, and the first censuses. The high visibility of single mothers among the poor was constant. But the explicit mention of female heads of household is scarce, except in the case of upper-class "virile widows" (Candido 1951). Indirect indicators suggest, however, that this is an old household pattern among the poor. For instance, many of the children born out of wedlock were abandoned in the *roda*--a religious charity for orphans. These children were registered in the parish churches as *expostas*. It is reasonable to infer that many of these children were left by mothers without a male companion, or a male supporter, i.e., by a potential female head of household.

Marcilio's study, based on baptismal records in the city of Sao Paulo between 1941 and 1945, shows that for each 100 children born, 39 were considered "bastards" (1974:159). Of total baptisms, about 16 percent were of expostas, and 23 percent were of illegitimate children. These figures are not necessarily an indicator of the rate of single motherhood. Many illegitimate children were born to a co-residential couple, or resulted from a stable concubinage. In many cases, illegitimate children resulted from concubinage between persons of different social classes. The mistress or the concubine commonly came from the lower classes. Thus, the probability that these women would be left alone with the child was high. This observation is supported by chronicles of foreign visitors. Single motherhood was explained by contemporary authorities and foreign visitors as follows: a male drive to polygamy; male irresponsibility toward their children (if inheritance and other interests, such as political parental solidarity, were not involved, as in the case of the poor); difficulty of the poor to meet the bureaucratic requirements of the Portuguese crown. In order to avoid bigamy, identity documents had to be procured from the metropolis or from the place of origin, an expensive procedure. Poverty was also mentioned in the sources as one cause of the abandonment of women by men, and of the fact that women had children out of wedlock. Mawe (cit. in Marcilio 1974:160), a British visitor, wrote in 1809 after a trip to Sao Paulo:

> Besides being poor, Brazilians, whose gentle qualities should be praised, enjoy pleasure, and they find in the women of the country, customs which facilitate it. They [Brazilian males] avoid being locked in marriages.

Demographic-historic studies add other factors to the understanding of the extension of single-mother families and concubinage, besides the "male's drive to pleasure" and refusal to marry. Marcilio (1974), for example, has described the sex imbalance in Sao Paulo, which led to a higher number of women, chiefly in the eighteenth century. Candido (1951) and Azevedo (1966) have discussed relations between masters and slave women, another basic cause for the expansion of the mother-children families. It is assumed that single mothers did not necessarily have the status of *de jure* female heads of household, because many of them lived in an extended family residential arrangement.

In the Brazilian socio-historiography the patriarchal family is important in the formation of the national identity; and its role in the power structure was central up to the beginning of industrialization/urbanization, when the authority of the landowner (*pater familias*) was to a certain extent replaced by that of the state and local government (Candido 1951).

The colonial production of goods, and chiefly of the export monocultures based on slavery, was organized in autonomous units whose structures resembled feudal fiefs, despite the integration of the economy into international capitalism. These plantation units were, *par excellence*, the seats of patriarchal families, and represented the class power component in the social meaning of family. Azevedo (1966) refers to these families in the Bahian region known as Reconcavo. Candido (1951) discusses their role in the area of *paulista* influence.

As previously noted, there is much more historical reference to the patriarchal family than to arrangements considered typical among slaves and the lower classes. Slaves and poorer folk engaged in consensual marriages, formed by *amasiados* (non married persons living together); the *mancebia*; concubinage; and in what Azevedo (1966:115) refers to as the "partial family", i.e., female-headed households.

A variation of the aforementioned type of *amasiados* is the *familia parcial*, described by Carmelita Hutchinson in the State of Bahia:

> It is comprised of households headed by women, commonly by an old woman who lives with one or two daughters and sons, without the presence or the permanent residence of husbands or *companheiros*. In this matripotestat family, just as in its similar form in Jamaica (Cohen), all the power and responsibility in relation to the children is left to the mother; practically no moral or economic responsibility is fulfilled by the fathers. They never lived in the household nor did they have any function to perform there; they are biological fathers of some of the children, but they are not heads of the household. The woman supported the children with their work as domestic servants, washerwomen, market sellers; and these women were supposed to educate and bring up their children (in Azevedo 1966:115).

Candido's (1951) conceptualization of the patriarchal family structure deserves to be cited at length. He takes into account the importance of the patriarchal family in the broader social context, and its characteristics as a pattern of domestic organization. He refers to the Brazilian patriarchal family of the sixteenth century as follows:

> The patriarchal organization of the family itself presented a double structure: a central nucleus, legalized, composed of the white couple and their legitimate children; and a periphery not always well delineated, made up of the slaves and *agregados*, Indians, Negroes, or mixed bloods, in which were included the concubines of the chief and illegitimate children (1951:294).

The legal nucleus was the core of the domestic organization, and from the beginning it developed according to moulds which persisted until a few decades ago. The chief's dominance was almost absolute, corresponding to the necessities of social organization in an immense country lacking police, and characterized by an economy which depended upon large-scale initiative and the command over a numerous labor force of slaves. It was a type of social organization in which the family necessarily was the dominant group in the process of socialization and integration, a group in which the distances were rigidly marked and regulated by hierarchy.

The patriarchal family was composed not merely of the married couples subordinated to the chief but included the household--that is, the servants, the retainers, the slaves, and the children of all, from whom were recruited the occasional mistresses and the concubines of the white men, and among whom lived the children born from such unions. As will be seen below, the nature of the patriarchal family relegated sexual and emotional satisfactions to the area beyond its legal orbit. On the other hand, since the whites were a minority until the end of the colonial period, perhaps it would not be exaggerating to say that until the nineteenth century, and for the population as a whole, procreation in general and the satisfaction of the sexual impulse occurred more frequently without than within the legal realm of the family.

In the above description, there are several elements which assist in the understanding of the objective basis supporting the extensive presence of single-mother families, and the intimate relationship between these and the traditional ruling-class patriarchal family of colonial times.

The patriarchal family (see note 2) was above all a political institution, based on a union arranged to consolidate wealth and power interests. Marriage among the upper classes was commonly contracted among relatives--between cousins, nieces, and others, as part of "parental solidarity" (Candido 1951) to strengthen the parental groups, and to protect patrimony. There was little room for romantic love, emotional satisfaction or sexual fantasies. Such a custom reinforced the practice of extra-conjugal relations, legitimized by the gendered double standard. Male adultery was simply a matter of litigation if the family wealth was endangered or the *pater familias* did not fulfill his economic obligations toward the family. By contrast, it was expected that an adulterous upper-class wife would be executed by her husband. The mistress or the concubine could not necessarily depend on the patriarch's protection for life, and many were left with the off-spring, contributing to the contingent of "potential female heads of household".

The linkages between the core formation--the patriarchal family--and the other types of family is described by Candido (1951:303) in these terms:

> The result was that the patriarchal family organization sheltered, in proportions larger than one may think, a deep countercurrent or irregularity in which the desires and sentiments sought to compensate for the obstacles to which they were submitted by the impersonal system of marriage. A patient and courageous work of investigation indicates the frequency with which unmarried girls bore children; it shows the occurrence of secret affairs between brothers-in-law and sisters-in law, cousins, uncles and nieces, godfathers and godmothers, and even mothers-in-law and sons-in- law. Under the heavy mantle of patriarchal authority there developed an unobstructed system of compensatory relationships.

No matter what the social class, women today commonly blame "male infidelity" for their decision to separate or to break the marriage contract (Garcia Castro 1987). That was not the case in the eighteenth century. Women's subordination to the husband's authority is not enough to explain why the *sinhas* (as mature or older upper-class women were called in the colonial times) and *sinhazinhas* (young upper-class women) did not leave the "unfaithful husband", returning to the father's house. Candido (1951:303) maintains that separation, except among the poor, was not common, because the patriarchal family "performed a function which was primarily economic and political". Thus, stability and continuity were defended, and emotional and sexual aspects put aside. Candido (1951:303) infers that this was the basic difference between the patriarchal family of colonial times and the contemporary family: "it was not primarily an emotional and sexual system, as is the case today". Not all

authors, and feminists in particular, would agree with Candido's understanding
of the functions of the contemporary family, but he poses a task worth further
exploration: to identify the roots of the potential and *de facto* female-headed
family.

In addition to Candido's suggestion that some female-headed households were
by-products of the patriarchal family rigidity, one must ask about the case of the
poor, considering that no property or power alliance was at stake. Referring to
the "lower classes of the new society"--the late 19th-century working class--
Candido argues that it was characterized by "stable monogamous" relations, and
that this was a drastic shift, considering the widespread practice of unstable
consensual unions of the previous centuries:

> Although the data are lacking it is possible to conjecture, for example, that only from the
> middle of the nineteenth century was there a tendency for the formation of a legal Negro
> family, along Christian and monogamous lines: in the regions of great concentrations of
> Negroes, however, such as Bahia and Maranhao, they remain intimately connected with
> primitive practices of domestic and sexual organization, *with the tendency to polygyny*, the
> dominant position of the woman in relation to the children, and the whole magical framework
> for regulating marriage, preferences, separations, and reparations (emphasis added) (Candido
> 1951:305).

To a certain extent, explanations of the changes and continuities in family
types dominant among slaves and free labor in the period of colonization in
Brazil follow the original debate developed for the case of Blacks in the
Commonwealth Caribbean. In brief, the original debate on the dominance of
mother-children families in that region suggested that: (1) this type of family is
related to "the survival of Africanism" (Herskovitz 1948 cit. in Brana-Shute
1982:1); (2) the origins of female-headed families should be discussed in terms
of the "social structure of slavery and plantation life" (Frazier 1939 and King
1945 cit. in Brana Shute 1982:5); and (3) explanations have to be sought in the
discussion of actual socio-economic constraints (Safa 1965, 1976), with the
"weak economic position of the male", which challenges his power position in
the family (Smith 1978, Safa 1965, 1976).

Smith (1978) also criticizes the literature's disregard of the question of power
and racial relations, and states that the internal domestic logic is not necessarily
pragmatically or economically oriented.

The effect of the social relations of production and domination on the slave
family, as well as on the free labor family, as reinforced by racial and gender
connotations, is a basic part of the explanation of the "partial" and mother-
children families in Brazil. As pointed out by Candido (1951), the Black domestic slave was a natural sex object of the master. This author also argues that the
patriarchal family model was imposed upon the lower classes as a norm, but one
which was not necessarily followed. The patriarchal family model was progressively altered due to "changes in the family functions" in the processes of

"urbanization, industrialization, proletarianization, immigration and acculturation" (Candido 1951:59).

Azevedo (1966) also agrees that the nuclear type of family progressively
became dominant in all social classes, although vestiges of the patriarchal family
are still found, chiefly in rural and less developed areas, e.g., the case of the
caipira family (originally from certain rural areas of Sao Paulo) described by
Candido (1964). Using anthropological research in the area of the Bahian
Reconcavo in the 1950s, Azevedo (1966:118) states that lower-class families are
less stable, chiefly due to male desertion. This observation is in accordance with
contemporary evidence for other Third World countries as well as for minorities
in the United States (Buvinic et al. 1978, among others). Azevedo does not rely
on a strictly economic analysis to explain this pattern among the poor:

> Because at the lower level of the social structure, illiteracy rates are higher, there are
> reminiscences of slavery and economic conditions are very low, the virginity taboo is less
> observed, and the legalization of unions is not too widely followed. This explains the higher
> number of *amasiados*, a type of consensual union of relative stability. These unions might last
> from one year to a lifetime (my translation, Azevedo 1966:118).

In Brazil, as in the Caribbean islands, this type of union is common among
the poor, and among Blacks, chiefly in areas where the concentration of slave
descendants is higher.

The figures illustrate the correlation between the predominance of free unions
and economic and educational backwardness.

> In 1950, in the State of Bahia (an area of concentration of ex-slaves, and with low levels of
> education and considerable poverty) there were more single mothers than in the states of
> Minas Gerais, Rio Grande do Sul and Sao Paulo (regions with higher indexes of
> development). . . . For every 1000 single women only 31 were single mothers in Sao Paulo,
> 56 in Minas Gerais, and 110 in Rio Grande do Sul, while in Bahia the number jumped to
> 244. Of 1000 women who had children, 191 were single in Bahia, 63 in Rio Grande do Sul,
> 32 in Minas Gerais, and 15 in Sao Paulo (my translation, ibid).

Recently the historian Mattoso published a book on the family in the city of
Salvador in the period 1800-1889. She calls attention to the widespread
presence of single mothers, not only among the poor, and discusses female
family headship in these terms:

> In Salvador, frequently women came to be by themselves. . . . and that is true of every social
> stratum. [A woman] was responsible for herself and her children, [and] she had a special role
> in an apparently masculine society. . . . On average these women were 40 years old, but
> those 19 years old and even those of 90 years of age were found to be female heads of
> household.

> Single mothers were especially prominent among Black slaves, and not all of them were

151

associated with interclass or interracial unions. On the contrary, in the past as in the present, the typical union is of endogamous type. . . . Couples living in concubinage were found among all racial groups, but mates were more likely to be of the same racial origin (my translation, Mattoso 1988:125).

Contrary to what the above suggests for Salvador, sources consulted for the case of Sao Paulo (Marcilio 1974; Candido 1951, 1964) indicate that in colonial times it was even more evident that female-headed households were an outcome of class and gender domination. For example, some female-headed households resulted from the common practice of interclass/interracial concubinage, a custom which often resulted in the abandonment of the poor woman and her offspring.

New Social Meanings of Female-Headed Households in Brazil

In the contemporary period (1950-1980) there has been a rapid increase in the growth of female-headed households in the State of Sao Paulo. This paper suggests a new social meaning of this household pattern as emerging from the process of proletarianization. This new pattern results in part from the industrialization/urbanization model which began at the turn of the century, but it also combines with previous traditional forms of organization of the economy. This section focuses on Kuznesof's (1980a, 1980b, 1986) research on the proportion of female heads of household at the turn of the century in the city of Sao Paulo.

Azevedo (1966) and Marcilio (1974) also call attention to patterns of nuptiality that suited that structural characterization for the poor: consensual unions and the exclusive "marriage by the Church", i.e. without civil legalization. These types of unions are also more easily broken (Azevedo 1966; Marcilio 1974; and Kuznesof 1980a, 1980b, 1986). Although such relationships were spread over different regions, data for the contemporary period show sharp regional differences in the levels of occurrence. For instance, in 1950, in the Northeast about 51.8 percent of the unions were legitimized by the Catholic Church, while in the industrial states of the Southeast region this type of union represented only 8.2 percent (Azevedo 1966:131).

The practice of "marriage by the church" actually encouraged bigamy, since the requirements for documents to certify that the brides were not previously married were not so strict as for civil marriage. Many of these unions ended with the abandonment of the woman whose union was only recognized by the church. Cases of bigamy have been documented among the poor by Azevedo (1966) for the rural areas of Bahia in the 1950s.

Azevedo's (1966) and Candido's (1951) historical-anthropological studies elucidate cultural factors entangled in the regional economic formations, supporting my thesis that female-headed households and single-mother families were and continue to be common among the poor.

From historical-demographic studies, factors related to the population structure and dynamics supply additional supporting evidence. Marcilio (1974), using parochial registers and census sources to study the period 1750-1850, and Kuznesof (1986) who used census manuscripts to study the period 1765-1836, provide for the city of Sao Paulo statistical data and analyses on the importance of the following demographic factors in the rise and persistence of households headed by women and/or single mothers at the turn of the century:

(1) Sex ratios favorable to women (registered in the end of the nineteenth century) favored the occurrence of female-headed households;

(2) The growth of rural/urban and Northeast/Southeast migratory movements, and differences in the sex and age composition of the migratory streams. According to Kuznesof (1986), during periods of growth in the exchange economy, as in 1802, while young and single men were going to the interior, widows and young single females were going to the city, stimulated by a new economic demand for female labor. The sex ratio declined from 83.77 to 74.52 between 1790 and 1802, which is interpreted by Kuznesof (1986:83) as: "A continuation of a pattern in which women remained in the city while men migrated into the new settlement areas of the captaincy to claim lands."

(3) The pattern of nuptiality--such as age at marriage, incidence of celibacy, age selectivity in the case of the bride, and population composition by marital status. Paulistano and Bahianio men preferred young women, and age differences from five to twenty-five years were noted by Kuznesof (1986:56): "The changes in the age/sex structure over the period 1705 to 1802 combined with these kind of marriage preferences meant that the marriageability of women over 20 declined substantially."

The percentage of female heads of household under age 44 in the urban areas increased from 43.98 in 1765 to 65.5 in 1863. More spectacular is the increase of unmarried mothers as a percentage of total mothers--from 34.3 in 1765 to 60 in 1836, providing strong support for the hypothesis that consensual unions were both more common and less stable in the early nineteenth century than they were in 1765 (Kuznesof 1986:163).

Kuznesof (1986) and Marcilio (1974) mention only *en passant* gendered cultural norms that influenced such figures. But both Azevedo (1951) and Candido (1966) provided a more detailed analysis regarding such things as the Paulistano and Bahianio men's reluctance to get married, chiefly when economic interests (as in the upper-class patriarchal family) were not related to marriage.

Kuznesof (1986) emphasizes that the shifts in nuptiality and other population patterns, and the growth of female-headed households, chiefly between 1765-1802, were linked to changes in modes of production. She combines an analysis of population dynamics, and changes in the kinship structure, size and composition of the household, with an analysis of the organization of the economy. Indeed it is in this work that the interplay between "economy, demography and family" proposed by Tilly and Scott (1978) is analyzed structurally, showing that those demographic factors are not independent of one another. Kuznesof is also the first to address specifically the case of female heads of household among the poor in Brazil (at the end of the nineteenth century).

Kuznesof's analyses confirm findings appearing in the literature on the family in Bahia to the effect that marriage between the sixteenth and the nineteenth centuries was not a universal practice. Consensual unions and concubinage were widespread among the poor. She also points out that there was a matrilocal tendency in residence patterns, and further provides insights on differentiation among female heads of households by social class. While female heads of household among the rich were commonly widows, among the poor single mothers predominated. This finding is also reported for Bahia by visitors and it appears in ethnographic studies as well (cit. in Azevedo 1966).

But a basic difference between Kuznesof's analyses and previous ones is that she premises her argument on the thesis that between 1765-1836, and chiefly between 1765-1802, there were notable structural changes in the Paulistana economy and in nuptial patterns, as well as an increase in female-headed households among the poor. She argues that observations made in 1765 show that the economy then was based on the domestic mode of production. It was a non-monetary economy, characterized by a small, predominantly nuclear family unit, engaged in "semi-nomadic subsistence forms of domestic production" which required mutual assistance among households and exchanges based on reciprocity through the system of kinship, and demanded both male and female labor, with small family units of production (Kuznesof 1986:175). Production for use favored integration between the processes of production and reproduction. This organization of the economy favored an increase in marriages and/or consensual unions. She describes the economy at the second and the third times of observation (1802 and 1836) as being based on exchange, on the establishment of urban markets, with the development of infrastructure--particularly the road of the *Serra do Mar*, useable by mule teams.

> For many low-income groups in 1836 the choice between a subsistence and an exchange mode of household production no longer existed. The lack of landed property and cash payments required for taxes or rents implied that, it was no longer possible to live in a completely self-sufficient manner within the district of Sao Paulo. (Kuznesof 1986:174)

She claims that the new forms of labor demand affected the nuptiality structure. The dissolution of consensual unions became more common, resulting in a large proportion of households headed by single mothers. Between 1765 and 1802 there was also an increase in celibacy, i.e. a higher proportion of both adult males and adult females who were not married at the age of 40. At the same time, there occurred a decrease in the age of marriage--"probably in response to improved economic conditions for the commercial class" (1986:73). In the period between 1802 and 1836 these tendencies accelerated. There was also a decline in fertility and an increase in child abandonment.

In Kuznesof's third observation point, starting in 1836, she noted that the previous tendencies toward an exchange economy were consolidated, but through cycles of depression within the economy. The transformation of a domestic subsistence-oriented economy to an exchange mode of production and the introduction of the money market had not resulted in the displacement of the household as the locus of production in the period (1765-1836). Industrialization was still based on the domestic production of goods. But labor recruitment became individual instead of family-based. The small predominantly nuclear unit of the subsistence economy was replaced by a more complex household economic organization, and women were employed as individual gainful workers. In 1802, female heads of household were chiefly found as home-based workers, "spinning from small garden patches of cotton, making clothes for slaves (about 53 percent in 1802), or employed in the service sector" (Kuznesof 1986:168). Kuznesof's conclusions do not favor a linear association between economy and household organization:

> It does not follow that changes in the household economy and structure would occur only in conjunction with the totally basic institution of an exchange for a subsistence household economy. To the contrary, there is reason to believe that the domestic group has much greater plasticity in any given society, in terms of composition and size, than has generally been recognized. (Kuznesof 1986:77)

Additional Remarks on the Growth of Female-Headed Households in Brazil

Several authors have called attention to the sharp growth of female-headed households in Brazil, especially in the period 1970-1980. As noted, however, this is not necessarily a new phenomenon. To demonstrate this, I have used Kuznesof's (1980a, 1980b, 1986) study of the city of Sao Paulo at the turn of the century, which documents the high proportion of women household heads, and notes how women's entry into the labor market also varied in accordance with the prevalence of certain family types.

Following Buvinic et al. (1978) I further noted that the concept of female heads of household hides different types of family arrangements. The proportion of widows, single mothers and separated women among female heads of household grew in the last three decades, especially in Sao Paulo. This pattern contrasts with that found in colonial Brazil, where the typical (non-widowed) female head was a woman living in a visiting union or in concubinage.

Older female heads of household and single mothers became more visible, and were likely to be more economically vulnerable. The same process is documented in other countries. Folbre describes the case of the United States as follows:

> Subsequent increases in the number of families maintained by women alone [in the late 19th and early 20th centuries] were not reflected in aggregate census data, which recorded the gender of the "head of the household". Few single mothers and children could afford to maintain a household of their own.... Relatively little historical research has explored the changing economic position of the elderly and single mothers with young children. But it seems clear that both groups became more economically vulnerable with capitalist development, not only because their opportunities for wage labor were restricted, but also because family obligations were loosened. (Folbre 1988:66)

In spite of the increase of female-headed households, the pattern of the couple-based family persists in Brazil. There are no data to support the "increased disorganization of the modern family" thesis, as posed by Smith (1963, cit. in Mayers 1970:20) for Brazil. It is clear, however, that there is gender differentiation in family formation. Men enter successive unions, while women are more likely to stay by themselves after the first union. Since children are also left with their mothers and/or are supported by them, these women are likely to assume the role of head.

My research on Brazil points to the inadequacies of the "development with poverty" thesis as a way of explaining the rise in female-headed households. Such a thesis suggests that there should have been a sharper rise in the number of such households in the 1960 to 1970 decade than in the more prosperous 1970 to 1980 period. Yet, it is precisely in the more "affluent" period, between 1970 and 1980, that the increase in female heads of household is more noticeable. During this decade, the increase in the numbers of women heads of household involved in the labor market was as impressive as the rise of female-headed households in the same period.

If these data suggest that it is risky to attribute the rise of female headship to economic conjunctures, we must nevertheless emphasize that such conjunctures do affect female-headed households, especially those whose immediate survival needs impel them into the labor market.

Indeed, although economic processes such as proletarianization and industrialization affect family formation and transformation, nuptiality patterns and the age effect should deserve more attention in analyzing the growth of female heads of household. This procedure moves the discussion away from the realm of "economic" explanations, and emphasizes demographic and life cycle variables.

To be young and childless are criteria that count in favor of women in the marriage market, and in the mating game. Considering that appearance and youth are part of a widespread ideology in Brazil, and that about 20 percent of the 1980 female population was between 15 and 39 years, it is not improper to assume that the probability of remarriage for female heads of household due to widowhood and separation was low: about 38 percent of female heads of household were older than 39 years in 1980. Female heads were on the average much older and more likely to be widows than male heads. In Sao Paulo, the average female head was 5 years older than the average male head.

The Colombian Case: Poor Wives and Poor Female Heads of Households, Daily Life Situations and Perceptions

General Overview

This part of the article explores differences and similarities in daily situations and perceptions among poor female heads of households and wives in poor neighborhoods in Bogota, in 1981. Some aspects of production and reproduction were taken into account, but before presenting details taken from interviews and survey analyses, a general overview on poor women's daily constraints and gender ideological traits is presented.

The results suggest an underlying similarity in the situation of poor women, whether they be wives or household heads, taking into account the process of reproduction, the sexual division of work, power and pleasure, and the relations between paid and unpaid work. Today's female heads of household are yesterday's wives and may be tomorrow's wives. Today's wives may be tomorrow's heads of household. That fact that both categories include mothers who are underpaid or whose work is not recognized as socially important results in the same social situation. Yet, despite the instability of marital relations, the accepted ideology of the family is an idealization of the unit of husband, wife and children, which in Colombia carries an emotional and cultural baggage that goes beyond the commonsensical understanding of the family as an institution and what we find emperically.

The results of my research question the universality of these common ideological assumptions:

1. That women are heads of household only because of economic constraints and never choice;
2. That women are heads of household because men are skipping out on their role as economic providers for the family; and
3. That female heads of household are necessarily worse off than wives.

The data collected confirm the high representation of female-headed households among the poor, but also note that in the labor market the occupational and income distribution of poor female heads of household was closer to that of poor male heads than to that of their wives. It is agreed that if there were more job opportunities and easier access to collective services, such as day-care centers, the number of female heads of household would be higher, since many poor wives declared they were not in this category by choice.

In Colombia in 1980, of a total of 5,033 single women about 10% were mothers. In a study of families with an average earning of up to 3 times the minimum salary for families, it was ascertained that about 20% of these families were exclusively supported by women (Rey de Marulanda, 1982).

Poor Women's Daily Lives in Bogota:
Some Dimensions of Production and Reproduction

On Perception and Usage of Some Public Services. Analysis of the perception and usage of some public services in certain neighborhoods included the following services: water, electricity, sewage, the distribution of combustibles, day care centers, schools and health centers. Aside from these items, women in the in-depth interviews complained about the lack of garbage collection, the poor quality of public transportation and the quality of the stores.

More complaints were registered about the service provided by health centers, as much regarding the long wait for medical attention as regarding the poor attention finally received. Criticism of health centers also focused on the doctor-patient relationship, the ways in which they failed to deal with the ignorance of the women about their bodies and how this was in fact reinforced by doctors. The women also complained about ways in which official family planning services were more concerned with the imposition of a birth control method, the I.U.D., than with reproductive education, or with providing women with alternatives from which they might choose.

Women also complained about the day care centers. A critical aspect is the orientation of state-run facilities, which were not necessarily attuned to the needs and expectations of the potential clientele. Many day care centers had schedules that were incompatible with the working hours of women and with school hours. Besides, many women found it difficult to put their children in the centers because of the complicated registration process.

Household Composition and Women's Labor Force Participation. Male heads of family were employed in the protected labor market in greater numbers than female heads. The notion that males are the only providers was rejected, as working wives predominated in the sample. The segmentation of the market by sex was apparent. Poor women were more likely to be found in less protected occupations with lower incomes, even though there were no significant differences in education or age between male companions and women interviewed.

About 48% of the female heads of family received less than the official minimum wage. Only 25% of the poor men were at such an extreme level of poverty. Wives earned the lowest individual incomes. About 65% of the gainfully employed worker's wives were found in the lowest category. Both groups of women had children, both were of the same age group (between 25 and 38 years old), both had the same educational level (just primary school), but cohabitation with the male companion created advantages for them in the labor force. For instance, typical occupations of female heads of families consisted of domestic service (per diem and per task), cleaning, office auxiliaries, vendors; whereas the typical occupations of wives included: seamstress in the home, other remunerated activities in the home, street vendors and workers in family businesses.

Considering also that there were no significant differences found between the two types of families in terms of the age compositions of children, and help from others in domestic activities, the hypothesis is raised that the role of mothers is not the only factor inhibiting equal competence in the female labor supply. Many wives interviewed stated that among their domestic activities they had to "take care of their husbands."

Female heads of family had more flexibility in terms of physical mobility, as they were concentrated in the kind of domestic service work that demanded commuting from their home to their place of employment. Wives predominated in paid occupations performed in the home. This was an important difference with female heads, for these activities (although more compatible with the domestic role of caring for the husband) comprised some of the worst-paid jobs.

It is common for husbands to react negatively to the fact that their wives work outside the home. Men used to criticize their wives because they were not "taking care of the children." But cases in which the wife was prohibited from working in the labor market were infrequent. Necessity brings cultural change, but even the women used to feel guilty for "leaving the children."

In summary, the domestic burden of the wives increased because they had to take care of the husband as well as the children, and the ideology that women's salaries were supplementary also supported their situation. To those women this ideology was necessary to maintain the internal power division in the family, and female heads used to say they had to fight for a better job since they were the only breadwinners.

Wives used to say "My husband works, I help." But since the salary is constituted at the family level, indeed the female-headed families were in the poorest situation, although with a little greater autonomy. At the same time, 83% of these families showed a per capita family wage that was less than half the minimum wage. About 60% of husband-and-wife families were in the same situation.

Mutual Support. It is common in Latin American literature to stress the importance of networks, and it is a widespread notion that the family is a "survival strategy". Colombian society is extremely oriented toward the family and by the family. So the family is not only a social institution but also an ideology or a way of thinking about reality.

Indeed many different types of mutual aid between neighbors and extended family members were detected, chiefly in cases of emergency. But as for all social relations, there were contradictions that should be noticed. To obtain favors and help from family members, friends and neighbors, one had to observe many codes of behavior, to be considered normal. Women had to behave themselves, to fit these behavioral codes in order to belong to these networks and receive their aid.

Single mothers suffered more from social coercion and their sexual life was constrained. Female heads and especially single mothers did not look for community aid, in order to avoid judgment on and repression of their private lives.

Because of the ideology of the "complete family" (husband-wife and children), women who are alone often perceive themselves as segregated. Their self-esteem is also affected. Single mothers used to tell similar stories in which they viewed the children they had outside wedlock as a "bad step," "an error," a "failure" or associated with "*an engano*" (an illusion).

Paid and Unpaid Work. When we refer to unpaid work no differences between the living situations of wives and female heads were found. When investigating the time spent in domestic activities, the following findings were significant:

1. The situation of the wives and female heads were similar in that they were both responsible for housework;
2. To make work at home and the time spent on it by women visible was a hard task for the researchers. Women did not consider as work a lot of the activities done at home, since they were naturally thought to be "women's things" (expression of an interviewed wife);
3. A basic point of difference between wives and female heads was in the use of free time, including weekends: female heads had more time for themselves, and more freedom to go out.

In poor neighboorhoods in Bogota, in the case of families with husbands, there was clearly another question of the internal division of power at the home level. While wives spent their weekends doing housework, being with children or talking to relatives, neighbors and friends, it was common for men to go out drinking, to "*rumbas*" (parties). For men in the working class, the possibilities for spending their free time were also reduced. The kind of work in which they were engaged demanded physical strength and took up their free time, and many just spent their weekends working at another supplementary job or resting. Women's free time was more restricted to the house. For women, home was a place of work and leisure and the home influenced the way in which they viewed their lives.

Some findings from the case study I conducted in poor neighboorhoods in Bogota are quite similar to those stressed by Figueiredo (1982) who developed a comparative study on female heads of households in two fishing communities in Colombia and in Brazil. Figueiredo pointed out women's double day, with responsibilities both for domestic chores and producing income for family survival. She also called attention to the concentration of women (wives and female heads of households) in the lowest-paid jobs in Colombia and in Brazil.

Unions, Biological Reproduction and Sexuality. The category of female heads conceals a number of different situations. There were single mothers, women with children who never lived with men, women who were abandoned by the fathers of their children, women who provoked the separation, and also women who had some stable relation with a man without living with him. Each case had its own history connected with the way each woman perceived reality. About 31% of women heads were single mothers. These women were more critical about their situation, but it cannot be claimed that their way of living was related to a deliberate aim toward liberation. On the contrary, these women, as did many in other situations, affirmed that they had a hard life. They commented on the hostility of the community.

Generally, separation in those cases where husband and wife lived together was associated with the progressive abandonment on the part of the husband of his economic responsibility, or else was due to the constitution of a new family by the man. But most commonly it was the woman who made the decision to end the relationship. Maria, one female head of household, told us she said to her husband: "Well, if you have another woman and if you do not bring more money to your children, I will not wash and iron your shirts, and I will not cook anymore for you." As a result, Maria's husband left and did not return.

Women were not passive in the process of separation. After separation, although they considered they were not in a better situation than when they were married, they were aware that this situation was caused by external constraints. According to my observations Colombian society is oriented toward the family, but about 90% of these female heads of household were the only family breadwinners.

Why Do Women Marry? In the survey, a common answer was: "I was in love." In the case study no more than 40% presented this reply. Another common response was that marriage represented a way to run away from the original family. As many married women as separated ones gave their children as the reason for not changing their conjugal situation.

In theory children are supposed to have a father, however, what is fully demonstrated by the lives of these womenheads is that this ideology does not have any empirical support. Separated women said that they were afraid to remarry since it was probable that the children would not be treated well by the new spouse. Children, as a private property of the family, belong to their biological father and mother.

The strict linkage between women and mothering is also reflected in their references to sexuality. Discussions about sexuality were interwoven with references to pregnancy, and the importance of young women knowing how to avoid it. Although there is in Colombia considerable diffusion of birth control services, they are available only for married women or women living in stable relationships. The state's policy is clearly to make the politics of birth control compatible with family morals.

It is difficult to separate discussions of sexual pleasure from those of pregnancy. The consensus of the interviewers was that the major categories which emerged from the discussion on sexuality were far from those they were concerned with--pleasure, autonomy of decision, and degrees of knowledge about different forms of sexual life. Although wives viewed sexual relations as a duty, they were more concerned with how to avoid pregnancy and how to decrease violence in intersexual relations.

One of the subjects which illustrated a new aspect of women's subordination was the use of contraceptive methods. To our surprise the majority of female heads did not use any contraceptive method, whereas among wives this was a common practice. These female heads did not use any contraceptive method for the simple reason that they did not have any sexual relations at all!

Sexual activity was only for biological reproduction or to satisfy the male companion. Discussions with these women about their mother-daughter relations suggest these women talked more with their daughters about sex. But the topic was the same: how to avoid getting pregnant.

In spite of the symbiosis between mother and child and the almost exclusive burden of childbearing upon women, men always had an important role in the decision to have children. Women said such things to the interviewer as: "He wanted to have a child", or "He would not allow me to kill his child". These were common reasons given for having children. While the role of such ideas as potential maternity or the impulse to be a mother are unclear, it was clear that child care was not only a women's economic and emotional duty, but also a form of compensation for unsatisfying male/female relationships. According to Maria Montoya (interviewee): "I did not care if he went away, I stayed with the children."

The ideology of property, basic to the concept of family organization, is represented in the relation between mother and children, even without any reference to a father. Indeed, it is a common reflection by anthropologists that this

is the strongest link. In the case of wives, it is interesting to note how they describe their sexual feelings toward their male companions. A refusal by a woman to have sexual relations is generally attributed by the man to her infidelity or to work outside the home. We did not find any case of a husband who attributed the tiredness of his wife to domestic work. Nor do men or women consider that a woman's lack of interest in sexual intercourse might be related to the types of sexual practices which are imposed upon the women. In terms of sexuality, wives and female heads of household reveal the same attitude: their having sexual intercourse is the result of a man's request.

Gender Ideology in Poor Bogota:
Who Are Female Heads of Household?

The ideologies of poor Colombian wives and female heads were very similar in many aspects: both agreed that the man should be the principal breadwinner. Women who are the heads of household today were wives before, and before marriage they lived in a family arrangement where they were subject to many constraints. Rosa, one of the wives interviewed, explains this better:

> Of course, I like to be married. When I was single it was slavery, I had to cook for all the family, since Mama was working. I had to help and to take care of my brothers. I could not go out alone, my brothers were always keeping one eye on me... What could I do? To marry is women's fate. I really did not want to marry, but Mama was very scared I would lose myself.

Poor Colombian female heads of household differed from wives basically in the following ways:

1. They were more vulnerable economically and also vulnerable socially. For instance, according to Ana, a single mother: "It is not good to have a man in the house, but when you do not have one, all men outside do not respect you... People do not respect a woman who is alone".

2. They differed in terms of decision making. Women living alone had a higher degree of autonomy, although this autonomy was limited by outside social constraints. They had a broader sphere of mobility and were not so circumscribed to the home space, as wives were.

3. They were more critical about the current patterns of sexual relations. According to interviewees, it was not necessarily the husband who should be the one to propose sexual relations, but in general their

sexual lives were as repressed as those of their wives.

Once a wife, a woman continued to orient her life to a great degree as though she were still a wife, and induced her daughter to assume the same role. These women did not have a life of their own. A mother is an example, not necessarily a person. The father was commonly referred to as the "head of the household", even when not living with the family.

Children were supposed to need a father. It was common to find cases where the father's authority was replaced by another male family member-- not only acting as an authority figure for the children, but also supervising women's behavior, to preserve their "honor." The church was also used to replace the absent father. One of the interviewees participated in church sessions so the "children would have someone to respect."

Poor Colombian wives and female heads worked hard. Like their husbands (when married), they lived in a rigid class society and poverty called for the labor of both. Women were treated as subordinated not only in the family, but in the labor market too, as well as in the neighborhood, in the public sphere.

Female heads of household demonstrated that they were able to support their children on their own. It was clear that women played an active role in family formation and transformation. If they were in a worse economic and social situation than wives it was not necessarily because a husband was fundamental in women's lives, but because the society in which they lived praised the "complete family". It should also be noted that these women were not generally proud of, or even conscious of, their own strength.

Final Remarks on the Colombian Case

The analysis presented here raises some general points for reflection:

1. Class and gender in Latin America are so interconnected that all struggles for liberation have to consider this interaction. It is not easy to separate what in a poor women's living situation was caused by her status as a woman and what should be attributed to her poverty.

2. For any society the ideology of what constitutes a family and what roles are expected of women and men is more complex than a simple statement about the preferred type of household organ-ization. The cultural emphasis in Latin America on the importance of female subordination, and the cultural need for women to live in households with a husband, is a major cause of the low self-esteem of female heads of households. For this reason many of these women would need help if they are to become aware of their gender subordination and the need to struggle against this.

More attention has to be given to the social system. The family is a social institution which is closely linked to historical formations, although some universal features could be specified. In a society such as Colombia, where women are faced with many restrictions and where poor women are more vulnerable to social oppression and economic exploitation, the family acts simultaneously to reproduce women's oppression and to provide women's economic and social support. As I have demonstrated, it is questionable to consider the "complete" family as the only "survival strategy". Women who were heads of household demonstrated that they were able to bring up their children and support themselves. It was more difficult to accomplish these tasks due to the lack of job alternatives and public social facilities, as well as social pressure against women without a male companion. Without a broader social transformation, it is hard to think of radical changes in female-male relations.

There is a need for social programs for poor women in Colombia, such as: adequate child care centers, supportive services to facilitate domestic work (such as public laundry services and neighborhood canteens), and programs of sexual education concerned not only with contraceptive measures, but also with the right to pleasure. Solidarity among women and gender consciousness raising are a must among the poor, and a must for a feminist agenda. The emphasis should be on the daily lives of poor wives and poor female heads of household. This perspective questions the selection of women heads of household as a distinct "target group" among the poor.

Female-Headed Households: Similarities and Differences Between Colombia and Brazil

Brazil and Colombia share a common fate as Latin American countries. Structural processes related to the type of development or underdevelopment which are associated with the growth of female-headed households include: unequal income distribution, proletarianization, migration, concentrated urbanization, gendered use of the labor force and gender stereotypes in the mating system. In Brazil as in Colombia the probability of remarriage is higher for men than for women, especially if women are in their 40s or above. The recent increase of women's participation in the labor force, the decrease in the fertility rate, and women's struggle against subordination and gender ideology are mentioned as factors associated with family dynamics, such as the growth of mother-and-children-based households.

At the micro-level, similarities between the Colombian and the Brazilian cases need to be investigated further, since there is a lack of qualitative comparative studies in Latin America on gender and family. Figueiredo's (1982) study is an exception, and she concludes that there are more similarities than differences among female-headed households with respect to participation in the labor force, victimization by the double day and double sexual standard, and low self-esteem, and low social recognition in both countries. (Her study was about two fishing communities in Brazil and in Colombia.)

On the macro-level the data also point to some similarities such as the higher participation of female heads of household than wives in the labor market, and women's participation in gender ideology. In both countries, women are more likely to consider that men are "natural" heads of household, even when they (women) are the principal breadwinners. In both countries, the official statistical system (censuses and national household surveys) contributes to the legitimation of this ideology, by using the term "head of household".

Macro-level analyses also point to differences between Brazil and Colombia. Despite the fact that women who are heads of households are more likely than men to be concentrated among the poor, in Colombia the proportion and growth of female-headed households among the non-poor is quite impressive. It is not the case in Brazil, although the growth of female-headed households is higher in this country than in Colombia. Despite universal tendencies characteristic of gendered/class-based systems, such as the fact that female-headed households are the poorest among the poor, more attention has to be given to national idiosyncrasies in order to understand how history, economy, culture and gender ideology are intertwined in the production and reproduction of female-headed households, and different meanings given to such an institution in each period, in each class and in each country.

Notes

1. See Buvinic et al. 1978; Youssef and Hettler 1984 in comparative studies on different Third World countries; Massiah 1980 for Jamaica; Merrick and Schmink 1983 for the Metropolitan Region of Belo Horizonte, Brazil; Barroso 1978 and Castro et al. 1979 for Brazil; Rey de Marulanda 1982, Garcia Castro 1987, and Velez and Kaufman 1985, for Bogota, Colombia; Gogna 1984 for Argentina; Scott 1984 and Rodgers Jr. 1986 for the United States; and Tienda and Salazar 1982 for Peru.

2. The concept of patriarchy, and that of patriarchal family, in the feminist literature, are indicative of asymmetric power relations between women and men. According to Eisenstein (1979:17):

> For radical feminists patriarchy is defined as a sexual system of power in which the male possesses superior power and economic privilege. Patriarchy is the male hierarchical ordering of society. Although the legal-institutional base of patriarchy was more explicit in the past, the basic relations of power remain intact today. The patriarchal system is preserved via marriage and the family, through the sexual division of labor and society. Patriarchy is rooted in biology rather than in economics or history. Manifested through male force and control, the roots of patriarchy are located in women's reproductive selves. Woman's position in this power hierarchy is defined not in terms of the economic class structure but in terms of the patriarchal organization of society.

Weber is the first author in the area of sociology to present a theoretical discussion on patriarchy, which in his work is one construct of his "sociology of domination". Patriarchy would be a traditional type of domination. According to Weber (in Toth and Wittich, 1978:1006):

Among the prebureaucratic types of domination the most important one by far is patriarchal domination. Essentially it is based not on the official's commitment to an impersonal purpose and not on obedience to abstract norms, but on a strictly personal loyalty. The roots of patriarchal domination grow out of the master's authority or his household. . . . Under patriarchal domination the norms derive from tradition: the belief in the inviolability of that which has existed from time out of mind.... In the case of domestic authority the belief in authority based on personal relations that are perceived as natural.

In its pure form patriarchal domination has no legal limits. It is transferred without qualification to the new master at the time of the old master's death or downfall. The new master also acquires the sexual disposition of his predecessor's women--possibly of his own father's.

3. In this table, potential female-headed households are calculated using the method described by Norrissey: "Present marital status is used as the basis for calculation. That is, women in the following marital status who are 15 years or older are grouped: widows, separated and divorced women, and single mothers. The proportion of potential female heads of household is the division of the number of potential female heads of household by the total potential number of households (married, widowed, divorced and separated males plus married, widowed, divorced and separated females)." (Morrissey 1985: 34) (See also Buvinic et al. 1978).

References

Aguiar, Neuma. (ed.). 1984. *Mulheres na Força de Trabalno na America Latina Analises Qualitativas*. Petropolis, Vozes.

_____. 1985. "Research Guidelines: How to Study Women's Work in Latin America." In J. Nash. and H. I. Safa (eds.). *Women and Change in Latin America*. (pp. 22-33) Massachusetts: Bergin and Garvey Publishers, Inc.

Ayala, Ulpiano. 1987. "Hogares, Participacion Laboral e Ingresos in Ocampo." Jose Antonio y Ramirez, Manuel, (ed.). *El Problema Laboral Colombiano (Informes de la Mission Chanery)*. Bogota: Consultoria General de la Republica, DNP-SENA.

Azevedo, Thales. 1966. *Cultura e Situacao Racial no Brasil*. Rio de Janeiro: Civilizacao Brasileira.

Barroso, Carmen. 1978. "Sozinhas ou Mal Acompanhadas: A Situacao das Mulheres Chefes de Familia." Paper presented at the Seminar A Mulher na Forca de Trabalho na America Latina IUPERJ. Rio de Janeiro.

Brana-Shute, Gary. 1982. "Family, Kinship and Household Studies in the West Indies. A Review." *Florida Journal of Anthropology*, Vol. 7: 1, 118.

Buvinic, Mayra, Yousseff, Nadia; and Von Elm, Barbara. 1978. *Women Headed Households: The Ignored Factor in Development Planning* (Available from Washington International Center for Research on Women. Washington.)

Candido, Antonio. 1951. "The Brazilian Family". In T.L. Smith and A. Marchant (eds.). *Brazil: Portrait of Half a Continent*. (pp 291-312.) New York: The Druden Press.

_____. 1964. *Os Parceiros do Rio Bonito. Estudo sobre o Caipira Paulista e a Transformacao dos seus Meios de Vida*. Rio de Janeiro: Livraria Jose.

Chaney, Elsa Mae. 1980. *Women in International Migration Issues in Development Planning*. (Available from Office of Women in Development. Washington.) AID REPORT 147, 8-46.

Chaney, Elsa Mae. and Schmink, Marianne. 1976. "Women and Modernization: Access to Tools". In J. Nash, and H. I. Safa (eds.). *Sex and Class in Latin America*. (pp. 150-183.) Amherst,

Massachusetts: J.F. Bergin Publishers, Inc.

DNP-Departamento Nacional de Planeacion. 1991a. *Estructura Laboral Rural y Participacion de la Mujer*. Bogota: DNP-Division de Programas Sociales Speciales. Working Paper

_____. 1991b. *Caraceristicas de la Poblacion Femenina Urbana y su Participacion en las Actividades Laborales*. Bogota: DNP-Division de Programas Sociales Speciales. Working Paper.

Eisenstein, Zillah (ed.). 1979. *Capitalist Patriarchy and the Case of Socialist Feminism*. New York: Monthly Review Press.

Faria, Vilmar. 1980. "Divisao Social do Trabalho, Especializacao e Crescimento urbano. O Caso da Macrometropole Paulista". In ABEP (Ed.) *Anais do II Encontro de Estudos Populacionais*. pp. 745-775. Aguas de Sao Pedro: ABEP.

Figueiredo, Mariza. 1983. "Estudo Comparativo do Papel Socio-Economico das Mulheres Chefes de Familia em Duas Comunidades Negras de Pesca Artesanal." Paper presented in ANPOCS meeting. Caxambu.

Folbre, Nancy. 1988. "Whither Families? Towards a Socialist-Feminist Family Policy." *Socialist Review*, Vol. 18; 4, 57-75.

Freyre, Gilberto. 1968. *Sobrados e Mocambos*. Rio de Janeiro: Jose Olympio.

Garcia Castro, Mary. 1989. *Family, Gender and Work: The Case of Female Heads of Household in Brazil (States of Sao Paulo and Bahia)--1950-1980*. Dissertation presented to the University of Florida, Sociology. Gainesville.

_____. 1987. *Mujeres Pobres como Jefes de Hogar y como Esposas en el Proceso de Reproduccion en Bogota: Identidad y Heterogeneidades*. Geneve: International Labor Office. Working Paper no. 156.

Garcia Castro, Mary, Feitosa, Lucia, Simoes, Celso, and Oliveira, Luis Antonio. 1979. *O Quadro das Familias em Domicilios de Chefes Migrantes e Naturais: Um Estudo Censitario dos Diferenciais nas Regioes Metropolitanas Brasileiras*. Rio de Janeiro: IBGE.

Gogna, Monica. 1984. "Participacion de la Mujer en el Mercado de Trabajo: Trabajo y Familia." (Preliminary Report.) Buenos Aires: Consejo Nacional de Investigaciones Cientificas y Tecnologicas (CONICET).

IBGE--Fundacao Instituto Brasileiro de Geografia e Estatistica. 1953. *Censos Demograficos-VIII Recenseamento Geral do Brasil--* 1970. Rio de Janeiro: Fundacao IBGE.

IBGE--Fundacao Instituto Brasileiro de Geografia e Estatistica. 1970 VIII *Recenseamento Geral de 1970, Instrucoes de Coleta. Documento Censo Demografico*. (pp. 1-8.) Rio de Janeiro: Fundacao IBGE.

IBGE--Fundacao Instituto Brasileiro de Geografia e Estatistica. 1973. *Censos Demograficos*-VIII *Recenseamento Geral do Brasil*--1970. Rio de Janeiro: Fundacao IBGE.

IBGE--Fundacao Instituto Brasileiro de Geografia e Estatistica. 1978. *Censos Demograficos*-VI *Recenseamento Geral do Brasil*--1960. Rio de Janeiro: Fundacao IBGE.

IBGE--Fundacao Instituto Brasileiro de Geografia e Estatistica. 1983a. *Censos Demograficos*-IX *Recenseamento Geral do Brasil*--1980. Rio de Janeiro: Fundacao IBGE.

IBGE--Fundacao Instituto Brasileiro de Geografia e Estatistica. 1983b. *Metodologia do Censo Demografico de 1980*. In IBGE. Relatorios Metodologicos. Vol. 4, 1-80. Rio de Janeiro: Fundacao IBGE.

Kuznesof, Elizabeth Anne. 1980a. "Household Composition and Headship as Related to Changes in Mode of Production: Sao Paulo 1765 to 1836." *Comparative Studies of Society and History*. Vol. 22, 78-108.

_____. 1980b. "The Role of Female-Headed Household in Brazilian Modernization: Sao Paulo 1765 to 1836." *Journal of Social History*. Vol. 13, 589-613.

_____. 1987. *Household Economy and Urban Development: Sao Paulo 1765-1836*. Boulder: Westview Press and Frederick A. Praeger Publishers.

Marcilio, Maria Luiza. 1974. *A Cidade de Sao Paulo: Povoamento e Populacao em 1750-1850 com Base nos Registros Paroquiais e nos Recenseamentos Antigos*. Sao Paulo: Pioneira-USP

168

Massiah, Jocelyn. 1980. *Female Headed Households and Employment in the Caribbean*. Women's Studies. West Indies University Press and UNESCO 2, 62-130.

Mattoso, Katia de Queiros. 1988. *Familia e Sociedade na Bahia do Seculo XIX*. Sao Paulo: Corrupio-CNP.

Mayers, John. 1970. *The Brazilian Household: Size and Composition*. Ph.D. dissertation. University of Florida, Gainesville.

Merrick, Thomas, and Schmink, Marianne. 1983. "Households Headed by Women and Urban Poverty in Brazil." In M. Lycette and P. McGreevey (eds.). *Women and Poverty in the Third World*. (pp. 244-271.) Baltimore: The Johns Hopkins Press.

Morrissey, Marietha. 1985. "Female-Headed Households in Latin American and the Caribbean." Paper presented at the meeting of the Latin American Studies Association-LASA. Albuquerque.

Profamilia. 1991. *Encuesta de Pravalencia, Demografia y Salud*. Bogota: Profamilia/DHS Rey de Marulanda, Nora. 1982. *La Mujer Jefe de Hogar*. Bogota: Universidad de los Andes CEDE.

Rodgers Jr., Harrell R. 1986. *Poor Women, Poor Families: The Economic Plight of America's Female Headed Households*. New York: M. E. Sharp.

Saboia, Joao. 1991. Pacto Inflacionario in Tavares, Maria da Conceicao, Teixeira, Aluizio and Junho Pena, Maria Valeria (org.). *Aquarella do Brasil*. Rio de Janeiro: Rio Fundo Ed.

Safa, Helen I. 1965. "The Female Based Household in Public Housing. A Case Study In Puerto Rico." *Human Organization*. Vol. 24: 2, 135-139.

_____. 1971. "The Matrifocal Family in the Black Ghetto: Sign of Pathology or pattern of Survival?" In C. O. Crawford, (ed.). *Health and the Family*. (pp. 35-59.) New York: The Macmillan Co.

_____. 1976. "Class Consciousness among Working Class Women in Puerto Rico." In J. Nash and H. I. Safa (Eds.). *Sex and Class in Latin America*. (pp. 69-85.) New York: Praeger.

_____. 1985. "Women In Latin America: A Decade of Change." In J. Hopkins (ed.). *Perspectives of a Region*. (pp. 50-86.) New York: Holmes and Meier.

Schmink, Marianne. 1986. "Household Economic Strategies: A Review and a Research Agenda." *Latin American Research Review*. Vol. 19; #3: 87-101.

Scott, Hilda. 1984. *Working Your Way to the Bottom: Feminization of Poverty*. London: Pandora.

Smith, Raymond. 1978. "The Family and the Modern World System: Some Observations from the Caribbean." *Journal of Family History*. Vol. 34; 337-360.

_____. 1979. "Caso das Fazendas de Cafe em Sao Paulo." In K. de Almeida (ed.). *Colcha de Retalhos. Estudos sobre a Familia no Brasil*. (pp. 39-90.) Sao Paulo: Brasiliense.

_____. 1986. "Sex and Occupation in Comparative Perspective." Unpublished manuscript. New School for Social Research. New York.

Tienda, M. and Saazar, Sylvia Ortega. 1982. "Las Familias Encabezadas por Mujeres y la Formacion de Nucleos Extensos. Una Referencia al Peru." *Demografia y Economia*. Vol. XVI: I, 64-89.

Tilly, Louise and Scott, Joan. 1978. *Women, Work and Family*. London: Holt, Rinehart and Winston.

United Nations. 1984. *Report of the World Conference to Review and Appraise the Achievements of the United Nations Decade for Women: Equality, Development and Peace*. Nairobi/New York: United Nations.

Vallejo, Martha Luz Henao, and Sierra Garcia, Oliva. 1991. *Pobreza Urbana y Distribucion del Ingreso en Colombia (periodo 1976-1986)*. Medellin: Centro de Investigaciones Economicas Universidad de Antioquia.

Vellez, Eduardo B., and Kaufmann, Daniel. 1985. "La Heterogeneidad de los Sectores Marginados: El Caso de los Hogares con Jefes Femeninos." In E. Bonilla (ed.). *Mujer y Familiaen Colombia*. Bogota: Plaza and Janes.

Werneck Vianna, Maria Lucia Teixeira. 1991. Salve-se Quem Puder! (Reflexoes Sobre a Politica Social no Projeto Collor). In Tavares, Maria da Conceicao, Teixeira, Aloisio and Junho Pena,

Maria Valeria (org.) *Aquarella do Brasil*. Rio de Janeiro: Rio Fundo Ed.
Youssef, Nadia H., and Hettler, Carol B. *1984*. *Rural Households Headed by Women: A Priority Concern for Development*. International Labour Office, World Employment Programme Research. WEP 10/WP, 31 Geneva.

8

An Ignored Population: Female-Headed Households Among Refugees in Africa[1]

Nana Apeadu

Over the last decade the international population of refugees has risen drastically, with the result that by 1991 it was estimated that 15 million of the world's population were refugees. Of this number approximately 4.6 million were in Africa. Although refugee statistics are constantly changing and are not consistently disaggregated by age and gender, it has been estimated that up to 80 percent are women and children. It has also been noted that female-headed households comprise a significant proportion of this population (United Nations Economic and Social Council E/CN.6/1991/4:5). This is of particular concern since under "normal" conditions women represent the most economically, socially and politically vulnerable segment of the international community (DAWN 1985), and in most contexts households headed or supported by women are particularly vulnerable.

This discussion will focus on Mozambiquan refugee female-headed households in Malawi. Limited comparative attention will be given to comparable female-headed households living in Zimbabwe. Malawi provides a useful context for examining this issue because it currently has the largest refugee program in Africa, and one of the largest refugee programs in the world. Since 1976 there has been a steady movement of refugees from Mozambique into Malawi. This movement rapidly escalated after 1989 to such an extent that by 1989 it reached about half a million persons (Kalyati 1990). A focus on Mozambiquan refugee female-headed households in Malawi usefully illustrates the problems confronted by poor third-world countries, which by virtue of their location as well as their socio-cultural linkages with populations generating refugees, find themselves hosting large numbers of poor refugee women and children.

This analysis underscores the importance of giving careful attention to culturally determined patterns of family organization and the content of male, female and children's roles. Further it shows that it is equally important to give attention to the impact of historical, political and economic forces in analyzing the emergence and functioning of female-headed households in Africa. It is argued that all of these forces must be taken into consideration in the development of appropriate programs and policies to alleviate the problems of refugees.

Three themes are explored in this chapter:

1. That in the African context it is appropriate, given the importance of women's economic roles to the well being of their families, that primary attention be given to developing income-generating and education projects for the refugee women, particularly those heading or supporting families.

2. That the lack of consensus on the numbers of female-headed households in the refugee population is related to the issue of the criteria to be used in determining household headship. This problem is more pronounced among the refugee population because: (a) there is a greater degree of shifting household composition, (b) the enormous numbers of people seeking asylum makes documentation of house-hold composition secondary to meeting life preserving needs.

3. That the low level of education among Mozambiquan refugees, high levels of male migration and escalating numbers of Mozambiquan refugees are all related to Portuguese colonial policies in Mozambique. These policies deliberately depressed educational opportunities for Africans, and set in motion adult wage labor migration. In addition, the relationship established between Colonial Mozambique, South Africa and Southern Rhodesia created the frame-work for the current civil war in independent Mozambique which has given rise to escalating numbers of Mozambiquan refugees.

The discussion which follows is divided into five parts: (1) a brief overview of the African refugee problem; (2) a description of the Portuguese colonial system in Mozambique prior to her independence, which emphasizes the role played by colonial policies in the creation of large numbers of rural female-headed households in Southern Mozambique prior to her independence in 1975; (3) a discussion of female-headed households in Malawi which gives special attention to the types of female-headed households there (Malawi and Mozambique both belong to the South African labor complex, and are characterized by high rates of male migration, which has had a significant impact on family structure and organization, particularly in rural areas); (4) a description of some of the conditions in refugee camps in Malawi, especially as they relate to female-headed households and women and children; and (5) needs and recommendations.

Overview of the African Refugee Problem

In 1991 Africa's 4.6 million refugees represented the second largest refugee population in the world. In this population 1.3 millon were from Ethiopia, 1.1 million were from Mozambique, 488,000 from Angola, 438,000 from the Sudan and 388,000 from Somalia (United Nations Focus, Refugee Women Factsheet, 1991). The majority of African refugees live in the horn of Africa, and are concentrated in the following countries: Djibouti, Ethiopia, Somalia, Sudan. Other large segments of this population live in Malawi and the countries bordering Liberia. Currently Malawi, a small landlocked country that has been designated as the fourth poorest country in the world by the World Bank, has the largest refugee program in Africa, and one of the largest in the world (Women's Commission for Refugee Women and Children 1991).

A review of the African countries generating and receiving refugees shows that refugees are moving from and settling in underdeveloped, poor countries that are experiencing low levels of economic growth and a high population growth (Kibreab 1985). In some instances these countries are also plagued by serious drought, famine, political upheaval and human rights violations. As a result, the influx of large numbers of refugees compounds these existing problems, by putting additional pressure on economic, social and political resources. The problems of refugees are compounded in these new settings because they must deal with many of the same problems faced by the nationals of these countries without the critical social supports of their home community.

Refugee Women and Children: Special Concerns

Two of the most serious problems facing women and children refugees are (1) the need for adequate nutrition and (2) the need for protection. In both instances separation from the previous institutional and social supports of their indigenous community has resulted in increasing their vulnerability to death through malnu-trition or various types of physical abuse. Malnutrition is the leading cause of death among refugees (United Nations Economic and Social Council E/CN.6/91/4:8; Johnsson 1989).

The overwhelming majority of women and children refugees have come from poor rural communities where women play an important part in the production of food and provision of subsistence goods for their families. Access to land, water, firewood and in some instances trading opportunities have been critical to their subsistence strategies. In addition, in these contexts they also often make decisions about the allocation of food within their households. As refugees it is precisely in these areas that their access is impeded. Without access to land and other subsistence resources they become dependent on external institutions for the essentials of life.

Decisions on the distribution of food, access to water and firewood in refugee camps are usually made by international organizations and national governments in consultation with male refugee leaders. These decision makers do not adequately understand the needs and circumstances of women and children. This results in food distribution procedures and content of rations that may not adequately meet their needs (United Nations Economic and Social Council E.CN.6/1991/4:8). It is important to keep in mind when reviewing this problem that it is usually occurring in a context where many of the women and children of the host country are also poor, lack adequate food and safe drinking water and are experiencing high rates of both child mortality and poor health. The additional pressure of refugees on already limited resources and lack of adequate international attention to their plight can act to create tension between the indigenous population and incoming refugees. The situation in Malawi represents a good case in point.

Malawi is a small, poor country with a geographical area of 118,484 square kilometers and an indigenous population of 8.3 million. It shares its longest border with Mozambique. Since 1976, as a result of the armed conflict in Mozambique, it has been host to a steadily rising refugee population. In 1986 the number of Mozambiquan refugees in Malawi was 70,000. It rose to 227,000 in 1987 and to about one half million by 1989 (Kalyati 1990).

Currently Malawi has the greatest density of refugees (defined as the number of refugees per square mile) of any country in the world. In some districts, particularly those in border areas, the refugees outnumber the nationals (op. cit.). However, despite this situation Malawi has never closed its borders to Mozam-bique. Some refugees upon arrival were immediately integrated with Malawians; however, not withstanding this hospitality, refugees are imposing a great deal of strain on the economy and resources of Malawi. They are contributing to defor-estation of the country by cutting down trees for building shelters and for firewood. Some refugees are growing vegetables in areas belonging to Malaw-ians, thus worsening the already existing land shortage. Further, they are overburdening the available social services such as hospitals, health centers, food markets and transportation (Apeadu & Karumuna 1989).

This situation was exacerbated by the calamities of flood and earthquake in 1989, as well as a severe drought. Thus the little food that was available had to be shared amongst nationals and refugees alike. In this context of high population density and land scarcity it becomes understandable why in most refugee camps access to land is impossible.

Most of the female refugees in Malawi are rural Mozambiquans. One of their major needs is access to land so that they can supplement their food rations with vegetables grown in their own gardens to combat malnutrition. This need, combined with the need for firewood for their own use and to sell and buy foodstuffs, has driven them to cross the border back into Mozambique to fetch firewood at risk of their lives.

Interviews with women in camps, most of whom were household heads, revealed that in addition to the problems of lack of adequate nutrition and services, they also have very serious problems in the area of protection. During their flight from Mozambique they encountered situations such as road blocks, persecution, trauma, torture and rape. Their problems continued when they reached their country of asylum in the form of inadequate and unsuitable service provision and protection (Apeadu and Karumuna 1989). The data gleaned from these interviews supports Johnsson's (1989) position and that of the United Nations High Commission (UNHCR), that more attention needs to be given to the protection of refugee women and children.

A number of refugee camps and settlements in Africa are located in remote areas where the lack of good roads and transportation make the refugees very isolated. In some instances the distance of the camps from the border leads to armed attacks. Further, most of these isolated areas are infested with mosquitoes. This results in deaths due to malaria and related diseases, which are highest among children. In addition to these problems, refugee women are vulnerable to rape, torture, and other types of physical abuse.

In part, inadequacies in this area stem from the way that the 1951 Convention on Refugees conceptualized the refugee problem when developing policy. First, they did not foresee that women and children would comprise a significant portion of the refugee population. In fact, not one woman was among the drafters, nor was the word "woman" ever mentioned. To the extent that gender is revealed in these legal terms, it is clear that the male refugee was in the mind of the drafters. Further, the 1967 protocol and the 1969 OAU Convention governing specific aspects of refugees in Africa, as well as the African Commission on Human Rights, are all totally male in composition. In spite of OAU's most progressive legal treaty, refugees and displaced women in Africa continue to be most often subjected to military attack, and even children are subject to forced recruitment by both government and rebels. The whole concept of political persecution has been perceived by the male-oriented society as more relevant to the fate of males rather than females.

Historical Background to Mozambiquan Refugee Problem

Why are there so many Mozambiquan refugees? Why have so many selected Malawi as their place of asylum? Is the forced movement of large numbers of Mozambiquans across national borders a new phenomenon? In addressing these questions, Marvin Harris's 1958 pamphlet, *Portugal's African "Wards" - A First-Hand Report on Labor and Education in Mozambique* provides a useful back-ground to the current situation in Mozambique. This section of the discussion draws heavily on this report because, due to the Portuguese policy of restricting anthropological and sociological research in Mozambique, there is little other first-hand documentation or analysis of the Portuguese colonial system in Mozambique or its consequences for family organization, education, and agricultural development.

Harris describes colonial Mozambique as a carefully administered colony, characterized by an apartheid-like system that was more severe than in South Africa. The indigenous population was insulated from provocative news from abroad, subject to corporal punishment and deportation, and vastly unequal access to education was used as a central pillar for keeping the system in place.

Portugal's overseas territories were organized and administered through a provincial system. Each of the overseas territories was considered to be a province of Portugal with the same juridical standing. The citizens within each province were said to have the same privileges and entitlements as citizens in the mother country. However, Mozambiquans in the colony were not granted citizenship unless they were able to speak Portuguese correctly, and to adopt the "habits and customs presupposed for the application of Portuguese common law". At the time of the writing of Harris's report, less than one-tenth of one percent of the African population had been granted citizenship since the application of the first Assimilation law in 1917 (Harris 1958:7). The overwhelming bulk of the population held the status of "indigenalto". This status was comparable to that of a minor ward. The ideology surrounding this status was that like children, "indigenaltos" were incapable of making decisions that were in their best interests. Thus the government had the responsibility of "protecting them and guiding them towards maturity of mind and soul" (Harris 1958:8).

This system of rule was administered by dividing Mozambique into eighty urban and rural districts, each governed by an administrator who executed all police and juridical functions. Control of the indigenous population was carried out through myriad devices, the most important of which were the passbook system (which regulated movement), corporal punishment, deportation and a carefully regulated system of African education designed to insure low academic competence. In 1950, as a result of these education policies, the Mozambiquan population had a 99 percent illiteracy rate (Harris 1958:16).

The underlying objective of this tightly controlled system of colonial rule was the control and deployment of African labor. In fact, African labor was the greatest natural resource exploited by the colony, and large profits accrued to Portugal from its use and sale. The stringent labor codes developed and implemented by Portuguese administrators allowed for two central patterns of exploitation to emerge:

1. Forced contract male migrant labor, in which any adult male between the ages of 18-55 was presumed "idle" unless he could prove other-wise, and was subject to recruitment by the government for six months of labor in the public interest. These workers were paid minimum legal wages for the region which varied from less than two dollars to five dollars a month. Others, despite the illegality of the practice, were conscripted by private non-governmental recruiters and were sent primarily to European farms and plantations. (See Harris 1958 for a detailed description of this system.) Still others were recruited through government agreements with South Africa to South African mines. Under these formal agreements with South Africa, the Portuguese government received a substantial portion of the workers' wages in gold at the official rate. They then paid the migrant workers in local currency, retaining the gold for their own use (Nelson 1985: xxvi).

2. Forced cotton production in the area north of Zambezi. This pattern of labor control acted to bind African males and their families to the land in a serf-like condition to produce cotton for the twelve Portu-guese private concession companies. The producers were forced to sell the cotton to the concession companies at a price far below the international market price. This pattern resulted in large tracts of land being taken out of agricultural production for family and community use, and being used instead for cash crops that did not generate enough cash to compensate for the lost subsistence crops. (See Harris 1958 for a detailed description of this policy.)

The consequences of these policies for this discussion are threefold. Harris computes that approximately seventy-five percent of adult males in southern Mozambique during this period were engaged in some form of migratory wage labor involving protracted absences from their rural homesteads and families. They did not earn enough to send remittances home; therefore the women left behind were totally responsible for supporting themselves and their children. Thus a pattern emerged in which high percentages of women in Southern Mozambique became heads of households as a result of government policies. Further, in a significant number of cases, men who wanted to avoid being placed under the contract labor system became "clandestine" emigrants to the Union of South Africa in order to find better wages and working conditions, thus becoming permanently lost to their home communities. The extraction of males from these communities disrupted traditional division of labor patterns, leaving women with exclusive responsibility for clearing land, and for planting and harvesting basic food crops. This reduced the productivity of homestead agriculture, and retarded the development of modern farming.

Portugal's policies in Mozambique were designed to generate as much profit as possible with as little investment as possible. Her own economic position did not allow for the development of Mozambique's vast resources. Therefore she used the strategic location of the country in relation to South Africa and land-locked Southern Rhodesia to her best economic advantage. The Indian ocean ports on the one hand, and rail transportation between Southern Rhodesia on the other, allowed the Portuguese rulers to establish economic ties that rendered Mozambique a service economy for South Africa and Southern Rhodesia. (See Rinehart 1985 for a fuller description of this process.) The colony depended on South Africa for imports of food, consumer goods, oil, raw materials and foreign exchange earnings (Rinehart 1985).

In the early 1960s the Portuguese government made the following changes in the regulations affecting the African population: 1) abolished the legal distinction between "indigenaltos" and the rest of the population; 2) abolished forced cultivation of commercial crops; 3) gave greater powers to local organs of administration; 4) made legal provisions for greater participation of Africans in government; and 5) increased expenditures on rural development, health and education (Reinhart 1985). At the end of a long armed struggle Mozambique became independent in 1975, but is still plagued by the legacy of its colonial experience. (See Rinehart 1985 and Kaplan 1985 for a detailed discussion of the legacy of colonialism and the economy.)

For purposes of this discussion, we see the emergence under colonialism of people being forced to leave their country to escape political pressures and the development of long-distance male migration which continues until today. Finally, although there has been considerable improvement in literacy rates, the impact of the colonial educational policies is still reflected in the relatively high illiteracy rates of both male and female Mozambiquans. In the early 1980s, the adult literacy rate was about 25 percent, and was markedly higher for males than for females (Rinehart 1985: xvii).

Female-Headed Households in Malawi

Malawi shares its longest border with Mozambique, and in the border areas the populations share many ethnic and sociocultural features; in some places they also speak the same local languages. Prior to the escalation in refugees, there had been significant movement of Mozambiquans in and out of Malawi (Kalyati, 1990). Both countries belong to the South African labor complex, thus both have experienced the impact of high levels of male labor migration. In Malawi this has contributed significantly to the high levels of rural female-headed households. For example, Spring (1986) reports that approximately one-third of rural households are female-headed, and that male labor migration has contributed importantly to the emergence of this household type (Spring 1986). Thus both countries have a long-standing tradition of female-headed households whose numbers are augmented through male migration. Spring divided female-headed households in Malawi into six basic types, each with its own consequences for the maintenance and functioning of the household.

1. Those in which the household head has never married. This category can be further divided into those that are self-sustaining and those residing with relatives.
2. Married women whose husbands are away for short or long periods.
3. Married women who have been abandoned.
4. Separated women.
5. Divorced women.
6. Widowed women.

She suggests that households headed by women, especially those who do not receive remittances, experience food deficits due to labor constraints, simpler farming systems and lack of agricultural services. However, those female-headed households whose husbands return at intervals, and/or send regular remittances, are comparable to male-headed households (Spring 1986:335). The key element then in the economic vitality of Malawian rural female-headed households appears to be not solely the sex of the household head or the intensive involvement of women in agriculture, but rather the degree to which they have access to male labor, or the fruits of that labor.

This finding further refines our understanding of the variables that lead to the well-being of women and children in various types of households. Increasingly, researchers working in Africa are giving closer attention not only to the resources held by households, but to the ways in which those resources are generated and distributed among family members. In this regard researchers have stressed the importance of moving away from Euro-centric models of family organization, family composition, and households in the analysis of African families (Spring 1986, Lloyd and Brandon 1991, Okonjo 1989, Desai 1991, Guyer 1981, Sanjek 1982, Frank 1988, Robertson and Berger 1986). This caution is of particular importance in understanding the degree to which family structure in and of itself affects the economic well-being of African women and children.

Both Guyer (1981) and Desai (1991) point to the incompatibility of the assumptions underlying the concept of "household" with the African reality. This concept, they argue, implies a domestic unity, with the unit exercising control over production and consumption. Several problems emerge when this model is utilized in the African context:

1. The model does not account for the flexibility in household composition, for instance, people coming and going on visits, seasonal migration, fostering arrangements;
2. It treats the household as a bounded unit, and as a result does not give adequate attention to the reality that individuals may exercise rights and be subject to economic obligations beyond the households in which they live;
3. It does not recognize that often husbands and wives do not form a unified production unit, and that wives' incomes are often separate from their husbands'. Further, Western conceptions of the content of male and female roles differ from those of most African societies. For example, in the African context women's economic roles are intricately intertwined with their roles of wife and mother. In most instances, particularly in rural societies, an important part of a mother's role is the provision of food and other subsistence goods for herself and her children.

All of these factors combine to create a very different form of family and economic organization, which has profound implications for the well being of women and children. For example, Desai, in examining the nutritional status of children in monogamous and polygamous marriages in West Africa, found that the nutritional status of children in these two types of families showed "a very small and statistically insignificant difference" even though the father's income was shared by more children. This was explained by the fact that women and children provide most of their own food, thus the reduction in the father's contribution had little negative impact (Desai 1991:1).

Spring (1986) also stresses the need to disaggregate household income between husbands and wives in order to adequately understand production and consumption patterns in African families. She states:

Studies have shown that mother's income rather than the overall household income is the significant factor in the status of child nutrition (Spring 1986:338).

In this regard she alerts us to the importance of recognizing that many factors influence the degree to which mothers can adequately meet the subsistence needs of their children, and also vary depending on the circumstances of the mother. For example, in rural areas, the following factors may critically influence the degree to which a woman can adequately feed her family:

1. degree of access to land;
2. the amount of time she spends cultivating her own crops, versus the time spent working in her husband's fields or engaged in other income-generating activities in which he is engaged;

3. the amount of control she has over her own labor and the labor of their children

4. the amount of land devoted to cash crops versus crops for family use.

All of these are important in determining the nutritional well-being of women and children. The discussion above suggests that variables beyond the type of marriage (polygamous, monogamous) and the sex of the household head come into play in determining the well-being of family members.

This has implications for addressing the needs of refugee women and children, especially in the areas of nutrition and education. It underscores the importance of giving close attention to culturally determined patterns of family organization, and the ways in which these influence the deployment of resources held by the unit in designing programs to meet the needs of families. Further, the discussion demonstrates the importance of providing income-generating projects and educational opportunities for mothers so that they can meet the needs of their families now and in the future. Most importantly it shows the inappropriateness of making assumptions based on the "ideal" type of western family form, e.g., that the provision of training and income-generating activities for men will automatically insure the well-being of the family unit.

In addition, this work demonstrates that family structure does not always predict the viability of the household. In the case of female-headed households it is not solely the structure of the family that causes poverty. Rather, this research strongly suggests that when mothers are given access to productive resources they tend to direct income generated from them to the well-being of their children (*Technical Reports in Gender and Development* 1989). Thus investment in the mothers heading these families is investment in the children, and given the reality that children and women form the overwhelming majority of the refugee population, attention to their needs benefits the whole community.

Mozambiquan Refugee Women and Children

In Malawi the refugee population has been estimated at approximately 800,000. The overwhelming majority are women and children, with children between the ages of 0-14 comprising the largest segment of the total refugee population (Kalyati 1990: 1,8). In thinking about the women and children living in refugee camps and settlements it proves useful to look at the process of forced movement and settlement. Refugees in camps and settlements are "survivors". Although they often represent a segment of the rural and urban poor, and often have left their homes with few if any possessions, they are the ones who were physically strong enough, and who had the social and in some instances material resources to travel from their home communities, often across long distances, to places of asylum. The refugee settlement or camp in most instances represents the last stop of a serial movement. They arrive physically and mentally exhausted and traumatized. Sometimes they travel alone, and sometimes in small bands or in groups.

While collecting data in Malawi on the refugee situation, the total surviving population of a village located about ten to fifteen miles from the border arrived. The group included extended families, women with children, many without husbands, and orphaned children. They arrived with the few possessions they could carry, and traumatized by the violent attack that had been waged on their village by soldiers who thought that they had been helping the opposition. While in flight, they traveled at night, always in fear of being ambushed, physically assaulted or killed. Some members of the group knew people in Malawi and spoke the same local language. In this instance, relationships of mutual assistance established in the home community could be partially maintained. For instance, the orphaned children had already been absorbed by families in the group, and injured members were being helped by the more able-bodied in the group.

In other instances where refugees had traveled alone, the resettlement in the new situation was much more difficult, because they were separated from prior social supports. Usually refugees try to settle in places where they know someone, but this is not always possible. There is always an active exchange of information among refugees, which has proven very useful in helping some of them find lost relatives and friends, and in some instances to partially reconstitute social network systems.

In Malawi there are roughly two patterns of settlement: (1) integrated settlement within Malawian communities, which most commonly happens when there has been a tradition of interaction between groups prior to settlement, and (2) refugee camps and settlements.

In some districts the refugee population has grown to such an extent that refugees represent between 23 percent and 61 percent of the total population of the district. The refugee female population is very heterogeneous; there are important variations in age, education, religion, family composition, culture and prior rural, urban experience. In addition they differ in their expectations and their possibilities for repatriation and resettlement. Thus although there are basic needs of all refugees, different refugee camps and settlements have their own special needs shaped by those of the population they serve. Moreover, there are significant differences in the sizes of camps and the numbers of men, women, and children served. Female-headed households represent a significant segment of the population; however, the problems of enumeration found in non-refugee situations are present in the statistical procedures within camps and settlements. These problems are compounded by the ever-changing numbers of refugees.

Some of the problems of accurate measurement arise from fluctuating household membership. Men may have arrived with their families, but have left the camp to look for work. Thus, although the unit may be recorded as male-headed, it is *de facto* female-headed. Makanya, in a discussion of Mozambiquan refugees in Zimbabwe, reports that it is relatively easy for men to leave camps for work on farms, plantations and in urban areas, and that in some cases men have gone as far as South Africa looking for work (Makanya 1990:3). Apeadu and Karumuna found a similar situation in Malawi, in which men leave the camp for two to three weeks at a time to work on tea plantations, others leave to find work as domestic servants for more extended periods, and in some instances the migrating men never return. Also there is the situation where families enter the camp with a male head in whose name food ration cards are issued. In many cases these men are working outside of the camp, and return to camp every two weeks to get the food rations for the family. Since they leave immediately afterwards, they appear present when in fact they are absent most of the time.

Other problems of accurate measurement result from the suggestion of Frank that despite the self-reliance of women in providing for themselves and their children, headship is a social status rather than an economic reality (1991). Thus males may wish to be recorded as heads even if they do not contribute economically. This problem is related to the broader issue of what constitutes headship, and the failure to reach consensus on the critical variables to be used in determining headship discussed in the introduction to this book. In the refugee context, if the critical variables used in defining headship alternate between marital status and residence, and economic support, a discrepancy would arise between the statistics gathered by enumerators using different headship criteria. For example, those using economic criteria as the crucial variable, in situations where the adult male is handicapped, and unable to contribute economically to the household, would list those families as female-headed. They would also list polygamous situations where each wife was solely responsible for the well-being of herself and her children as female-headed. However, if marital status and/or residence was used as the critical variable, both of these units would be listed as male-headed. This variation in criteria is partly responsible for the disparities in the statistics on female-headed households among the refugee population. Another problem that arises in this regard is the failure to consistently collect data on family composition. As the following chart shows, the records document the numbers of men, women and children, but it is impossible to determine from these records the relationships among these individuals. This problem is compounded by the rapidly changing number of refugees. For example, Kalyati states that in 1989 "UNHCR officers stationed in Districts hosting refugees reported an average of 17,500 refugees being registered per month" (Kalyati 1990:2). With the volume of refugees pouring into Malawi, it is certainly understandable that given the enormous needs and various problems, it would be difficult to keep accurate and up-to-date records on family composition. The tables below, drawn from site visits in

Malawi during November and December of 1989, give some indication of the numbers of men, women, and children served in refugee camps and settlements, and of the variations in camp size and settlement patterns.

District: Chikwawa
Location: Kunyinda
Brief description of the setting: Malawians and Mozambiquans live side by side. They share the same skills, language, and cultural background. The Malawian rural communities have absorbed the Mozambiquan refugees into their population. They are integrated, but not self-sufficient.
Refugee Population 32,166
Women 8,806
Children 17,913
Men 5,347

District: Mulanje
Location: Muloza
Brief description of the setting: One of the oldest and most densely populated camps in Malawi, situated 2km from the Mozambiquan border. This camp hosts refugees from the neighboring Mozambiquan township of Mulanje whose life style is urban. The camp layout is typical of an African slum.
Refugee population 30,365
Women 8,371
Children 15,151
Men 6,964

District: Ntcheu
Location: Mulangeni
Brief description of the setting: In this district refugees form 34 percent to the total population (Kalyati 1990).
Refugee population 148,128
Women 37,896
Children 82,664
Men 29,788

District: Dedza
Location: This settlement has fourteen camps spread along the western side of the district.
Brief description of the settlement: The refugee population is

29 percent of the total population of the district (Kalyati 1990). The refugee population is integrated into the Malawian villages. The largest concentration is in Mphati where there are IGA activities for women.

Refugee population 148,069
Women 39,360
Children 82,137
Men 38,862

These statistics demonstrate that children significantly outnumber adults among the refugees, and that women consistently outnumber the men in each settlement. In reviewing these statistics it is helpful to keep in mind the 1980 Mozambiquan population statistics. Although outdated, they provide a rough profile of the population. At the time the Mozambiquan population was 12.1 million, dis-tributed as follows: 42.5 percent was under 15 years of age, 42.2 percent were between the ages of 15 and 44, 11.9 percent were between the ages of 45 and 64, and only 3.4 percent were over 65. The average life expectancy was 45 years and the ratio of men to women was 100 males to 105 females. Females exceeded males in all categories except children 15 years and under (Kaplan 1985: 80). If these rates have not been radically altered it is not surprising that children 14 years and under comprise the largest segment of the refugee pop-ulation.

The brief descriptions of these few camps show that there are rural-urban differences within the refugee population, and different patterns of settlement in relation to the indigenous population. These differences have important impli-cations for the subsistence strategies employed by refugees and the types of services and programs needed by those hosted in each settlement.

Refugee Female-Headed Households

There are important variations in age as well as the conditions that lead women to assume the role of heads of their household or providers of primary economic support to their families. Among the refugee population, although there are no firm statistics on the number of female-headed households and estimates of their percentage of population vary widely for the reasons cited above, it is widely agreed that they constitute a significant segment. Female-headed units within the refugee population can be roughly divided into the following categories: 1) Widows (divisible further into two categories: (a) women with dependents whose husbands are victims of civil war or were murdered by bandits or rebels, and (b) women whose husbands are missing and presumed dead, but may sometimes return unexpectedly); 2) divorced women with dependent children; 3) separated women with dependent children; 4) abandoned women with dependent children (in these cases the women arrived with their husbands and were abandoned after settling in the camp); 5) young unmarried women who have taken over the responsibility of younger brothers, sisters or other minor relatives because of the death of their parents; 6) elderly or disabled women who have become heads of households with or without dependent children because of the frequent absences of husbands or adult male family members. Each of these situations has different consequences for the women and children in these families and calls for different patterns of support.

Female-Headed Households: Current Conditions, Needs and Recommendations

Within the refugee camps and settlements, culturally determined sexual division of labor patterns persist, despite radically changed conditions. Although there are ethnic variations between groups, the general pattern is basically similar. Women are engaged primarily in domestic activities such as family care, fetching water and firewood, washing, food preparation, caring for the sick and finding necessary items for the household. Men carry out tasks such as building shelter, and when possible they are engaged in income-generating activities such as carpentry, tailoring, or tinsmithing. Many also leave the camp to look for work. However, given the separation of refugees from their home communities, the social context and resources needed to carry out many former productive tasks such as farming, craft production and trading have been severely diminished. Thus, although the division of labor pattern has been maintained, the productive activities which undergirded family subsistence have been severely curtailed.

Given the importance of women's economic activities to the well-being of their families and in particular their children, the separation from the needed resources to carry out their economic roles has had serious consequences particularly in the area of nutrition and health. Further the time and energy women spend performing domestic and family care activities has been greatly increased. They often must go further to collect water and firewood, and sometimes these tasks must be repeated more frequently. Caring for the sick has become a major task, given the increased vulnerability of children and other family members to illness. Finding the needed condiments, and ways to purchase them while trying to stretch rations until the next food distribution period, makes the process of food preparation more difficult.

For female-headed households where no adult male is present, these problems are intensified. In these households, mothers must also carry out the essential tasks that are usually the responsibility of men, thus increasing their already heavy work load. In addition, unlike households where men are involved in income-generating projects that may if shared increase the budgets available to women for food and other subsistence goods, single mothers are limited to the resources that they can individually obtain. This situation is most critical in camps or settlements where they have no friends or family that they can depend on in times of crisis.

Moreover, women who are alone with their children are far more vulnerable to physical abuse, rape and other indignities than women who are attached to households with adult male family members. Some of the specific needs of women, particularly women heading households, in the area of income generation are discussed below.

Income-Generating Activities

Employment should be recognized as a protective issue. Increasing the self-reliance of refugee women will have a positive effect on the whole community. As producers in the host country, refugees can represent an asset rather than a liability. This can lessen the burden they place on their hosts and reduce tensions between nationals and refugees. When they return home they can take with them new skills and experiences that can contribute towards their nations' development.

In order to allow the full participation of women in training programs, literacy classes and income generating projects, serious attention must be given to introducing appropriate technology to reduce the time and energy spent in carrying out domestic activities, particularly in the areas of provision of food, fuel and water. A review of income-generating projects designed for refugees in Malawi and Zimbabwe reveals that although there are a variety of programs, they largely serve men. In part this is related to the enormous time and energy that women must spend carrying out domestic and family care activities. However there appears to be another problem which contributes to this imbalance. The projects tend to be male-oriented. Interestingly, the social constraints on women learning and doing such work as carpentry, black-smithing, or shoe repair are not confined to the refugee population. They are reinforced and perpetuated by the aid agencies whose male workers bring with them their own stereotyped views of women's work.

In the areas of crafts and specialized trades, men are better able to gain access to the resources necessary for carrying out the specialties that they brought with them such as building, shoemaking and carpentry. In many instances fathers are training their sons in these trades. Some examples of the types of projects offered to women are: sewing, knitting, baking, basket weaving, poultry raising. In discussions women have expressed an interest in having challenging coopera-tives where they will be sure of earning regular cash income, or obtaining certif-icates of skills learned that they can take home with them when they are repatri-ated.

We suggest, based on field experience, that there should be more income-generating projects for women and girls, and that attention should be given to training at least a few women in the basic concepts of marketing, management, accounting, bookkeeping, costing and pricing. Further, opportunities for training should be offered to women interested in obtaining skills in nontraditional areas such as maintenance and repair of equipment, carpentry, etc. In addition, given the reality that refugees are in a new setting and might not be able to take advantage of existing opportunities, even if they have the prerequisite skills, because of lack of information or start-up capital, efforts should be made to provide these resources to both men and women so that they can become more self-reliant (see Kalyati 1990).

Education

Studies of Mozambiquan refugees in both Malawi and Zimbabwe have revealed that the literacy rates of refugees are generally lower than those of the host countries' populations; and that the literacy rates of female refugees are significantly lower than those of male refugees (Makanya 1990, Kalyati 1990). For example, in Malawi "it was observed that out of every ten women interviewed one or none is literate (as compared with three out of every ten men)" (Kalyati 1990:8). In part this is a result of the colonial education policies which deliberately limited educational opportunities for the African population. Since independence Mozambique has been plagued with economic problems and civil war; these problems, combined with the culturally affirmed very low marriage age for girls, have created a situation where women have much lower academic attainment than men. In schools within refugee camps, girls tend to leave school at lower levels than boys. They also tend to get married at very young ages, often between the ages of 12 and 13.

Given the positive correlation between mother's education and child survival in Africa, and the low education of women and high child mortality rates among refugees, the education of mothers should be seen as a critical intervention strategy for improving the well-being of children. Without the ability to read instructions and other types of information related to general family health, mothers are seriously handicapped (See Segal, Nyirongo, and Misuko 1991).

In Malawi there are serious efforts underway to raise the literacy rates of refugees. In 1990 there were 566 functional adult literacy classes, and women's participation in these classes was higher than that of men (Kalyati 1990).

Conclusion

This overview of the Mozambiquan refugee situation has stressed the need to give serious attention to historical and cultural factors in assessing the special needs of refugee women and children, particularly those living in female-headed households. It is argued that given the important economic roles that women play and the critical relationship of their economic contributions to the well-being of their households, that more attention needs to be given to the development of income-generating projects and education of women in the refugee camps.

Further, the discussion suggested that the lack of consensus on the number of female-headed households among the refugee population is related to issues concerning the critical variables to be used in determining headship, e.g. marital status and residence versus economic contributions to the household. These problems are compounded by the fluctuating membership of the households as a result of male labor migration.

The discussion has alluded to the similarities in causation of high numbers of female-headed households in Malawi and Mozambique, suggesting that the economic hegemony of South Africa in this region is reflected in the family organization of both countries in the form of high rates of adult male migration. Thus in addition to sharing many sociocultural traits, they also have similar patterns, particularly in rural areas of *de facto* female-headed households.

In this instance the well-being of the "left behind" women and children is closely related to the degree of access they have to their migrating husbands' income through remittances, and/or to their labor on return visits. Finally we suggest that there is a need to look beyond family structure to the system of financial and social supports available to refugee households headed or supported by women in assessing their needs and developing programs of assistance. The focus on the actual activities of household members and the strategies utilized for survival will give a clearer view of the types of resources they actually have access to, and the types of problems they encounter in their struggle for survival as refugees.

Notes

1. I would like to thank Alem Habtu and Anne Okongwu for their valuable comments on earlier drafts of this article.

References

African Commission on Human Peoples' Rights Election of Eleven Members, 29 July 1987, pursuant to Article 31 of OAU Charter on Human and Peoples' Rights. Twenty Three Ordinary Session of Heads of State and Government. Addis Ababa, Ethiopia.

Apeadu, Nana. 1991. "Resettlement: A Woman's Issue; Refugee Women, Liberia, Mozambique, Rwanda." Unpublished paper presented at the 34th Annual meeting of the African Studies Association, Nov 23-26.

Apeadu, Nana and Stella Karumuna. 1989. ILO/OAU Consultancy Mission in Malawi: Report to ILO/OAU.

Apeadu, Nana. 1988. "The Forgotten 80%: The Plight of Refugee Women and Children in Africa." Unpublished Manuscript.

Blac, Anne and Cynthia Lloyd. 1990. "Women's Childrearing Strategies in Relation to Fertility and Employment in Ghana." Working Papers, No. 6 *The Population Council*.

Desai, Sonalde. 1991. "Children at Risk: The Role of Family Structure in Latin America and West Africa." Unpublished paper presented at the DHS World Conference, 5-7 August.

Frank, Odile. 1988. "The Childbearing Family in Sub-Saharan Africa: Structure, Fertility and the Future." Joint Population Council and International Center for Research on Women Seminar, Series on Determinants and Consequences of Female-headed Households.

Guyer, Jane. 1981. "Household and Community in African Studies." *African Studies Review*, Vol. XXIV, No. 2/3 June/Sept, pp. 87-137.

Harris, Marvin. 1958. "Portugal's African 'Wards' - A First-Hand Report on Labor and Education in Mozambique." American Committee on Africa, pp. 1-37.

Johnsson, Anders B. 1989. "The International Protection of Women Refugees: A Summary of Principal Problems and Issues." *International Journal of Refugee Law*, Vol. 1, No. 2, pp. 221-232.

Kalyati, Esrath. 1990. "Refugee Women and Children in Malawi: Some Issues." EGM/RDWC/1990/CS.2/Rev.1. Prepared for Expert Group Meeting on Refugee and Displaced Women and Children, Vienna, 2-6 July.

Kaplan, Irving. 1985. "The Society and Its Environment," in *Mozambique: A Country Study*. Edited by Harold Nelson. Area Handbook Series, Department of the Army, Washington, D.C.

OAU Convention Governing the Specific Aspects of Refugee Problems in Africa September 1969. Addis Ababa, Ethiopia.

OAU Charter on Human and Peoples' Rights. June 1981.

Okonjo, Kamene. 1989. "Rural Development in Nigeria: How Do Women Count." *African Marburgensia* XXII, No. 1, pp. 32-51.

Protocol of 1967 Relating to the Status of Refugees. January 31, 1967.

Rinehart, Robert. 1985. "Historical Setting," in *Mozambique: A Country Study*. Edited by Harold Nelson. Area Handbook Series, Department of the Army, Washington, DC, pp. 1-71.

Robertson, Claire and Iris Berger. 1986. "Introduction: Analyzing Class and Gender: African Perspectives" in Claire Robertson and Iris Berger, eds. *Women and Class in Africa*. New York: African Publishing Company. Pp. 3-24.

Sanjek, Roger. 1982. "The Organization of Households in Adabraka: Towards a Wider Comparative Perspective," *Comparative Studies in Society and History*. Vol. 24, No. 1, Jan.

Segal, Margaret, Naomi Nyirongo and Doris Misuko. 1991. "Education and Its Impact on Family Health: Implications for Refugee Programming." Prepared for the Sub-Regional Seminar on Strategies for Combatting Illiteracy and Equalization of Access to Education and Educational Opportunties Among Displaced Persons in Southern Africa. Malawi, 14 March.

Sen, Gita and Caren Grown. 1985. *Development, Crises and Alternative Visions: Third World Women's Perspectives*. Norway: Verbum.

Spring, Anita. 1986. "Women Farmers and Food in Africa: Some Considerations and Suggested Solutions" in *Food in Sub-Saharan Africa*. Eds., Art Hansen and Della E. McMillan. Boulder: Lynne Rienner Publishers, Inc. Pp. 332-349.

Technical Reports in Gender and Development: Women's Contributions to the World Economy. 1989.

UN Convention Relating to the Status of Refugees. 28 July 1951 (A/Conf. 2/108).

United Nations Economic and Social Council 1990. "Priority Themes: Peace, Refugee and Displaced Women and Children." E/CN. 6/1991:4.

United Nations Department of Public Information. 1991. "Refugee Women Factsheet." *United Nations Focus.*

United Nations High Commission for Refugees. July 1991. *Guidelines for the Protection of Refugee Women.*

Women's Commission for Refugee Women and Children. 1991. New York.

9

Women-Headed Households from the Perspective of an Egyptian Village

Lucie Wood Saunders and Sohair Mehanna

The near invisibility of women-headed households in statistics on Egyptian society throughout most of the 20th century raises questions about incidence as well as functioning, causes, and consequences. Such households are of particular interest in a society where extended families persist in rural areas, many rural households continue to be units of production, and great value is placed on family relationships; thus preferred arrangements leave little space for women living alone or with their children. Some recent studies have shown the functioning of these households when they result from labor migration (Taylor, 1984; Brink 1991), but those resulting from widowhood or divorce have received little scholarly attention. Such women and their children must face different economic problems and make somewhat different adjustments as they respond to the choices available to them.

Here, the focus is women-headed households in a village in the Egyptian delta in 1962 and 1978[1]. These households did not result from labor migration during either period; they are primarily the result of widowhood and divorce. The questions we raise here are whether such households are short-term, how women cope with their economic situations, whether the households reflect a degree of choice on the part of the women and if so, what are the bases for choice; whether the women are economic and moral wards of their kin in Youssef's terms or operate somewhat independently, and how? (Youssef 1978:77)

To anticipate our conclusions, coping with poverty was a predominating concern for the women-headed households in this village. They differ in this from women whose husbands were labor migrants; the latter expect upward mobility and their ability to achieve it depends on having their husbands rejoin them when the periods of employment end. The women reported on here were like the wives of labor migrants in having more autonomy in their daily lives, and unlike them in seeming to have somewhat more control over their children's lives.

Background and Demographic Data

The data that we interpret are drawn from a long-term ethnographic study of a village in the Egyptian delta about 90 km northeast of Cairo. We worked in the village, Tafahna al Ashraf, in 1961-62, 1965, 1978 and 1979. Small in the range of Egyptian village sizes, it had a population of about 2,200 in 1962 and 1978; the seeming stability was an anomaly which reflected the emigration of about 100 nuclear families from the village during the 1960s as settlers in a state project to reclaim marshland. The agricultural land adjacent to Tafahna measured 642 feddans (1 feddan = 1:038 acres) and in 1962, about one-third of it was in medium-sized estates owned by townsmen, most of whom managed the estates themselves. Less than half the village men in a survey of a random sample of households named farming as the primary means of livelihood in 1962 but more than half did in our survey in 1978. While agriculture, including animal husbandry, was the primary resource, capital-intensive mass production of poultry funded by village capital, invested individually or in partnerships, had refocussed economic strategies by 1978 (Saunders and Mehenna 1986:83-86). In 1962 cotton was the cash crop of choice, but it had been replaced by rice in 1978. Women and men worked in agriculture as laborers or in household farming if they had enough land. Women and men also raised animals, and women kept household poultry.

The population of the village is Muslim. Marriages continue to be arranged by parents, and residence immediately after marriage is patrilocal. Though the proportion of extended family households declined between 1962 and 1978, brides expected to remain in these households until the deaths of their husbands' parents, unless pre-marital agreements specified that they should live separately, or they moved to another place. Thus, mothers expected that sons and their wives would care for them when they were old, while earlier in the domestic cycle, a husband's mother expected to enjoy the control of her household and the women there. If a woman is widowed prematurely, she may stay unmarried with her children in her husband's home, or leave and remarry. A divorced woman is expected to return to her natal home and to remarry. In brief, the organization of household production and the interpretation of kinship responsibilities tended to return widowed and divorced women to their natal households and remarriage.

There were 28 households headed by women in Tafahna in 1962 and an additional 30 women lived alone[2]. In 1978, there were 30 households headed by women; two of these were temporary because the husbands were in the army. An additional 22 women lived alone. The proportion of women-headed households to the total number of households was 6.9% in 1962; in 1978, 7.4% of households were headed by women, excluding the women alone. If we include women alone, 13.9% of headed households were women-headed in 1962 and 12.5% in 1978. In 1962, 8.9% of all women lived in women-headed households and 7.3% did in 1978.

The proportion of all persons living in these households is low compared to the total population because all of these headed households are small or relatively so. Thus in 1962, 93 women lived alone or in women-headed households: Of the 30 women-headed households, 18 had no adult men present; 5 had adult sons living in the house, 8 had sons in the army. In 1978, 75 women lived alone or in women-headed households.

In 1962, there were 25 males in female-headed households; in 1978 41 males lived in female-headed households. In eight of these households, sons and in two cases, husbands, are counted as members though they are absent from the community serving in the army. The range in size of women-headed households was from one to seven persons with no significant difference in our counts for 1962 and 1978.

The age range of members of female-headed households was 3 years to 70 with no significant difference in range in 1962 and 1978. The heads of households were aged 20 or above. Characteristically, these households are composed of a youngish adult woman with her young children, or a slightly older woman and her nearly adult children; occasionally, households include the grandmother, a divorced daughter, and grandchildren. All heads of households have been married at least once. The solitary women were an older population and typically widowed or divorced; in 1978, 4 of the 22 solitary women never married. One household, a different one in both years, was matrilocal, consisting of a woman, her married daughter and the daughter's husband from another village.

Women-Headed Households

The women alone and women-household heads represented a range of household income resources in 1962, and represented the village range, excluding the top level in 1978. Woman-headed households cluster at the lower end of the scale of household income; solitary women are among the poorest villagers, with one or two exceptions. The range of economic statuses that the female-headed households represent indicates a variety of strategies as we shall show.

Static enumerations of women-headed households at two different periods conceal the processual nature of the phenomenon. Woman-headed households are a possible phase in the village domestic cycle when there is an untimely death of a husband or divorce. The expectation is that young widows or divorced women will return to their parents' homes, then remarry quickly; their children usually go to the father's relatives. When a woman has children and her parents are dead, she may not marry, however, and in time she will become head of an extended family when her first son marries and his bride comes to her house. The 13 households in which there were adult sons, either in the army or living at home, in 1978 were close to achieving this goal; so were those with adult sons in 1962. There were a number of extended family households with the older mother present which had grown recently out of woman-headed households. The transitional character of women-headed households points to some of the complexities with which women must come to terms; on the one hand, the interest of their natal family members, and perhaps their own, in their remarriages; their children's interests in remaining with their mothers and avoiding step-child status, a most dreadful condition in village ideology; coping with making a living in a single-income household in an economy in which economic viability usually depends on the work of more than one adult, and strategizing to accumulate funds for marrying children off.

Coping: Getting a Living and Work

The status of a woman alone or an adult woman in a woman-headed household is secondary to economic status in determining women's resources, work, and standard of living. With the exception of four women in 1962 and two in 1978, the women in these households were in the poor or marginal sector of the population. The poorest were dependent mainly on other villagers' charity, recompense for running errands or doing other small services, and government payments, which were made to more people proportionately in 1978.[3] Women smallholders cultivate their own land themselves or with their children's help; they are more likely to have cattle as well as household poultry than landless women, but their children are likely to work for wages occasionally or regularly. Landless women who are able-bodied work for wages in agriculture, and they may combine this with working as servants or for pay for occasional household services. The children of landless women work for wages, with youngest daughters least likely to do so because they do housework. Working children in women-headed households bring their wages to their mothers or grandmothers at the end of a day's work and it is used for household expenses. Landless women and smallholders may be peddlers, either selling directly in the markets or house to house, and a few also buy eggs or dairy products from other villages which they sell in town to traders. The rich women alone were landowners who lived on their rent.

Landless women and women with minute holdings struggle to provide food for their households and clothing annually for their children. Some, particularly old women, spoke of eating nothing except the leaves of a plant that grows wild with bread and salt in 1962, a time when old women particularly were concerned about hunger and food. Conditions had eased slightly for women alone by 1978; nearly all had poultry and thus some income from egg sales; people did not talk about food scarcity, though clothing for their children remained a problem. At both times, women owned their houses or a share of them which they had inherited from their parents.

Being Alone and Being Kin

Relatedness is an important means of allocating responsibilities in Egyptian village life. This study indicates three ways in which this impinges on women living without husbands. The first is mutual help, the second, the responsibility for funding childrens' marriages, and the third, inheritance. While there is an understanding that kin should help each other, kin aid to women-headed households varies with the economic condition of the kin and whether they live in the village. In theory, brothers do not have financial responsibilities toward their sisters after marriage, except for providing them with a share of familial inheritance. Divorced or widowed women have the right to return to live in their natal homes if they own a share of them, though their brothers live in them with their conjugal families. In such cases, the sister usually has a separate room, budgets separately, and eats separately.

A woman's kin do not have formal responsibility for her children because this is a patrilineal system. Siblings help usually with presents of grain, meat at feasts and in visits, thus showing their appropriate kin concern. One woman, divorced for eight years, and living with two daughters and a son, all under 13 years old, said: "I have three brothers and two sisters and they often visit me at the feasts, they send me rice and 1/2 kilo of meat. As for my neighbors, they help me all the time. And my brothers send me an ardeb of rice and an ardeb of wheat after each harvest" (An Ardeb = about 5 Bushels). This woman supported her household with her seasonal work as an agricultural laborer, the occasional work of her children, the income from the sale of 8 ducks and the eggs from 9 chickens; additionally, she has a lamb and a ram which are her means of building up funds. Another speaker whose income is from buying and selling butter gives us another view of kin assistance:

I would not like to live in the same house as my brothers because I would not like to see my children humiliated by them. My brothers are in Tahreer province -- each has taken land and cultivated it. The others are white-collar clerks in the government, but no one asks about us, not even when I had a car accident two years ago and went to the hospital.

This woman has two daughters and two sons living with her; of her oldest daughter who moved with her husband to Cairo, she says:

Even my daughter doesn't come to visit me except when she quarrels with her husband. Otherwise, her husband doesn't permit her to visit me. Needless to say she doesn't send money since she is hard up, too... my neighbors are kind.

What we see here is a pattern in which these women are the recipients of charity rather than being participants in a mutual aid system. Here women alone interact with relatives and neighbors. But they have little to give and need to receive. Relatives shy away from their needs, living marginally themselves; neighbors help as they can, nothing more is expected from them, and women alone help neighbors out with household tasks occasionally.

Women with children have the responsibility for funding their children's marriages. One woman described how she did this. She first sold the wheat crop from the smallholding (1/2 acres) that she and her children had inherited together from her husband. She also sold the water buffalo and borrowed LE5 (about $12 at that time) from her sister. She gave the bride price with this, and her oldest son was married. During the wedding celebrations, people gave money amounting to LE16 as well as presents of sugar, rice and macaroni. She used some of this food for the wedding feast and sold the remainder and used the money to buy a buffalo calf. In about two years, she found a wife for her second son and agreed to pay LE50 as a bride price. Again she sold the water buffalo for LE40 and the cotton crop for LE10 and was able to give the money. During the celebration for this son's marriage, she received LE17 in cash which she used to repay the debt she still owed her sister, and in addition bought another buffalo calf. Later, she financed the marriage of her third son with this buffalo; meanwhile she married again herself, but her husband died in less than two years, and she lived with her children. She and her sons arranged her daughter's marriage, and the mother sold her share of land in order to provide a large quantity of presents for her. Thus she became a landless woman through meeting her responsibilities for her children's marriages.

The case of the rich widow in 1962 illustrates the impact of inheritance claims on the lives of more affluent women. This widow was a resident owner of a large amount of land by village standards; she and her daughter lived in a big house which was furnished rather elaborately. She came to the village from Cairo after her divorce from her second husband, who seems to have married her at least partly for her money, and in fact succeeded in acquiring part of her wealth. Her daughter was married young, but she quarreled with her husband and returned to live with her mother. The daughter's husband neither sent for her, nor would he divorce her, so she was immobilized. The two women lived in social isolation, except for their servant and an old woman, a distant relative, who did errands for them. The problem that concerned them was that the sons of the widow's brother were the legal heirs to most of her property, so the best solution for them would be for the daughter to marry one of them, but she could not unless her husband would divorce her, and he would not agree to do this without payment. They haggled to reduce this amount, and invited one of the brother's sons to help them with their affairs, and to advance the idea of the marriage with the daughter, eventually succeeding in both. Relatives were not a resource for them, but one of the difficulties with which they had to cope.

Intergenerational Impact of Women-Headed Households

In 1962, there was very little difference in the education of children in women-headed households and others. Village children did not go beyond primary school; many did not even go that far, and most of the adult population was illiterate. Children learned to cultivate and boys learned to do unskilled labor, while girls learned housework. By 1978 Tafahna children were completing preparatory and secondary school in nearby villages, and 1% of the adult population had completed post-secondary training. The last group would have full employment in white-collar positions; secondary graduates could anticipate some kind of salaried employment.

The children in women-headed households did not become educated. In 1978, only 3 boys and 2 girls in these households had completed primary school. Of the 107 village children (82 boys and 25 girls) in preparatory school in 1978, none were from women-headed households. This difference reflects the demand for children's work and the inability of women-headed households to meet the auxiliary costs of schooling. The long term consequences are that their children are in a disadvantaged position relative to others in terms of job options.

Discussion and Conclusions

While the case of women-headed households in Tafahna is of some inherent interest, its significance is that it is an indicator of the extent of the phenomenon in rural Egypt. Information on incidence of these households has not been compiled from the Egyptian censuses (including the 1986 census), but some information is available from community studies. Thus, in Mush'a, an agricultural village in the south of Egypt, a household survey showed that about 8% of households were composed of women and children only (Hopkins 1987:70). In a sample survey of 79 women in a village close to Cairo, there were 8 households without adult men because the husbands were working abroad (Brink 1991: 201). A study of family life in Cairo notes that there are women-headed households resulting from widowhood or divorce and living in poverty, but does not include statistics (Rugh 1984:189-195). Another indicator of the potential for the formation of women-headed households is statistics on widowhood and divorce, though not all of these women form women-headed households. National statistics show that 15.6% of all Egyptian women were widowed or divorced in 1976; this was a decrease from 1960 when 20.6% of all women were divorced or widowed. In the 1986 census of Daqahliya

Province, where Tafahna is located, 14.1% of all women were divorced or widowed.

The incidence of women-headed households in Tafahna may be compared with national statistics available from other North African and Middle Eastern countries. In Tafahna, as noted above, such households were 12.5% of the total if women alone are counted, and 7.4% if they are not. Statistics from Tunisia show that 10% of all households are women-headed, and that 17% are in Morocco; elsewhere in the Middle East, 7% of the households in Iran are reported to be women-headed; 5% in Kuwait, 13% in Syria and 10% in Turkey (United Nations, 1991: 26-29). These data refer to the 1970s, and those for Morocco and Turkey reflect the impact of labor migration. That labor migration also has increased the incidence of women-headed households in Egypt is demonstrated in specific studies (e.g. Brink 1991; Khafagy 1984; Taylor, 1984). Incidence of women-headed households in Middle Eastern countries continues to be lower than in many other regions, reflecting probably the continued viability of the household as a production unit.

The functioning of women-headed households in Tafahna shows the economic problems they face in different categories. Most are poor and so are their kin therefore support by their natal families is not a viable option. Instead these women cope through multiple strategies involving agriculture, animal husbandry, and wage work. Some also receive charity or government subsidy; none in Tafahna, and relatively few in rural Egypt, are in the unskilled labor force that leaves home for work. We see this as reflecting improved rural economic conditions, and on this point we differ from those who interpret rural Egypt in terms of a continually declining economy, though most women-headed households remain in marginal conditions (Saunders and Mehenna 1988: 25-28). Women-headed households elsewhere in rural Egypt appear to manage through similar strategies. At present, women's labor is still in demand for agricultural tasks in the delta despite the mechanization of men's work in plowing and harvesting (cf Toth 1991:218-219; 230-231). The products of household poultry and animal husbandry are also in demand as consumer spending rises. These are marginal strategies often and additional economic support from government may be necessary to alleviate the pressure that women alone experience.

The question remains of whether women alone in Tafahna have greater control over their lives. Brink shows that the wives of labor migrants make decisions on many matters that their absent husbands would usually have handled, a finding also indicated in a study of the wives of migrants in Giza (Brink, 1991; Khafagy, 1984: 18-19). Tafahna women stated clearly that they prefer to stay alone because of their children's well-being as they grow up; when they do this, they seem to have somewhat more choice about their children's lives. Younger women, or course, are freed from subordination to their husband's mothers, and all are free of daily supervision of their movements. These women all involve kin in decision making, but they seem to have some leeway in deciding whose advice to seek. The case of the wealthy widow shows how property may circumscribe rather than broaden choices.

It should not be assumed, however, that the existence of women-headed households necessarily leads to creating new patterns for all women. Historical evidence suggests that such households existed in the past, with many villages being made up of women, children, and the infirm in 1841 when about one-sixth of the population was away from home doing forced labor (Tucker 1979). Whatever impact this kind of household has must have existed for some time. Second, ethnographic work on Egyptian country women indicates that wives are managers of their households in daily budgeting and organization of work. In Tafahna in 1962, most wives said they received and allocated household funds to daily use and savings. Neither adult men nor boys kept wages for their individual use, a pattern that was beginning to change by 1978 when more men were keeping money. Since wives are household managers, their roles are similiar to those of divorced and widowed women, a point that is sometimes misunderstood by people unfamiliar with the realities of Muslim societies. Women-headed households lack the income of an adult man and we argue that this becomes the defining factor in their conditions and expectations. It exacerbates their conditions as one descends the economic scale.

The meagre compensations of women living alone do not yet lead to reevaluating their condition in the villagers' view. They are pitied, not emulated, and such households are regarded as the consequences of disasters, not choice. This view receives cultural expression in the idea that old women alone are most likely to give the evil eye, presumably because they are so lacking in the good things of life, whether material or social. Thus, the small pleasures these women may have in their daily lives remain invisible in the cultural construct. If the economic circumstances of their lives ease, they may be able to value more highly the greater choice that they have in their daily lives as they manage their resources, cultivate and tend poultry, decide on children's marriages and strategize to fund them and, with expanded economic resources, plan to educate their children.

Notes

1. We gratefully acknowledge support for field work in 1961-1962 and 1965 by the Social Research Center, American University in Cairo, and support in 1978-1979 from the Smithsonian Institution foreign currency grant FC#70945800 and a CUNY PSC/BHE Grant #11780.
2. We made village censuses in 1962 and 1978, enumerating the people in each house, their ages, relationships to the head, and places of birth.
3. Widows and divorced women may qualify for the government relief program, which is part of the national social insurance system. The monthly award in 1980 was LE10 (Tadros, 1984). In Tafahna, women went to the umda (village head) for help in arranging for payments. He was prompt in attending to their requests but village awards in 1978 were about LE4 monthly and LE

202

1 in 1962. We do not know whether this reflected lower relief in rural areas. These amounts alone would not be enough to feed a woman and 2 children.

References

Brink, Judy. 1991. "The Effect of Emigration of Husbands on the Status of their Wives: an Egyptian Case", *International Journal of Middle East Studies*, 23: 201-211.

Hopkins, Nicholas. 1987. *Agrarian Transformation in Egypt*. Boulder: Westview Press.

Khafagy, Fatma. 1984. "One Village in Egypt", *MERIP Reports*, #124, vol. 14: 17-21.

Rugh, Andrea. 1984. *Family in Contemporary Egypt*, Syracuse: Syracuse Univ. Press, 1984.

Saunders, Lucie Wood and Sohair Mehenna. 1988. "Smallholders in a Changing Economy: an Egyptian Village Case", *Peasant Studies* 16:5-29.

Saunders, L. and S. Mehenna, 1986. "Unseen Hands: Women's Farm work in an Egyptian Village", *Anthropological Quarterly*, 59: 105-114.

Tadros, H. 1984. *Social Security and the Family in Egypt*. Cairo: The Cairo Papers in Social Science, American University in Cairo.

Taylor, Elizabeth. 1984 "Peasant Wives", *MERIP Reports* 124:3-10.

Toth, James. 1991. "Pride, Purdah, or Paychecks: What Matters in the Gender Divison of Labor in Rural Egypt?" *International Journal of Middle East Studies*, 23: 213-236.

Tucker, Judith. 1979. "Decline of the Family Economy in Mid-Ninetecenth Century Egypt", *Arab Studies Quarterly* 1: 245-271.

United Nations. *1991. The World's Women 1970-1990: Trends and Statistics, Social Statistics and Indicators, Series K, No. 8*. New York: United Nations.

Youssef, Nadia. 1977. "The Status and Fertility Patterns of Muslim Women", In *Women in the Muslim World*, L. Beck and N. Keddie, (eds.) Cambridge: Harvard University Press, Pp.69-99.

10

Female-Headed, Female-Supported Households in India: Who Are They and What Are Their Survival Strategies?

Joan P. Mencher

Introduction

Until relatively recently, most of the work on female-headed households has tended to focus on Latin America, the Caribbean, and Africa, and to ignore societies such as China, India, and Bangladesh, which have been associated (at least ideologically) with relatively strong extended families and extreme male domination. This chapter examines and assesses the available literature on female-headed/female-supported households in India, and presents materials on such households in rural areas in Tamil Nadu and Kerala, two of India's southern states, collected as part of a larger study of women and rice cultivation.[1] What the Kerala and Tamil Nadu data show is: (1) that in those households headed by women where there are no other earning adults or where a daughter is the sole support of aged parents, the families are among the poorest of the poor, or in other words that the most important characteristic of the poorest households in our sample is that in most cases they are dependent on only one income (especially if that person is an uneducated female worker); (2) that among the poor, household income is rarely supplemented by contributions from relatives in cash or kind; (3) that there is considerable regional, class, caste, and religious variation in the situation of female-headed/ female-supported households, and that these differences need to be explored in detail if programs are to be initiated to help these families.

In most of India (excluding Kerala), the cultural ideal has been that of the patrilineal extended family. However, as actually observed, more than half of the population in India live either in nuclear households, or ones with at most 1 or 2 extended kin. The proportion of extended households to the total number of households varies from state to state (and by district within each state), as well as by caste and religious group (Kolenda 1968). When a female lives in an extended household she is less likely to become its sole or even main support, because even if her husband should die or become infirm, or fail to provide for her, she can expect to be supported by the other adult males of her husband's household. If however there is no son, or an only son dies, and there are no other adult males of working age, a woman may end up having to support not only her children but also her aged parents-in-law in a North Indian village, or even in Tamil Nadu. However, such households are often recorded as being headed by the father-in-law even if he is physically unable to contribute to the maintenance of the family.

Female-headed households constitute a significant proportion of the population of India. The total population of the country as of the 1981 census was about 658 million people. If we assume that female-headed households account for approximately the same proportion of the population in 1988 as in 1971, i.e. 9.43% of households (see Visaria and Visaria 1985:56), then roughly 60 million people now live in such households. Even if we assume that only one third of these are in the poorest of the poor category (since some belong to landowning households or households with other assets, or have other earners in the household), that would come to 20 million people, more than the total population of many another third-world country. These figures are shocking. Clearly such households need to be taken into account. The policy implications are glaring.

It has been argued that most of the female-headed/female-supported households in India consist of elderly widows with grown sons, and thus are not necessarily among the poorest of the poor. However, my own field data as well as data from other areas indicate that this is not always the case, and that there is a great need to disaggregate these data. The figure of 20 million includes widows with small children, as well as some women with small children living alone as a result of desertion, divorce, or male migration. In addition many "male-headed households" are supported primarily by female earnings. This chapter explores the incidence of female-headed/female-supported households in selected areas.

Who Is the Head of the Household?

Before proceeding further, it is necessary to clarify what is meant by the terms "female-headed" and "female-supported" and show why the latter term is needed. A household can presumably be defined as a social unit composed of those living together in the same dwelling place. But taking into account the day-to-day economy of the household--that is, how the household is supported-- can be more complicated. Field work over the past 25 years shows that the simple question "Who is the head of the household?" will normally reveal who makes major decisions or exercises authority, but will often fail to provide information about who *supports the household*. Thus, a woman might be the main support of a household, but her infirm husband might still retain decision-making power, and dominate the household in other ways. In such cases it is common for the wife herself to identify the husband as the household head. Unpacking the concept of headship (see diagram 10.1) indicates its multiple dimensions.

A full discussion of this subject is outside the scope of the present chapter (see Mencher 1992a). Nonetheless, it is important to mention here because of the baggage that has traditionally been incorporated into the concept. Figure 10.1 shows 4 major aspects of headship: (1) authority or power, (2) sources of economic support, (3) decision making, and in some instances (4) control over and possession of minor children in case of divorce or death. These present a multi-dimensional picture that has come from explorations of "female-headed" households cross-culturally. It should be noted that each of these aspects is discrete in some societies or situations. The same individual does not necessarily fulfill all of the functions that we traditionally associate with the concept of headship even in Asia, though there may be general patterns noted. Where we do have detailed data, we find that even in traditional societies there is some degree of variation in headship.

This chapter focuses on *female-supported* as well as female-headed households, because it is primarily concerned with the question of the survival of households, though reference is also made to issues of power and authority. In looking at the material from India, it is especially useful to note the distinction between female-headed and female-supported households, though many households are both. The issue of household support can be more complex, as Figure 10.2 shows. In nuclear households or where the nuclear unit is semi-independent within a larger unit, households start with some assets, which may come from either side in the union of a man and a woman. Furthermore, support can include goods as well as cash. Support can also include services which if they were unavailable would require cash, such as child care when a woman is working. Even if a man is the only one ostensibly working, the family may require food grown by a woman in a kitchen garden even to survive. Or a man might have economic responsibilities in his mother's or father's household that sometimes take precedence over the needs of his wife and children. In modern situations, women often have to juggle a wide variety of income sources in order to survive and reproduce.

Even in households with two earners, a husband and a wife, females tend to use most of their earnings for household purposes except when they need the funds to pay for food to enable them to work, whereas males withhold more for their own personal uses (Mencher 1989). This holds true in Kerala, Tamil Nadu and West Bengal, among the poorest households as well as among those which are somewhat better off. Clearly there are individual differences, and some men do give a higher percentage of earnings to their homes than others.

Figure 10.1 Components of Household Headship

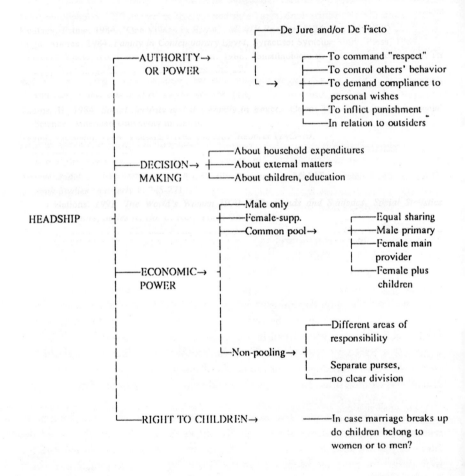

Figure 10.2[a]

WIDOWS	MARRIED WOMEN
*(1) with small children/aged adults (2) with small children & working adults (3) with working adult daughters (no males) (4) with adult sons/daughters who work plus their spouses	*(1) with husbands who are ill or too old to work, no other working adults *(2) with husbands who refuse to contribute much to household, no other working adult *(3) with husbands working away from the village, only rarely sending home money, no adult children, or other working adults

↑   ↑

FEMALE-HEADED/FEMALE-SUPPORTED

↓   ↓

DESERTED, DIVORCED, SEPARATED   **UNMARRIED WOMEN**

*(1) with small children, no working adults
(2) with small children plus one or more other working adult
(3) with adult sons/daughters who work, plus their spouses

(1) daughter important contributor and other household members also working
*(2) daughter main support of old parents, perhaps small contribution by father or mother
*(3) daughter supporting 1 or 2 parents plus other younger siblings

*Indicates exceptionally poor household types
a. This diagram leaves out single person households, that is households consisting of only a single female and no other people.

The question of "female-headedness" raises a number of questions for which the answers are not available at the present time. These include: (1) whether or not there is a correlation between the age at marriage and the proportion of female-headed households; (2) whether in the Indian context a household can be considered female-headed if there is any male in the household older than the main female earner; (3) what economic activities in the household are involved in the assumption of authority; (4) in the absence of a father, at what age (or at what stage in the formation of his family of procreation) a son replaces the mother as family head; (5) whether a woman is considered the head of the household if the husband has left home to get work.

Regarding this last point, the wife might be making decisions on a day-to-day basis; on the other hand, she clearly can have problems getting agricultural loans if all of the land is in the husband's name. In some of these cases the households might be male-supported (by remittances), but in other cases the wife might be supporting the household, with only small amounts coming in from the husband. This is especially true where the husband has to spend a large amount of what he earns for his expenses, which is often the case when the husband works in one of the big cities of India such as Bombay where accommodation of even the crudest kind is costly.

General Materials on India

When it comes to India, very little systematic research has been done on female-headed/female-supported households compared to parts of the world like the Caribbean. Furthermore there is little statistical material available. Most of what is available consists of detailed descriptions of specific situations, or census materials based on a 20% sample survey.

The *National Sample Survey* (NSS) has collected materials which can be used in investigating the incidence of female-headed households, but very little has been done with this, the exception being a study of Maharashtra and Gujarat by Visaria and Visaria (1985). An additional problem is that in writing about India, there has been a tendency to restrict attention to households headed by widowed, deserted, or divorced women. These, along with households where men are absent from the village on a more-or-less permanent basis, are the only female-headed/female-supported households which show up in the census and the NSS materials.[2] (Households with a husband or male living at home were not included for a variety of reasons.)

Using the all-India Social and Cultural Tables, which are based on a 20% sample survey of all households, the Visarias report that for both the 1961 and the 1971 censuses there is considerable variation among the different states of India in the percent of female-headed households (1985:54-57.) While the 1971 all-India figure for urban and rural areas combined is 9.43%, the figures for the different regions[3] show significant variability. These go from relatively high figures like 26% in Goa-Daman-Diu, 17% in Kerala and 14% in Tamil Nadu, to lows like 6% in Assam, Haryana and Jammu-Kashmir. Apart from the northeast tribal belt and Himachal Pradesh, all of the higher-ranking places are in the south, and all of those with very low incidences are in the northwest where the extended family is the more common cultural practice, as compared to southern or central India (Kolenda 1968:190).

The northeast is a bit more peculiar, and we do not yet have a clear explanation of the variations there. Orissa reports a 9.18 percentage of female-headed households, which is not too surprising considering the proportion of tribal groups in the population, as well as the amount of out-migration of males to places like Calcutta and even rural areas of Bengal. It follows Maharashtra (10.32), an area from which there has been considerable migration to Bombay. However, Assam and West Bengal report lower levels (6.03 and 7.68), though not as low as the northwest. Why it is this low in these two states is hard to say at the present time. On the basis of field work in West Bengal I observed that many men in a Burdwan village who worked in either Calcutta or Burdwan would visit their village home once every two to four weeks. It is possible that if they had come during the period between March 10 and March 31, 1971, their households might have been included by the census as male-headed, even though on a day-to-day basis the household was normally headed by a woman. As far as support was concerned, whether they were male-supported, female-supported or supported by both depends on social class, how much of his income the man had to spend to live in the city, and his personal proclivities.

The breakdown of female household heads by age is also interesting. In most states (excluding Jammu-Kashmir and Himachal Pradesh), the number of households headed by females over 50 is about double the number of those with female heads under 30. According to the Visarias, the 1971 census shows a rise in the proportion of female-headed households with age in every state, i.e. older women are more likely than younger women to be heads of households. This is not unexpected, since women tend to be married to men ten or more years older than themselves, and thus a woman in her 50's could have a husband well into his 60's or even 70's. Nonetheless, there are some female-headed households reported for every age category. The all-India figure reports 6.07% of households with the head under 30 as being female-headed. The highest proportions in this category are found in Himachal Pradesh (18%), Goa-Daman-Diu (15%), Jammu-Kashmir (11%), and Kerala (11%). It is interesting that Himachal Pradesh and Jammu-Kashmir tend to reverse the all-India pattern in showing marked drops for older women, whereas the Goa and Kerala patterns follow the all-India picture. We are uncertain as to the causes of the Himachal Pradesh and Jammu-Kashmir pattern, but suspect that this reflects the fact that women tend to die at a younger age in these areas than in the south.

The proportion of female-headed households having a living spouse also shows considerable variation by state (Visaria and Visaria 1985:58-59). Taking only rural areas, the highest is Kerala (6.8%), followed by Goa-Daman-Diu (5.5%), and Karnataka (3.5%). Looking at rural households with the head under 30, we find that the highest again is Kerala, where 14.8% of female heads of households under 30 have living spouses. The husbands in such cases are most likely migrants, both to other parts of India and to the Middle East. Following Kerala come Assam (13.0%), Goa-Daman-Diu (10.1%), Karnataka (8.2%), West Bengal (7.3%), and Madhya Pradesh (7.2%). For the category of households with female heads over 50 having a spouse, the highest is again Kerala (3.8%), followed by Goa-Daman-Diu (3.2%) and Karnataka (2.1%).

The pattern for urban areas also differs among the states with the highest proportion again reported for Kerala. The position of Kerala is no doubt a reflection of the far superior health care available in Kerala, more than any other factor.

The Visarias note that female-headed households tend on the average to be smaller than male-headed ones (1985:60-62). This is partly the result of the obvious lack of the male. In addition, if the husband dies before a woman's childbearing years are over, then taboos on females remarrying and on bearing children out of wedlock also operate to restrict the size of the household. Indeed, this is one striking difference between regions such as India and many parts of the western world (including the Caribbean). Women are simply not allowed to bear children out of wedlock in most of South Asia. If a young girl becomes pregnant before marriage, she either has an abortion immediately or is married off as fast as possible, preferably before her pregnancy shows to outsiders. In the rare case where the pregnancy goes to term, she is expected to give the child up for adoption or abandon it. If a widow or deserted woman gets pregnant, she would normally have an abortion as soon as possible. We are dealing here with a society that has absolutely no tolerance for the overt expression of female sexuality outside of marriage. This is equally true for low-caste and high-caste women.

In *Towards Equality*, the report on the status of women in India, one of the reasons noted for the high rate of female suicide in Gujarat was illegitimate pregnancies. The study also notes that a large number of women were pushed into prostitution as a result of getting pregnant before marriage or when their husbands were absent (1974:99). We also hear of cases of pregnant girls being killed by their fathers, even if the pregnancy was the result of rape. There are homes for girls who get pregnant, but they are few and far between.

The Visarias' discussion of the size of female-headed households seems to suggest that because they are smaller, they are better off than they might be otherwise, but the data they are using cannot take into account social class. In their Table 5, they show that 706 out of 1000 male heads of household report their main activity as cultivation. In Kerala it is 411 and in Tamil Nadu 606. For female-headed households, they show that only 494 of 1,000 are reported as engaged in cultivation, with 289 in Kerala and 399 in Tamil Nadu. "Cultivation" however is a misleading term. It refers to those who cultivate their own land (including holdings of all sizes), but leaves out the landless. Thus, more female-headed households are either landless laborers or involved in "other" activities (i.e. not household industry or cultivation)--which we presume includes a wide range of menial work. The Visarias report that the proportion of female-headed land-owning households varies inversely with the size of land-holding (1985:64).

The Visarias' more detailed analysis of Gujarat and Maharashtra NSS data shows that female-headed households are mostly concentrated in the lowest expenditure categories, which presumably means that they are among the poorest, as elsewhere (1985:71). Their main conclusion is to call attention to the inadequacy of the data and the need for micro-level studies.

Apart from the Visarias' work, there were two earlier studies of female-headed households carried out, one by M. Krishna Raj and Jyoti Ranadive in a village in Thane District of Maharashtra, and the other a survey of a Community Development Block in Andhra Pradesh. In the Maharashtra village, widowhood accounted for the majority of female-headed households, though many females were in fact in charge of farm management and day-to-day activities because so many husbands are commuters to Greater Bombay. This study also indicates that there is a higher incidence of female-headedness among Christians. In the study in Andhra Pradesh, Parthasarathy (1982) found a clear link between poverty and female-headedness.

In the early 80's, the International Labour Organization sponsored a series of studies of female-headed households in different parts of India. The pro-gramming implications of those studies are discussed in the Singh article in this volume. However, the theoretical results of two of the studies are available and should be mentioned here. The first was a study by Ranjana Kumari in the eastern region of Uttar Pradesh, in the district with the highest recorded number of female-headed households in the state, i.e. Jaunpur District. Apart from general information, she also collected detailed data from four villages with diverse socio-cultural groups where she found a 12.5% incidence of female-headedness (1989:95). Some of her data stand out as being significantly different from other available studies. For example, she found many of the female-headed households were quite large, and were either joint families or extended families. Most of these result from male out-migration or multiple male deaths.

Kumari examines some of the survival strategies of female-headed households in this area and notes the socio-cultural constraints faced by upper-caste females in such households compared to intermediate-caste and scheduled-caste women who have the option of doing manual labour for others (1989:77). As we shall see, this is different from the south, primarily because the upper-caste females are more likely to be educated and have options not available to illiterate or semi-literate women.

On the whole, out-migration was more significant than widowhood in this study, and cases of desertion or separation were few. It was interesting that she found 10 cases where the females were heads because "of being more able and competent than their husbands" (1989:95). The other causes of female-headedness noted were due to: "(a) handicapped male (12 per cent); (b) male not contributing to family fund (4 percent), and (c) male not willing to work (10 per cent)" (1989:95). Castewise, the incidence of female-headedness was more among the Scheduled and Intermediate castes (46 per cent and 28 per cent respectively) and less among Upper Castes (26 per cent). Among Muslims they did not come across any female-headed households, which is in sharp contrast to our Kerala data. Forty percent of their female-headed households were headed by women between 40 and 55, and 36 percent by females between 25 and 40. All were involved in agriculture as laborers or cultivators, though many had secondary occupations which varied by caste and landholding group.

They found that the average family size among the female-headed households was large but the number of people available to earn a living is low (1989:55-56). On the other hand, this study more or less corroborates the conclusions of other studies (that female-headed households have in general a very poor physical resource base including land and essentially belong to the economically deprived sections of the population):

> 30 per cent of the female-headed households were landless, . . . 36 per cent of them had landholdings of less than 1 acre. . . . Only 6 per cent of them had land holding exceeding 6 acres. . . . If households with more than 6 acres . . . are excluded, then the average land holding size for these households come to 1.26 acres (1989:59).

They also point out that households headed by widows fit into all socio-economic categories, that households with male out-migration were mostly marginal farmers belonging to intermediate and scheduled castes, that all of the deserted women were from scheduled castes, and that households with handi-capped males were either marginal or landless, belonging to intermediate or scheduled castes. Households where males were unwilling to work were mostly better off i.e. they owned more than 2 acres (1989:60). In this study population, poverty was more common among the separated/deserted cases and less among cases of out-migration, widowhood, and able and competent females (1989:63). Kumari's data on survival strategies is similar to the materials presented below for the south of India.

Devaki Jain also carried out a study under the auspices of the International

Labour Organization. Though only some of the papers from her study have been published, they are useful. Her group chose a number of sites for study with the intention of revealing the causal factors in the formation of female-headed households in each area. They chose to work in a matrilineal village in South Kanara District of Karnataka, a village with out-migration in the Himalayan region of Almora, and villages that combined poverty and abandonment in West Bengal (Birbhum and Midnapur Districts), an area with a high percentage of scheduled castes (in Gorakhpur), some villages in Bharatput District of Rajasthan, and a site with an intensive modern development input involving many village households in Bangalore District of Karnataka called Kanakapura (1990:5-6).

In each site they included a few villages. In each site except Almora they had five times as many male-headed households as female-headed ones. From secondary data Jain notes an increase in occurrence of female-headedness moving from north to south which she relates in part to a greater frequency of nuclear households in the south, and widow remarriage to the brother of the dead husband in some parts of the north (1989: 8). In the intensive survey, which covered 299 female-headed households and 295 male-headed households, she noted great heterogeneity even within regions, classes and castes. Variation

by caste ranged from 25% in Karnataka to 8% in West Bengal. . . . [But] in the Allaya-Santhana. . . villages of Matriliny in Karnataka, it is 45% amongst Scheduled Castes while in [two other villages] elsewhere in patrilineal parts of Karnataka it is 19% (1989: 9).

She also notes that while both male and female-headed households tend to be poor, women tend to own less land. The point is made that female ownership of land is an extremely pressing issue both for female-headed households and for females living in male-headed households. It should be added here, that it is not enough that land be in the name of a woman it is essential that females have management rights, including decision-making rights over the land, in their own names.

The remaining studies all focus on widows. The incidence of widowhood varies in terms of caste, class, region of the country, and the age of the woman. The implications of these variations remain to be explored. One recent article on widowhood in Purulia District of West Bengal by Chakrabarti appeared in the *Eastern Anthropologist* in 1990. The study is based on households from 12 villages in the district, and they were compared to census materials for 1961, 1971, and 1981. This data shows a significantly higher ratio of widows than that reported in census materials. Of their sample, 13% of the widows were under 34 years of age and another 16% were between 35 and 44. One out of every third household had a widowed female in it. They note that among the Muslims and low-caste Hindus, younger females who were widowed tended to remarry. This is forbidden to higher caste Hindus. In this area few widows are heads of households, except for the case where there is an adult son, and in these cases the son is the de facto head of the household.

The other study by Jean Dreze on *Widows in Rural India* is based on field work in Uttar Pradesh, Gujarat and West Bengal though where relevant it also makes use of National Sample Survey materials. He notes: "the number of widows in India is comparable to that of male agricultural labourers. Not all of them suffer from acute deprivation, but many do" (1990:1). The study notes that up to the age of about 60 the risk of being a widow is almost twice as high in the south of India as in the north-west. This is only in part related to the lack of ascribed leviratic unions in the south. Rather, Dreze hypothesizes that it is primarily the result of lower survival chances among women who are widowed in the north compared to the south. Certainly the data which are presented below point to the economic viability of households headed by widows in the south even if they are quite poor. The study by Dreze points quite clearly to the many kinds of social injustices and sufferings experienced by large numbers (though not all) widows. It points to various kinds of family neglect, and notes that while not all widows suffer economically, the vast majority do unless they have a grown and earning son and maintain a good relationship with him.

It is clear that much more all-India work needs to be carried out on female-headed households. Some research is currently underway but it will be several years before any of it is published.

Data from Rural Kerala and Tamil Nadu
(with Some Reference to West Bengal)

The data presented here for Tamil Nadu and Kerala come from rural areas. In looking at rural women and their households and discussing female-headed households as a subset of these households, it is important to divide the sample by socio-economic class. While finer divisions are both possible and meaningful, the sample has been divided primarily into two categories, landed and landless. (Among the landless are included those marginal landowning households whose mini-holdings are insufficient even for subsistence, and whose members therefore must still work for other income, usually through day labor.) While there is certainly some overlap between these two categories in terms of the kinds of problems found among women living without husbands or other adult males (due to labor migration, divorce, desertion, or death), they also differ in essential respects, and for this reason are considered separately here.

These households tend to fall into 4 major categories:

1. widows with young children, or older widows without adult sons or sons-in-law in the home;

2. women whose husbands are unable to work either due to illness or

old age, and who lack other adult male workers;

3. women who have been deserted by their husbands (or even an occasional women whose husband, while earning well and living in the house, refuses to give her anything for household maintenance);

4. women supporting aged parents, who may not be able to do much work themselves. In these households, often there are younger siblings being supported. Such households have been found in Kerala villages, occasionally in Tamil Nadu, and in three out of eight of the sample Bengal villages. The higher incidence of these cases in Kerala no doubt reflects the tradition of matriliny there, but the fact that they appear elsewhere clearly indicates that daughters feel obligations towards their parents, even when the status of women is lower. In West Bengal they are reported to be a growing problem in urban areas such as Calcutta where lower middle-class families without sons may be forced to rely on a daughter's earnings to support both the parents and younger siblings (see H. Standing 1985).

The extent of widowhood is in part the result of marrying girls to men 10 or more years older than themselves, and is in part related to the hazardous conditions of work in rural areas, along with relatively poor rural medical care (except in Kerala).

Landed Households

The existence of land or other assets *per se* does not prevent a woman from becoming the sole support and head in her household. What does play a part is whether or not the couple are embedded in a larger extended household. Where that is the case, the death or absence of the husband can result in the woman's becoming considerably worse off than the other females in the household. To begin with, in patrilineal households, the husband's brothers and their wives, and to some extent even the parents-in-law, are less likely to treat a woman well if the husband is absent. If she has no children, or only daughters, in the south she is more likely to return to her natal family if at all possible. But if she has children, especially sons, she must continue with the extended family or risk her sons' loss of patrimony. However, if the extended family has broken up and split its assets before the husband dies or deserts, then the woman is normally left on her own to manage.

Even when a woman has land and other assets there are many obstacles she might have to face. To begin with, if she has only daughters, the husband's kin can try to get her land away from her by all kinds of legal and illegal devices. Usually they do not succeed, but sometimes they do, or at least they manage to make life hard for her. If the husband has had more than one wife, it is often especially complicated for the wife who survives.

For example, Patti married her husband after his first wife had died, and he had given his son from the first marriage his share of the property. Patti bore three daughters, who were married off before her husband died, but had no sons. After her husband's death, she managed the land that she inherited from him with the help of a very trusted tenant who farmed the land on a 50/50 share-cropping basis. Patti still spent considerable time in the fields checking on everything. Being a Brahman, she could not work in the fields herself. When I first met Patti in 1962, her stepson was constantly trying to take the remaining land away from Patti by a variety of legal maneuvers. At that time, Patti had living with her one of her granddaughters who had been deserted by her husband, along with her (the granddaughter's) daughter and son. This grand-daughter with her two small children helped Patti to supervise the work of the tenant. Patti's land was supporting these four household members.

Several years later, Patti sold her land and took a house near a different daughter, and was trying to live off the profits from the sale of the land, because she could no longer bear the treatment of her stepson who lived near her village house. This kind of harassment is not uncommon. Lower-caste widows without small children might remarry, but many do not because of the fear that the first husband's relatives might try to take away the inherited land from their children, or because of the fear of the second husband mistreating the children. Women with only young children and no adult males often manage their farms quite well. While they have to hire males for ploughing and other activities only carried out by males, they are often very well informed and efficient in their farm management. Factors that affect their economic situation relate obviously to (1) the size of their holdings, (2) which crops they can grow, (3) whether the land is rain-fed or irrigated, and (4) how many mouths they have to feed. One finds female-headed and female-managed landowning households that run the gamut from a small number of well-off, comfortable and well-educated households to the larger number of households teetering on the edge of starvation.

Other factors that affect the economic well-being of the household have to do with whether or not there are male relatives in the village who can be trusted and who help. For example, one middle-class woman in a Tamil village had her father and elder brother in the village. While she managed her lands herself, she could count on them to market her produce for her when better prices were available outside the village. (In general women are free to sell their produce within the village, but tend to leave outside marketing to males.) Since many marriages are within the village in Tamil Nadu, women who lose their husbands are likely to get greater support from their own natal kin.

Among the land-owning households, both small and large, there are numerous female-headed households where the women in charge (even if they have grown sons) take the major responsibility for farm management. The proportion of female-headed households varies greatly from village to village, even within the same *taluk*. What can be said without question is that they exist in all villages and that in some their numbers are sizable; furthermore, many of them number among the more innovative and enterprising of the farming households. The most serious difficulties for women in managing their own land are not related to lack of physical strength, but involve special problems in dealing with the outside world. The main times these women need help seem to be (a) to buy essential inputs, for which they need to go to shops -- normally outside the village and to bargain with people, or to go to the government depot and deal with the male officials there, and (b) to sell their produce, if the merchant does not come to their house or nearby. (Where merchants come to the house, women are able to sell, often driving fairly hard bargains.) These are male domains and women alone do not feel welcome, though some women will go if they are accompanied by a male relative or farm servant. Apart from these two domains, some women are able to deal with the problems of supervision and still get good yields (Mencher 1984: 7-8).

For really small land holders, the loss of a household male can be more serious, because ploughing and the marketing outside the village are the responsibilities of the male household head. More importantly, if the man owned a plough and belonged to a community that did its own ploughing, and did not have much work on his own land, he might go out and do ploughing work for others. (At a time in the year when there was little work for women, male ploughing wages could be important. Apart from harvesting, ploughing is the highest paid manual task in agriculture.) Furthermore, if the family belonged to a high caste, it might be awkward for the woman to begin to do manual work for others even though no one might object to her doing it on her own land.

In Kerala, where there was a tradition of matrilineality among some of the landowning castes and communities (see Gough 1961), one finds even greater reliance on a woman's own kin to help when she loses her husband. This is even true among women belonging to groups that were patrilineal earlier, e.g. Muslims and Ezhavas in areas where they were patrilineal. However, the loss of a husband can greatly tighten the household's income, since the husband is often the only source of non-agricultural funds--which can mean the difference between living on the edge of starvation, and being well-fed and well-clothed.

Some Land-Owning Cases and How They Manage

Case 1. Saroja is a widow. She belongs to a high-ranking agriculturalist caste. She has a son who is a teacher in a neighboring village, an unmarried daughter, and a son in school. They own 2-1/2 acres of land. Her husband used to work as a car driver in Madras. She supervises the work in her own fields, and manages to earn a little extra by supervising others' fields during the harvest. She sends her sons when they are free to learn about agriculture. Her son purchases all inputs, but she does the spraying of pesticides, helps in sowing, and pays the laborers. Her son also helps at times. She is, in her own words, deeply devoted to agriculture, and once attended a conference at the block office. She says, "I supervise all the work, transplantation, weeding, etc. Especially I am careful in noting the duration of the transplantation work. I also watch how much time a worker takes for doing a certain job. I do this in my own field and in others' fields." She engages a head laborer who is in charge of hiring others. She pays him 1/12 of the produce, so he is eager to get good workers to increase the yield. She does not do any manual work herself.

Case 2. Saradamma lives with one son and her brother's daughter. She started to manage her land when her husband was ill. After his death, she sold some land to pay off debts. Since then, she has run her farm quite efficiently. "I go to the fields and supervise. I do everything that a man does. Sometimes I even go and sell, sometimes I send an agent. I also listen to the radio and go to seminars or training camps whenever the *Mathersangam* (women's club) sends me." She has 7 acres, 4 of wet rice and 3 of "dry land" given over to peanuts. Saradamma herself managed to get a borewell to change some of her dry land into wet. Her mother and her mother-in-law both used to supervise agriculture. Saradamma supervises all work now, though as her son grows up he is helping by going to shops for inputs. She attended a 4-day training program in the nearby town, where she learned all about seeds for different types of soil.

Landless and Marginal Landowning Households with Female Heads

In every village studied a number of landless and marginal female-headed households belonging to each of the categories listed on diagram 2 have been found. In addition, in most there are also a number of single females (usually widowed or deserted) living alone. These single-female households usually developed as a result of one of the following sequences: (1) all of the woman's children died young; (2) she had no sons, and her daughter's husband(s) or mother(s)-in-law did not want her to live with them; (3) she quarreled with her son and daughter-in-law, who moved away and left her alone; (4) her sons migrated and left her behind.

Except for the rare case where a son sends remittances, all of these landless or marginal women are exceptionally poor. Many cannot compete in the market for agricultural labor because of age, so they must survive through a combination of gleaning after the harvest or working in the home of a middle-class family (only possible if the woman is not an untouchable), or begging. In many instances these women are abused and even insulted by other poor villagers, who cannot really afford to give them anything. Widows in general are considered inauspicious in Indian culture, and single aged widows without any income are often considered to be the most inauspicious, being living symbols of the worst thing that can happen to an Indian woman.

Furthermore, in every one of the sample villages at least one and often many households may be found containing middle-aged or younger adult males who are unable to work. In part this is due to the precarious nature of manual work, leaving relatively young males liable to accidents of all kinds, e.g. falling from trees, sustaining serious injuries from vehicles or machinery, severe fevers that damage nerves or leave people without strength in arms or legs, etc. If the disabled man's family is part of a joint household, then there are still other male workers and they are not totally dependent on female income; but if they are living separately or if there are only old people and young children apart from one main couple, then this throws the household back on the earnings of the woman.

Some Marginal and Landless Cases

In the following four cases, there are husbands living in the households:

Case 3. Ayesha's 53-year-old husband is the ostensible household head. However, Ayesha's earnings support the household, which includes a daughter of 16 and two sons of 13 and 12. Her son of 19 works in a restaurant in Madras, but sends little money. The husband has been ailing for some time. During the year of the study, he spent more than Rs. 200 on medicines (out of a total household income of Rs. 1,374). He works when he can, but this is not often. He is the head of the household in the sense that he makes all decisions and even many purchases.

Case 4. Mami is 62. She lives with her husband of 78 who is too old to work. She had only one child, who died soon after birth. She is her husband's second wife. He has four children from his first wife, but none of them support him, though occasionally he gets a little money from one of the sons. Mami and her husband live primarily on the money she manages to make as a casual laborer.

Case 5. Kuppamma is about 40. Her husband of 45 has not worked for the past two years because he is an asthmatic patient. She has a son of 19 who works in a shop and sends home about Rs. 30 to 40 a month, but that is not enough to feed a person. She has another son of 16 who is what she calls "irresponsible" -- "I sent him to a hotel to work, but he does not send me anything. Only when he is sick he comes home and I have to spend for his medicine." She also has a 14- year-old boy who works as a servant for a wealthy farmer. He gets a little money and tea each day. She also has two sons of 12 and 8 in school. She is a very enterprising woman who moved to a different village after her husband stopped working, so that she could at least get the moral support of her sister. At one point she tried bringing up a goat to sell its young, but it was stolen. A large amount of her earnings go for medicines. Having taken many decisions and being a strong personality, she is clearly the family head despite the existence of her husband in the household.

Case 6. Mahalakshmi's husband is a TB patient. About two years before our study, he had left the household "due to the opinion of the family." He visits once or twice a year, but contributes nothing. She has a son of 28 who studied up to the 7th grade and was unemployed during our entire study. In addition, she has a daughter who started tailoring training, but discontinued the training because she could not afford the fees. The only other person earning was her 14-year-old daughter, who works as an agricultural laborer. There is also a 12-year-old boy in the house who goes to school. She is the main support of her household which belongs to a relatively high caste (Kallar). Perhaps it was due to caste dignity that the son and older daughter refuse to work as agricultural laborers, though the mother and younger sister are willing to do it.

In the following nine cases the main earner or informant does not have a husband living in the household:

Case 7. Vallachi was widowed when her husband was hit by a car while walking back from the fields. She lives in a very traditional village in Tamil Nadu which is still largely controlled by one big landowner despite land reform. Her household income looks fairly high, but this is deceptive. She has four children between the ages of 11 and 16, all four working. The oldest is a girl of 16 who works along with her mother in the fields. Actually, she works more than the mother. The other three, all boys, are working as cowherds. While their cash income is very little, they are fed by their employers. However, none of the children were able to stay in school long enough to even become literate.

Thus, while the household manages to get enough to eat, in terms of their future none of the children can even aspire to more responsible or higher level manual work such as running or repairing tractors, or factory work, since nowadays any such job requires literacy.

Case 8. Janaki is a widow of 47 whose oldest child is a girl of 18. This girl also works in the fields, but the two younger ones do not work. Her older son occasionally tries to catch some fish for them to eat. Otherwise, he does nothing. He studied up to the 4th grade but then failed. Her younger son is in the third grade now, even though he is fairly old for that grade. The household of four live on the wages of mother and daughter, which comes to Rs. 960 a year or less than $100. At the time our senior research worker interviewed them, they were all just recovering from some sort of a stomach ailment and the family had to spend close to Rs. 100 for "English" medicines. It was clear from looking at them that they were malnourished and had little resistance to disease.

Case 9. Pariyani has been deserted by her husband. She has two children and also supports her elderly mother. She originally lived in her husband's place, but returned to her own house shortly after marriage. A few years later, her husband left the house with her sister. She had three children but the youngest died. She is living in half of a house inherited from her own mother. Her brother and his family live in the other half of the house. Her daughter studied up to the 4th grade, then she was put to work. Her son studied up to the 10th. grade, but then failed his exams and has no work at present. So the mother and sister are supporting the son of 17 and the old grandmother who lives with the daughter. They used to have a goat but it had to be sold when the son required an operation.

Case 10. Janaki is a widow with two children, a boy of 13 and a girl of 12. The girl is studying in the seventh grade and doing well, but the boy stopped school in the 5th grade. He does not work at all since there is no work available for him. Janaki works for one main landowner, but when he has no work for her she will work for anyone; in the off season she gets work carrying stone and wood. She is worried about not earning enough. She also had three deliveries, but lost one child due to illness.

Case 11. Annapattu is a widow. She gave birth to eight children, three died, and one daughter is married. She is living with 3 daughters and a son. The oldest daughter passed 10th grade and is learning typing; the other two girls and the boy are studying in the local school. The entire household lives on her earnings. She has to pay Rs. 10 a month for her daughter's typing classes as well as bus fares. She is constantly borrowing from her employers and then repaying with work. She also suffers from the fact that in her village certain activities require a husband/wife team, so she gets no work when those tasks are called for. She says that at times she has to depend on relatives for food. "It is difficult to get rice gruel even once a day. Sometimes I even have to beg from my own elder sister or brother."

Case 12. Ambarakal Kalikutty is 38. She had five children, but two died and one daughter of 18 is now married. She is a widow. Her husband died at 43. She is living with her son of 12. Her daughter, who is studying in the 9th grade, is living with her brother. "My brothers are educating Nalini. They give all financial help for her studies, but I feel bad because they have financial problems of their own. I alone am educating my son and working. I could have gone back to my native place and stayed with my brothers but it was my husband's last wish that I stay here and bring up my son here. So, even if I have to suffer many difficulties I do not want to go from here." Though unstated, it is also clear that if she were to return to her own natal home, she would lose the house and house-site that she is living in to her husband's relatives. Since she wants to pass it on to her son, she has no option but to manage on her own with her meager earnings.

Case 13. Kunjukudiyumma is a Muslim divorcee. She is living with 3 children, a daughter of 16 and two sons of 10 and 13. Her oldest son is living with his father and his present wife. She also lost 3 children. She gets nothing from her husband for her maintenance. However, some of her neighbors have household members working in the Middle East and when they visit, she gets old clothes from the neighbors when they get new ones. Her husband sold all her ornaments and used to beat her. Her older girl only studied for 2 years, because she had to look after the younger children. The two younger ones are both students. They get old books from neighbors. The older boy who lives with his father refuses to study. She is the main support of her household, though when he visits her, the older son takes day work and gives her his wages. However, she cannot count on these wages and they are not reported in our survey materials.

Case 14. Thanka lives alone. She is 26 and never married. Her father's brother and his family live nearby, but she has no one in her house with her. Her only sister was married a few years back. She works as a temporary laborer for whomever will hire her. She started to work at the age of 10 and helped to support herself and her sister from the time her parents died when she was 9-1/2.

Case 15. Nabeesa lives with her daughter and her daughter's son. She herself has two sons living in the Masjid (mosque) and studying to become Muslim priests. Nabessa is the main earner in the household. Her daughter's husband has gone away for work, but he doesn't send much money or visit often. (We suspect he may have another wife.)

These cases of rural female-headed or female-supported households serve to show that there is considerable range in the actual life situation and the strategies pursued by landless and marginal households where the main economic support is from females.

The Poorest of the Poor

The starred categories on figure 10.1 represent those types of households which are likely to be exceptionally poor. In most cases they are the households with no other working adults, or with adults who only make a meager contribution. Table 10.1 is also informative in this regard. Households with low numbers in the brackets are the poorest in their respective villages; households with higher numbers are better off. This is of course relative. They are not being compared with landowning households, but with other landless ones. Those households in the poorest of the poor category in Kerala account for 16% of the total sample of landless households and 54% of the female-headed households. For Tamil Nadu, based on the 3 villages on the table, the figures are 7% for all landless households but 50% of female-headed landless households.

Most of the households with women who have only small children and no other adults to earn, or where a daughter is the sole support of aged parents, are among the poorest. However, we also find very poor households scattered among the other categories. I am not arguing that only female-headed/female-supported households are extremely poor, but rather that they tend to be among the poorest. Other factors may serve to make households with earning husbands poor, such as the wife's inability to get work due to age or ill-health, recent childbirth, lack of knowledge of agricultural tasks, caste/status pressures that keep her from doing certain tasks, etc. Further factors include situations where both husband and wife have small earnings.

The most important characteristic of the poor households in our sample which have only female earners supporting children and/or elderly adults and/or invalids, is that in most cases these people are almost completely dependent on the earnings of a single individual. Thus if anything happens to that person, there is no alternative provider to fall back on. Furthermore, in contrast with many other societies, household income is rarely supplemented by funds from relatives. Relatives such as elderly parents might help by looking after small children, or doing housework, or washing clothes, i.e., by providing services. But because there is no work available for invalids or the disabled that they can do in their own homes, they cannot make a direct contribution to family survival.

We are discussing here households that live very close to the poverty line, defined in India solely in terms of adequate nutrition, leaving out other aspects of life such as clothing, shelter, education, recreation, etc. Thus, loss of employment often means starvation. When there are only working females in a household, there is no way to get any income during those times in the agricultural cycle when there are only male activities being performed--for example, during the time of ploughing (unless transplanting is also going on).

When males belonging to this sector of the rural economy migrate in search of work, they normally tend to get work at the lowest level of the urban or modern economy. As a result, they are often unable to save much money to send back to their households. It is only the slightly more educated male who can send back a steady amount of money each month. Most of the landless and marginal male migrants are only able to send back occasional gifts of money. An illustrative case is a woman in a Kerala village whose husband was working in Coimbatore in a restaurant as a cleaner (bus-boy). She worked as an agricultural laborer, supporting three small children in the village, feeding them, and paying for their school books and clothes. Occasionally, the husband would send her Rs. 50, and at one time he actually sent her Rs. 100. The arrival of such funds might be the occasion to buy replacement clothes for a child, or to repair the house, but they could not be counted on regularly enough to help

Table 10.1 Landless Female-Headed Households in Some Kerala and Tamil Nadu Villages

Type of Household	KERALA						TAMIL NADU		
	Alleppey (1) # of Cases Rank*	Alleppey (2) # of Cases Rank	Palghat (2) # of Cases Rank	Cannanore (1) # of Cases Rank	Trichur (1) # of Cases Rank	Trivandrum (1) # of Cases Rank	South Arcot (2) # of Cases Rank	South Arcot (1) # of Cases Rank	Thanjavur (2) # of Cases Rank
1. *Widowed, separated, or divorced*									
a. with only small children or alone	1 (3)	5 (1,3,5,6,7)	1 (2)	4 (1,2,4,5)	5 (2,3,5,7,8)		2 (1,2)	2 (1,3)	2 (2,3)
b. with only one other female income					1 (18)	1 (5)			
c. with small income from other relative	1 (13)		1 (1)			1 (17)			
d. with sizeable income from sons, daughters, and/or several other relatives			3 (7,23,26)	5 (9,18,21, 22,24)	1 (17)	3 (12,14,20)	1 (6)	2 (19,23)	2 (12,15)
2. *Women with nonworking husbands, or husbands earning very small amounts*									
a. only wife's income (or husband's negligible)	1 (6)	1 (4)	3 (3,4,6)		2 (1,6)				
b. wife's income plus some salary income from husband or some pension									
c. wife's income plus some income from daughters						3 (13,15,16)			
d. wife's income plus some income from sons and daughters, and possibly other males						4 (24,25,29, 31)	1 (25)		

Table 10.1 (continued)

Type of Household	KERALA						TAMIL NADU		
	Alleppey (1) # of Cases Rank*	Alleppey (2) # of Cases Rank	Palghat (2) # of Cases Rank	Cannanore (1) # of Cases Rank	Trichur (1) # of Cases Rank	Trivandrum (1) # of Cases Rank	South Arcot (2) # of Cases Rank	South Arcot (1) # of Cases Rank	Thanjavur (2) # of Cases Rank
3. *Daughter main informant*									
a. Daughter sole earner, supporting elderly parents				1 (3)	2 (4,10)	3 (1,2,3)			
b. Daughter main earner, but one or both parents have some small wage income and/or pension		1 (21)	2 (8,9)			1 (10)			
4. *Total Number of Cases*	32	29	27	30	32	31	27	32	32

* In each village the households have been ranked according to total household income, with 1 representing the poorest household.

household members fill their bellies.

It is only in Kerala, with its higher level of literacy and with a high rate of migration to the Middle East (a phenomenon that may be undergoing change since hostilities broke out in that region) that any significant improvement in living standards in out-migrating households has occurred. Yet even in Kerala, not all migration necessarily leads to increased income for the household.

Considering only the household types with a star in Figure 10.2, it can be seen that the female-supported households fall into four general categories, based on their household composition. Their strategies are similar, but those with boys in the age range 7 to 12 or so also have the option (at least in some parts of Tamil Nadu and in West Bengal) to put them to work as cowherds for well-to-do land-owners. This kind of work used to be available in Kerala, but is not longer available, in part due to land reform, in part to over-population and the general lack of adequate work for adults. In addition, the introduction of noon feeding in the schools as well as the tremendous emphasis placed on education in the State, has removed any incentive on the part of parents to seek work for young sons. This also holds true to some extent in the eastern part of the old delta in Thanjavur district of Tamil Nadu. To what extent it has been changed in other parts of Tamil Nadu as a result of a former Chief Minister's noon feeding program is hard to estimate, since these data were all collected prior to the start of that program.

In the past, the need for income from young sons has meant that in at least some female-supported households, male children of 7-12 were forced to stop school to take up work as cowherds in order to feed themselves. This was especially the case where the mother, though working, was not earning enough to feed her children. Both in Tamil Nadu and Kerala, young girls in such households have always been expected to take up work as maidservants in well-to-do households where, though they might not earn much, they would at least be fed. Where government policy, as in Kerala, has provided noon feeding, and for the poorest children free school books and a clothing allowance, more of the girls have been kept in school. Having to take these children out of school has obvious implications for the child's future employability in any but the most menial of tasks.

Most of the female-supported households in the sample were in a kind of perpetual debt. Though this was also true of many other households, it was most striking in the case of the female-supported ones. Most required loans which were hard to pay back, though they would pawn any remaining jewelry before taking any kind of a loan. Out of 30 households for which detailed data exists, 12 had loans from their main employer, often with no official interest, but they were paying them back in service and could be expected to work longer hours or be more "loyal" if they had a loan. Only one seems to have borrowed from a relative (perhaps because relatives also tended to be quite poor), and only 3 from other villagers. Most of the loans were used to buy food. In only one case was a person able to use a loan to buy a productive asset, i.e., an animal.

Strategies Employed by Women Supporting Households

In both female-headed and male-headed households, the proportion of their income that women contribute is always very high (see Table 10.2). However, in female headed households without earning sons or sons-in-law, it is the only source of income. There are a number of variables that affect these women to cope. First and foremost among these is the ownership of productive assets. In rural areas this means primarily land, but also animals such as cows, female buffaloes, goats, and fowl, and for widows belonging to artisan communities (e.g. goldsmiths) the deceased husband's equipment which they can hire out to others. Other variables include (1) the caste of the household, and what kinds of work have been traditionally allowed to women of that caste, and to what extent nowadays women of that caste are observing such caste taboos; (2) the women's age and health; (3) the amount of training she has had in agricultural work; (4) her education, which can in some cases provide her with entry to low-level alternative employment, e.g., as a local government midwife, school teacher, clerk, etc.; (5) her relationships with extended kin both within and outside the village, and the extent to which she can count on them for non-financial kinds of help such as connections or consideration for a job, making contacts to obtain a loan for a cow, etc.; (6) family relationships with local big shots and politicians, as well as with the well-to-do in the village, and finally (7) an intangible element which includes the woman's own resourcefulness. Yet it is clear that in the long run, only alternative income-producing activities, tied to contemporary and future industrialization, will make any kind of fundamental difference in the lives of these women.

Summary and Conclusions

The relationship between female-headed/female-supported households and poverty in India is complex, and we certainly need to learn some of the underlying reasons for the wide variations between regions, e.g., the difference between a state like West Bengal that has only 7.68% of female-headed households and ones like Himachal Pradesh and Karnataka that have about double. However, data seem to indicate that a number of variables play a part, such as occupation, age, caste, religion, education, etc. There is a great need to clarify these variables further and to see to what extent such things as education can be used to improve the economic condition of these households.

The data from Tamil Nadu and Kerala show some of the ways in which the category of female-headed households can be disaggregated, and point out that some of them are poorer than others, i.e. that households with only one earner are poorer than those with more than one. Not only are they poorer, they are also at greater risk of starvation when the earner falls ill or if she becomes too

TABLE 10.2   Earnings Versus Contributions to Household Maintenance

	Informant Earn.	Cont.	C/E	Husband Earn.	Cont.	C/E	Ratio of wife's to husband's earning	Ratio of wife's to husband's contribution
KERALA								
Cannanore-1	1138	962	0.85	1954	1249	0.64	0.58	0.77
Palghat-1	-	854	-	-	645	-	-	1.31
Palghat-2	1065	990	0.93	2039	1406	0.69	0.52	0.70
Malappuram-1	435	421	0.97	1219	1020	0.84	0.36	0.41
Trichur-1	-	467	-	-	377	-	-	1.24
Trichur-2	786	688	0.88	1787	1294	0.72	0.44	0.53
Alleppey-1	752	691	0.92	748	569	0.76	1.01	1.21
Alleppey-2	530	438	0.83	743	541	0.73	0.71	0.81
Trivandrum-1	1027	938	0.91	2214	943	0.43	0.46	0.99
Trivandrum-2	1420	1209	0.85	2235	1141	0.51	0.64	1.06
TAMIL NADU								
Chengal-Anna-1	-	301	-	-	155	-	-	1.94
Chingleput-2	-	265	-	-	216	-	-	1.23
South Arcot-1	699	693	0.99	1449	1226	0.85	0.48	0.57
South Arcot-2	587	566	0.96	935	667	0.71	0.63	0.85
Thanjavur-1	-	468	-	-	490	-	-	0.96
Thanjavur-1	1173	1099	0.94	1653	1478	0.91	0.71	0.74
Madurai-1	564	556	0.99	1240	938	0.76	0.45	0.59
Kanya Kumari-1	-	369	-	-	365	-	-	1.01
Kanya Kumari-2	599	570	0.95	1297	808	0.62	0.46	0.71

Districts within each state are listed from north to south. In six villages data on earnings were not collected.

old to work.   While it is true that a man living alone might run the same risks, this is much less likely to happen.   A man who is widowed is extremely likely to remarry within two years, unless he is very old, in which case he is likely to have adult children.   Nonetheless, the occasional elderly male living alone should also be included here.

The data also show that female-headed and female-supported households can be found in all socio-economic classes, though obviously those in the lowest socio-economic classes are at worse risk of starvation.   Field work in villages in these states also brings out the fact that in every village there are a number of females, often aged women, living alone. If they do not own land, they are often the subject of public derision as they try to survive by gleaning, begging, and doing occasional errands.

It has also been noted that a migrant husband need not necessarily mean an economic benefit for the entire household. In some cases, migrant males send home sizable amounts of money which materially help the household, but in other cases, especially if the man has migrated to an urban area within India, the remissions may be small and so unpredictable that they can only be used to pay for an occasional luxury, not for daily food. We again need to learn more about this on the micro-level.

There is no question that there is an urgent need for increased employment for rural women, especially those who are the main supports of their households. It is not an accident that the International Labour Organization funded a study of female-headed households. But one organization's work is clearly inadequate. There is no question that it is essential for the women in these households to find ways of increasing their income, especially during the slack seasons of the year when there is no agricultural work available for them. In addition, for those unable to work all of the time due to old age, ill health, or a child's ill health, there need to be some sort of economic back-ups, either work that can be done at home that is not too strenuous and still brings in some income, or else some sort of last resort government help. The old age pensions for agricultural laborers in Kerala are a start, but clearly much more is needed.

It is also a problem that these households are scattered throughout India's villages and in urban pockets. In any one village there might be no more than 6 or 7 such households, and any help given to them is likely to be resented by those whose households are only marginally better-off with both male and female workers.

Government schemes such as noon school feedings and the disbursement of scholarships for clothes and books for indigent children are important, and certainly old age pensions have been of help where they have been obtained. But more than anything else, most of the women have asked for alternative employment, especially in the months when there is little work in the fields. In addition, work for the disabled that they can do on a piecework basis at home would also help landless and marginal households considerably.

Both the landless and those with very small holdings would benefit greatly from vastly increased and improved loan programs (with less redtape) for the purchase of cows, goats and chickens which can be cared for in the homes. And certainly all of these women would benefit from access to good water near their homes, both for cooking and drinking as well as to grow small kitchen gardens to supplement their diet (especially if also given help to fence in these gardens to protect them from their household goats). It is essential to recognize that agriculture is a female as well as a male concern, that there are women supporting households through agriculture both as workers and as small landowners, and that taking their concerns into account may involve a great deal of rethinking of programs and plans.

As noted in the beginning, there are close to 20 million female-headed/ female-supported households in India taking a very conservative estimate. They are not all elderly widows, the impression that seems to be prevalent in much of the writing. Some are young widows with small children, some women with small children resulting from desertion, divorce, or husband's working away from home. Data on the incidence of each type needs to be explored from a regional and even district perspective, taking into account both socio-economic status, religion, and caste. Not all of these households have been female-headed throughout the life cycle of the household, but many have been for a significant period of time. Often this is the period of time when children are being reared and when the nutrition of the household can be critical for maturation and education. Clearly, along with programming for these women, additional research is needed to learn more about them.

Notes

1. This chapter is based on research carried out over a period of 25 years, starting in 1958, when I first worked in Kerala. The chapter draws on my earlier work in Kerala and Tamil Nadu, as well as a large study of women and rice cultivation I carried out in collaboration with Dr. K. Saradamoni of the Indian Statistical Institute, New Delhi, funded by the Smithsonian Institution and the Indian Council of Social Science Research. That study included 10 villages each in Kerala and Tamil Nadu, and 8 villages in West Bengal. The author acknowledges the support of the Smithsonian Institution, the Indian Council of Social Science Research, and the Research Foundation of the City University of New York.

2. Some of the households where males have migrated are probably included in the category of female-headed households in the 1961 and 1971 censuses reported by Visaria & Visaria, but the percentage of such households is hard to evaluate. It might account for the size of the Kerala and Himachal Pradesh figures, but it is possible that this is not the entire story.

3. The small northeast states and all Union territories apart from Goa have been left out. The reasons for leaving out the northeast include the fact that most of the population in these areas are former tribals with very different cultural values, because the authors are much less familiar with the region, and because it is an area of low population density. The reason for leaving out the Union territories is because each is atypical in some way.

References

Census of India, 1981, Series I. India Part IIB (i) and (ii).

Census of India, 1971, Series I. India Part IIB (i) and (ii).

Census of India, 1971, Series I. India, Part C (iii), Vol. 1, Social and Cultural Tables.

Chakrabarti, Prafulla. 1990. "Widowhood in Purulia," in *The Eastern Anthropologist* Vol. 43, No. 2, pp.125-52.

Dreze, Jean. 1990. *Widows in Rural India No.* 26, Booklet of the Development Economics Research Programme, London School of Economics.

Gough, E.K.G. 1961. "Nayar: Central Kerala; Nayar, North Kerala; Tiyyar, North Kerala; and

Mappilla: North Kerala," in Schneider and Gough, eds. *Matrilineal Kinship*, U. of California Press.

Jain, Devaki & Mukul Mukherjee. 1989. "Women and Their Households: The Relevance of Men and Macro Policies-- An Indian Perspective," Institute of Social Studies Trust, New Delhi Manuscript.

_____. 1989. "The Determinants of Disadvantaged Households Headed or Maintained by Women: Considerations of the Life Cycle," Institute of Social Studies Trust, New Delhi. Manuscript.

Kolenda, Pauline. 1968. "Region, Caste and Family Structure: A Comparative Study of the Indian 'Joint ' Family," in M. Singer and B. Cohn, eds. *Structure and Change in Indian Society*, Wenner Gren Society and Current Anthropology, Chicago.

Krishna-Raj, Maithreyi and Jyoti Ranadive. n.d. "The Rural Female-Heads of Households: Hidden from View." SNDT Women's University, Working Paper.

Kumari, Ranjana. 1989. *Women-Headed Households in Rural India*. Radiant Publishers, New Delhi.

Mencher, Joan. 1989. *South Indian Female Cultivators*. Michigan State University, Working Papers on Women in International Development No. 645. 1989.

_____. 1992. "Who's the Head of the Household? Cross-Cultural Perspectives on the Definition of Household Headship," in Kamala Ganesh and Nukhet Sirman (eds.) *Anthropological Perspectives on Teaching and Research Concerning Women*. In press.

Towards Equality. 1974 Report of the Committee on the Status of Women in India. Government of India, Ministry of Education and Social Welfare.

Visaria, P. and Visaria L. 1985. "Indian Households With Female Heads: Their Incidence, Characteristics, and Level of Living," in D. Jain and N. Banerjee, eds., *Tyranny of The Household*. Shakti Books, division of Vikas, New Delhi.

_____. 1986. "Prospective Changes in the Age and Gender Structure of India's Population and Their 'Socio-Economic Implications'," in *Sociological Bulletin* Vol. 97-116.

Youseff, N.H. and Carol B. Hetler. 1983. "Establishing the Economic Condition of Women-headed Households in the Third World: A New Approach," in Buvinic, Lycette, and McCreevey, eds., *Woman and Poverty in the Third World*. Johns Hopkins U. Press.

11

Female-Headed Households in Rural Bangladesh: A Survey

Mahmuda Islam

Introduction

Female-headed households are a new phenomenon in the rural society of Bangladesh. Due to their very recent origin, information on their nature, extent, problems and issues is very scanty. Systematic study and research on these households are in the rudimentary stage.

The present survey attempts to work out a conceptual framework for identifying the female heads of households in the rural culture. From a brief review of the history of the origin and growth of such households in Bangladesh, the survey moves on to an analysis of the socio-economic background of the female heads and their roles in the production, distribution and management of household resources.

Methodology of the Survey

The survey is based on a study undertaken in three villages of Bangladesh during September-November 1987. A total of sixty-two households were identified as female-headed. Relevant data were gathered by questionnaire. In addition to data collection, the life styles and activities of the women in the relevant households were observed during stays in the villages. The members of the households, especially the female heads, were induced to participate freely in the process of interview and observation.

Conceptual Framework

Due to their comparatively recent origin, the conceptual issues involved in defining a female-headed household have not yet been settled and an accepted meaning has not emerged. As a starting point, female-headed households may be conceptualised from the operational standpoint in the context of Bangladesh.

In this context, the head of a household may be taken to be that member who exercises, directly or indirectly, control over the resources and the earning potentials of the household and who is recognized as such by all the members. The crucial determinant of headship is the ability to control and dispose of the resources of the household, not the ability to produce those resources. Thus, the head does not necessarily produce income for the household directly.

The emphasis on control rather than production of resources is necessary because women are traditionally restricted to performance of domestic chores (not economically measured) and are prevented from engaging in income-generating activities, which in the rural setting consist of agricultural activities in the field away from the home. Thus the female head, due to social inhibitions, may not directly participate in farming activities or engage in a vocation or occupation outside the home. The household income would thus arise from other members, whether from agricultural or other sources. If, however, all the members hand over their earnings to the non-earning female adult member of the household, who then assumes control over the produce of the household lands and the other earnings of the members, this can be considered a female-headed household. In this case, the members of the household defer to the authority of the adult female member in matters of the disposal of household income and resources, which by implication gives her the authority to make all important decisions concerning the household. Thus a household is female-headed either (a) when the woman is the major earner with control over the income and resources of the household, or (b) when she has control and authority over the resources of the household, including the earning of other members, without herself directly engaging in income-earning activities.

Genesis of Female-Headed Households
in Bangladesh

By tradition, man is the "natural" head of the household. The woman, subordinate and inferior to man, is a domesticated member under the domination and guardianship of the man, who may be father, husband, adult son, or any other male member of the kingroup. In some isolated cases, widowed mothers live as dominant persons dictating the domestic affairs of their sons. But the control is limited to such family affairs as socialisation of the grandchildren, behavior of the daughters-in-law, and birth and pregnancy rites. As regards external relationships, management and disposal of the productive resources and handling of cash, the authority remains with the sons who also hold the ownership of the landed property. Such cases cannot be considered female-headed households.

Due to the relatively insignificant frequency of female-headed households, census documents have not taken any notice of them. In 1982, a Sample Survey

235

conducted by the Bangladesh Bureau of Statistics reported for the first time data about distribution of households by the sex of the heads. According to this survey 15.4 per cent of the households (6.9 per cent urban and 16.5 per cent rural) were headed by women. Census 1991 is in the offing; the report which is expected by the end of this year does not contemplate inclusion of data regarding gender distribution of household headship.

The proportion of 15.4 per cent is quite impressive in the context of the historical trend and represents the result of the socio-economic developments through which the country is passing, especially since the seventies. Some of the factors that contributed to the emergence of female-headed households may be discussed briefly.

Liberation of Bangladesh and the Plight of the Women

Bangladesh achieved independence in 1971 after a bloody nine-month-long war which saw many women violated. Many women were widowed without any adult sons to look after the family. These women were without any means of livelihood, and responsibility for them had to be taken by the Government. A Bangladesh Women's Rehabilitation and Welfare Foundation was set up with the purpose of providing these women a means of livelihood, by engaging them in gainful employment or a vocation. With that end in view the Foundation gave women training, financial assistance, and public support. Many women found gainful employment through the Foundation and became the primary bread-winners of their households. In the meantime, the Decade of Women and Women in Development Campaign reinforced the endeavors of the Foundation. These efforts therefore did not remain confined to war-affected women only, but were extended to women in general. Various projects and programs were taken up by the Government and the NGOs, with a view to create more and more opportunities for income-generating activities by the women and to train, equip and encourage women in general, and rural poor illiterate women in particular, to engage in income-earning activities. As a result of these efforts, women in increasing numbers began to earn independent incomes from various economic pursuits. In this process, many women took over the headship of households.

Landlessness and Marginalisation of Agriculture

In 1983-84, nearly 40 per cent of all rural households were agricultural labor households, and 68.8 per cent of the rural population were either landless or had marginal holdings of less than 0.405 hectares. In the absence of land, the authority derived from the ownership of household land by men is nonexistent. As a result, the emergence of women as heads of household was facilitated. Women of the landless households could now enter the labor market to earn a living.

Urban Migration

Landlessness forced many rural people to migrate to urban centres in search of jobs. These migrants were primarily the males who left their wives and children back at home. Though the husband had close links with the household, his absence prevented him from performing many of the duties of the head. This was especially true where the husband or the earning adult male was serving in the Middle East far away from the home country.

Nuclearisation of the Family

The traditional joint family is on the wane. In 1982, 52.2 per cent of the households and 54.3 per cent of the families were nuclear in structure. In contrast to the traditional social system, nowadays deserted, divorced or widowed women and women whose husbands have become incapacitated for work can no longer fall back upon the kingroup. They have to somehow find their own means of subsistence and in the process take charge of their households.

Female-headed households in Bangladesh can be classed in the following broad categories:

1. Households with no adult male member living;
2. Households whose oldest male member (usually the husband) is living but is incapacitated by illness or disability;
3. Households whose adult earning male member is gainfully employed outside the country for a long period, but continues to remit money to the households;
4. Households in which the husband is not living, but other grown-up earning members surrender to the authority and control of the adult female member.

Socio-Economic Background of Female Heads of Household

Households headed by women are overwhelmingly poor and landless or nearly landless, and female heads are usually illiterate. They are also past their youth. Nearly 80 per cent of the female heads surveyed were between the ages of 30 and 50; none were below 20, and only 5 per cent (3 in all) were above 60. Younger women could not take charge of their households because the society still resists headship by younger women. Although the traditional practice of domestication of women has been relaxed to some extent by the rural society, the practice is still relatively rigorously applied to younger women, for the sake of maintaining the moral tone of the society. On the other hand, elderly women usuallly retire from home management after fifty, partly because they lose their working ability and partly because adult sons set up separate households, and aging mothers become dependent on the sons and even sometimes on daughters for subsistence.

Widows have the greater opportunity of heading households. In this survey, 47 out of 62 female heads were widows. Next in line were the deserted women (10 in the survey). There were no unmarried or divorced women in the sample. There were no cases of women who had never married, which is understandable. Such women remain under the guardianship of the parents or the kingroup until they are married. They are married at puberty or early youth and enter the households of their husbands as dependent members. On the other hand, divorces usually take place at the early stages of marriage and before children are born to cement the union. Under the Islamic tradition, such women are normally remarried. They return to the parents' households waiting to be remarried. Deserted women are very unfortunate; they cannot, under the present system, remarry unless they can obtain a divorce.

Poverty is the single most dominant characteristic of the rural female-headed households. Out of the 62 female-headed households, 56 (90 per cent) are landless or near landless and 38 (61 per cent) are totally landless. The women who head these households also came of landless households and were married into similarly landless households of the husbands. Both the kingroups of the father and the husband of these female heads live in poverty. None had the economic means to absorb the households of the unfortunate daughter or the daughter-in-law. It is due primarily to poverty that these women could not get the shelter of the kingroup and had to earn their bread by the sweat of their brows.

Due to their poverty-stricken upbringing, most of the female heads got no opportunity to learn the three R's and 48 of them are illiterate. Only one female head had reached the secondary stage of education; the others dropped out of primary school. Poverty and illiteracy went hand in hand to keep the female-headed households depressed.

Why are there no well-to-do female-headed households? In our sample, only four female-headed households own 0.81 or more hectares of land, which in Bangladesh is enough to provide a moderate living for a medium-sized rural household. Landowning households do not find the necessity of supplementing household income by the labor of their womenfolk. The surplus farmers in fact need the unpaid labor of their womenfolk for processing agricultural produce at home. In rural Bangladesh, those who have sufficient land aspire to aristocratic status, a crucial symbol of which in the popular mind is adherence to the Islamic injunction regarding seclusion and domestication of women. This practice was found to be more widespread among the richer households, while it was almost non-existent among the landless. It was therefore difficult for the women of the richer households to move outside the household and to engage in income-producing activities. Normally, when the husband in a landowning family dies or otherwise becomes unable to maintain the household, the family is absorbed into the households of the kingroups who look after their property, resources and survival. Ownership of land thus acts as an inhibiting factor for the growth of female-headed households.

On the other hand, poverty and landlessness promote the emergence of female heads of household, because these women have no prospect of falling back on the households of the kingroup, but at the same time have considerable leeway to move outside the household and earn their own livelihoods. For these reasons, three-fourths of the female heads surveyed directly were participating in income-earning work, and 29 (47 per cent) of the households were subsisting on the income earned by the female heads alone.

Marty Chen (1986) identified three broad economic classes of rural households on the basis of the labor and income of the women members: surplus level, subsistence level, and below subsistence level. Women in the surplus households work at unpaid family labor, while those in the subsistence-level households work at unpaid family labor as well as paid village labour. The women in the below-subsistence level households primarily work at paid village labor and also seek employment outside the village. The women in the last category have the greatest tendency to take over the headship of households when circumstances so require. The women in the first category seldom rise to headship. In our samples, female heads of households belong predominantly to the below-subsistence class. Taking into account the circumstances analysed above, the situation is likely to be similar everywhere in rural Bangladesh.

Strategies Pursued by Female-Headed
Households for Their Survival

All the female-headed households in the survey had originally been under the headship of men. "Abnormal" situations such as the premature death of the husband or desertion thrust the headship on the women. These women were born and brought up in an environment of male-dominated households and had lived under the control of men. They are conditioned to respond to man's authority and to play second fiddle. All of a sudden, they faced a complete reversal of fortune which transformed them from a position of subservience to a position of authority. This transformation was of a radical nature and imposed on the women, the household and the community a difficult process of adjustment, rearrangement and restructuring of the established institutions, customs, traditions and conventions.

On assumption of the new role, the female heads had to immediately tackle the need to provide the basic necessities of life; and the overwhelming majority of them responded by directly taking up income-earning employment. Some of these women were already working part-time for income. They now became full-time earners, and 29 households became dependent entirely on the income of the female heads. In the other households, the female heads made arrangement to supplement their own income by the income of their children and agricultural income.

Wage labor performed mainly in the middle-class or well-to-do households is the occupation of the majority of the working women. The employment is irregular, and payment of wages is either on a daily or a piece-rate basis. Work extends from daily domestic chores to the processing of paddy into rice. Some of the women earn by such activities as poultry raising and goat rearing. Some engage in petty trade. For example, they prepare indigenous snacks and sell them from the household or in the market through adult sons or kin relations. (Normally, women do not go to the market place to sell their products.) Income from these occupations is quite low. Because women are employed in unskilled jobs and their job opportunities are very limited, they do not have access to the organized labor market and their mobility is restricted within the village or the neighboring villages. They are not supposed to work in the fields. Normally, the female heads seek to keep their economic activities confined to the household or engage in occupations which can be performed in other households.

In 6 households, sons supplemented the incomes of their mothers, surrendering their earnings to the mother who controlled all the income. In 12 households, the working female heads derived some income from whatever cultivable land the household possessed.

In the three villages surveyed, the female heads of 15 female-headed households did not themselves earn any income. In three households, the husbands lived in the Middle East and sent remittances to their wives from time to time. Due to the long absence of the bread-earners from the households, the wives entered into the overall charge of the households and assumed control over the resources remitted by the husbands. In eight households, the earnings of the sons and the income from land provided sustenance to the households, the female heads controlling the income and the resources without themselves contributing any income to the household funds. Only four households subsisted entirely on the income from land.

Problems and Prospects of the
Female-Headed Households

One basic difference between the male-headed households and the female-headed households is that the male head has both ownership and control of the household property, i.e. the land and homestead. The female head has control but not ownership of the land, which is the most important productive resource in the village. Under the Islamic law of inheritance, a widow is entitled to only one-eighth of the deceased husband's property, a daughter gets half of what a son is entitled to, and all the residue after the share of the widow and the daughters goes to the sons in addition to their normal share. Theoretically every wife is likely to bring some landed property to the husband's household after the death of her parents. But daughters seldom claim their share in the patrimony and thus do not bring land with them. In these circumstances, when the husband dies, the surviving widow does not succeed into the property, although she may succeed into the headship of the household. Another important difference is that the male head either cultivates the land himself by engaging in agricultural operations like ploughing, sowing, etc., and/or supervises the conduct of these operations by hired labor/share cropper; but the female head does not engage in direct operations nor undertake supervision herself in the field during the agricultural operation. Her control over the cultivation is indirect, through her male relations.

Due to their inability to engage in or supervise cultivation, women heads had to either lease out the land on fixed rental or to settle for crop-sharing arrangements with sharecroppers. Income from these arrangements yielded lower income than from self-cultivation. They also did not get their due share of the produce from the sharecropper due to the lack of supervision. In negotiating leases or sharecropping arrangements the female heads did not participate directly, but had to depend on the services of the sons or kin relations who acted as intermediaries. The women were thus disadvantaged in dealing with the land.

Women heads of household decide on matters related to the buying, cooking, and serving of food. Besides food articles, the most important daily necessity is kerosene oil for light. Clothes are purchased usually once (or at most twice) in a year. Purchases and occasional sales of domestic products pose a problem for the women. Many of them go to the local grocers. But the grocers charge a higher price than the market price, and their stocks are limited. Women normally entrust marketing to sons, close male kin, or even neighbors. They are not happy with this arrangement, as they do not get their choice of items and suspect that whoever is entrusted with the shopping takes a hidden commission. Women engaged in poultry-raising, goat-rearing, and petty trade complained that they did not get fair prices when using middlemen. When advised to go to the market themselves, female heads said that it was neither possible nor proper due to the social norms.

The sons and daughters in a female-headed household start working at a much earlier age to relieve the hard-pressed female head. In traditional households, the girls begin helping their mothers in the domestic chores at an age younger than the age at which the boys start accompanying their fathers to the field. But in female-headed households, the sons have to seek jobs almost as early as the girls start helping their mothers. Girls in the female-headed households are thus less discriminated against vis-à-vis the boys than in the traditional households.

The traditional household is characterized by a clear gender division of labor between the man working outside the home for an income, and the woman performing domestic chores as free labor. In the female-headed household, this division is narrowed down and the two functions are combined in the female head who earns as well as doing the domestic chores. She has taken over the traditional male responsibility of earning the livelihood, and at the same time has retained the traditional female responsibility of keeping the house. She is therefore heavily burdened with extra work. The burden of work is much heavier on the woman who heads a household than on the woman who has a subordinate position in the traditional household. Many of the earning heads, therefore, did not relish their newly acquired position.

Interaction with the Village Community

The village community led by the elders of the well-to-do households maintains social control. None of the village leaders is a woman. The general attitude of the village elders towards the earning female heads is one of caution. The situation is considered a necessary evil for which a solution does not exist. They adhere to the traditional attitude of inferiority of women, and guided by the tradition they have now concentrated on a watchdog role, trying to see that the public dealings and economic activities of these women do not seriously affect the social structure and norms of the village. The female heads therefore live in constant danger of offending the community and have to be very cautious in performing their new roles.

In the villages, local problems and issues and inter-household disputes are settled in meetings attended by the leaders and male heads of the households. Female heads do not attend such meetings. If they have any grievance, they have to approach the community through households of their kin-group who will represent them in the meetings. The female heads are therefore disadvantaged in their social relations and are victims of discrimination.

At the community level, the female heads continue to have a subordinate position in their relation with kin and in-law groups and the neighbors. They cannot directly negotiate the marriages of their sons and daughters, but have to do so through male relations. They cannot engage in marketing operations in public places. In spite of being heads of their households, they cannot deal on equal terms with the male heads of households. Freed from patriarchy at the household level, these female heads are still subject to it at the wider social level.

Concluding Remarks

For inevitable socio-economic reasons, female-headed households have

242

emerged and are likely to continue. Existing female-headed households reveal the following important features:

1. Poverty is the main contributing factor in the emergence of female-headed households.
2. In female-headed households, the female heads usually participate directly in income-earning activities and are the main breadwinners of the households.
3. Though freed from the control of the male at the household level, female heads continue to be subjected to patriarchy at the community level.
4. Female heads often feel helpless, as they live below the poverty level and are often powerless in the face of the higher level of patriarchy.
5. Economic considerations have brought forth the female-headed households, but such households need to be promoted by an educative programme of changing social attitudes regarding the inferiority of women.

References

Bangladesh Census of Agriculture and Livestocks, 1983-84. 1985. Bangladesh Bureau of Statistics, Ministry of Planning, Statistical Division, Government of Bangladesh, Dacca.

Bangladesh Sample Survey. 1982. Bangladesh Bureau of Statistics (BBS), Ministry of Planning, Statistical Division, Government of Bangladesh. Dacca.

Chen, Marty. 1986. "Poverty, Gender and Work in Bangladesh", *Economic and Political Weekly*, Vol. XXI, No. 5.

Quddus, Md. 1985. *Rural Women in Households in Bangladesh: A Case Study of Three Villages in Comilla*, BARD, Comilla.

Statistical Pocketbook of Bangladesh. 1990. Bangladesh Bureau of Statistics Ministry of Planning, Statistical Division, Government of Bangladesh, Dacca.

12

Defining and Targeting Female-Headed Households for Development Assistance in South Asia

Andrea Menefee Singh

Introduction[1]

In recent years, research on female-headed households has shown us that their statistical incidence is surprisingly high and that their numbers are apparently increasing in both developing and industrialized countries (Youseff 1984). We have also found that there are multiple causes for this phenomenon, ranging from changing patterns in family relations, to migration, to the major structural adjustments occurring in the international arena. It has been demonstrated that the incidence of female-headed households is almost invariably under-reported in official statistics, largely due to methodological and definitional problems (Van der Kemp 1988). A lot of work has gone into developing a clear and com-prehensive definition in order to obtain more accurate statistics (Kelles-Viitanen 1988), but this has not yet begun to solve the problem. Census counts are done only once in ten years, and those in charge of census operations are often reluctant to introduce new questions or training procedures for data collection. In the meantime there is a need for action, a need to do something to address the special needs and constraints faced by the women who carry the burden of family survival on their shoulders alone.

In this paper, I argue that it is now possible to move from research to action, presenting the examples of several successful technical cooperation projects now being executed by the International Labor Organization (ILO) in South Asia. The paper will first discuss some of the definitional problems and their implications for designing programmes. It will then focus on targeting strategies and identification of some of the special problems and constraints faced by female-headed households. These will be relative to the design of specific components or types of activities which would need to be included in programmes meant to benefit female-headed households. Fourth, the paper will describe various strategies which have been used to target and assist female-headed households in the South Asian context. Finally, some conclusions are offered regarding the wider implications for policy and action.

Definitional Issues

A large number of criteria for defining female-headed households have been suggested in the literature (see Van der Kemp 1988 for an excellent discussion). Different definitions appear to have arisen both out of different micro-level research experiences as well as out of different data needs in terms of application. By way of example, the following definitional criteria may be said to be among the more common[2].

(1) Demographic Criteria: This usually refers simply to marital status and assumes that widowed, divorced and separated women are heads of their household, while unmarried women may or may not be, depending on their age and place of residence. In some cases, the physical absence of a spouse or presence of another male adult resident in the household may be taken into consideration on the assumption that a woman is head of household only when an adult male is not present.

(2) Legal Criteria: These are similar to demographic criteria, but may be more complicated because in many societies marriage and authority in the family may be defined differently according to relation (eg. personal laws based on religious customs rather than a universal civil code), according to customary law, or may be complicated by factors such as the practice of polygamy which may result in multiple residences.

(3) Relationship to Land: The legal ownership or tenancy of property in general, but especially of agricultural land in rural areas, may be used to define headship, regardless of patterns of residence.

(4) Decision-Making Criteria: These usually assume that the household head is the person who has the highest authority to make decisions, and usually involves a subjective judgement attributing weightage to different types of decisions.

(5) Customary Criteria: These take into account prevailing or ideal cultural patterns and perceptions of deference and authority within the family and wider kinship groupings.

(6) Designation by Respondent: In the absence of a clear definition of head of household, most censuses and surveys simply ask the respondent to identify the head of household. Without a clear definition, it is difficult to know what exactly is being measured in such cases.

(7) Multi-variate Criteria: The use of several different and often overlapping criteria is common, especially in micro-level case studies (see Kumari 1989). The result is only measurable on a cumulative level, often including numerous subjective judgements, and in aggregate it is again not very clear what one has measured.

(8) Economic Criteria: Perhaps the most important economic criterion is identifying the person who is the "principal earner", regardless of age, sex, relationship, etc. In the Indian Census, the household head has been defined as "the person who bears the chief responsibility for maintenance of the household" (and additionally since 1981 as the person who "takes decisions on behalf of the household", thus mixing criteria). The distinction between earnings and actual contribution to the household and family maintenance is of critical importance, but may be very difficult to measure, especially in subsistence societies where cash income may play a relatively minor role in family survival.

Given the confusion prevailing about the definition of head of household, and the inadequacies noted above in measurement, it may not be surprising that at the field level each project feels a need to evolve its own definition which is appropriate to its particular circumstances. This is at least partly because the objective of the definition is to identify the target group or those individuals who should qualify for assistance, rather than achieving precision in statistical measurement. Further, elements of all of the above criteria often need to be taken into account in order to identify problems, constraints and areas for possible intervention.

Nonetheless, economic criteria, including earnings as well as contributions to family maintenance in cash and in kind, are given the greatest importance. This is because the projects are often governed by the larger objective of targeting the rural or urban poor (with definition of the poverty line being determined by locally accepted norms), and the activities envisioned, at least initially, are therefore largely economic. In the case of the ILO projects which will be discussed below, the title of the multi-country umbrella project is "Self-employment Schemes for Female-Headed Households" which makes it quite clear that the need for enhanced employment opportunities and income by female heads of households is already assumed.

Targeting Strategies

Targeting female-headed households for assistance involves two levels of identification: first at a very general level and second at the level of the individual. For practical considerations it is first necessary to identify ways to reach "catchment areas" in which there may be disproportionate numbers of female-headed households. One problem is that women falling into the usual demographic categories presumed to be female heads of households (i.e. widows, divorcees, separated and unmarried women) are not necessarily poor, and do not necessarily lack an economically active adult male in the household who contributes substantial support, or otherwise sufficient economic support, for example, from remittances. Being a minority of the total population of adult females in most countries in the South Asia region, and being dispersed throughout the population, it is extremely inefficient to try to identify and reach needy female heads on a household-by-household basis.

The ILO projects provide examples of four different strategies to target clusters of female-headed households in the initial stages of project design (for more detail see Empowering Women 1989, Self-Employment Schemes ILO Terminal Report 1990, and Krishnaraj 1990):

(1) In India, it is known that the impoverished eastern region of the state of Uttar Pradesh (U.P.) has long had a pattern of male-only out-migration to large urban centers in the country which resulted in large numbers of *de facto* female heads of household being left behind in villages in addition to women who are heads as a result of demographic factors (see Menefee-Singh 1983 and Saxsena 1977). Parvarthan, a non-governmental organization (NGO) with an established presence in several villages in this region, was provided financial support and technical guidance by ILO to develop activities specifically for women who were heads of households in these villages. The strategy of identifying geographic areas with heavy male out-migration, can be undertaken initially simply through use of census data or other sources of information on sex ratios in migration streams.

(2) In Nepal, the ILO used a similar though slightly different strategy. In this case, a series of ethnographic studies on the status of women in Nepal (Acharya and Bennett 1981 and Bennett 1981) facilitated the identification of an area with a high proportion of disadvantaged ethnic groups in which the women and children carry out the major part (about 60 percent) of family farm work. In addition, a fairly large number of men were said to have migrated out in search of seasonal wage labor or permanent employment. A consultant visited the area in order to identify suitable villages for the project. However, she found migration to be on the whole less important than demographic and economic factors in defining headship. This strategy thus combined the use of secondary sources with additional investigations before deciding on a geographic location.

(3) In Bangladesh, the project linked up with the Vulnerable Group Feeding (VGF) programme of the World Food Programme (WFP) in which food grains were distributed to "distressed women" over a two-year eligibility period. A survey of the beneficiaries of this programme has revealed that the majority (about 61 percent) were female heads of household and were also from the poorest groups. Since the WFP programme covered over 8 to 10 villages at each distribution center, the link-up to this programme provided a quick and efficient way to reach a large number of female-headed households from the poorest groups.

(4) Also in India, another strategy was tried out, namely the identification of an occupational category of poorly paid and predominantly female workers. The occupational category was home-based piece-rate workers, several thousand of whom had already been organized by the Self-Employed Women's Association (SEWA). Group discussions and simple surveys carried out by SEWA had revealed that a disproportionately large number of these homeworkers were the sole or primary earners for their families. Many of the women would not be considered heads of household according to demographic or physical presence criteria of definition, but it was found that home-based work attracts many desperate women workers whose spouses are unemployed, irregularly employed, disabled, chronically ill, or, in some cases, simply irresponsible in contributing towards the maintenance of their families. The specific category of home workers initially targeted for assistance were *beedi* (cigarette) rollers, garment workers and *chikan* (embroidery) workers.

Once these general targeting strategies had been worked out, several questions arose at the field level in operationalizing technical assistance. Does one offer assistance to all female-headed households or should there be a further process of selection? In Bangladesh, it was decided that since the project objectives were to promote self-employment, only those women who were able-bodied, interested and motivated to take part in economic activities would be covered under the project. In India, SEWA members were, in a way, already self-selected in terms of motivation by having displayed the courage to join the organization. In eastern U.P., better-off women were also eager to take part in project activities. In order to maintain good relations within the community, it was decided to include all interested women in certain activities such as those related to social development (e.g. health and non-formal education), but to limit economic support to the poorest and those most in need. In Nepal, this question did not arise since widespread disparities in wealth apparently did not pertain in the villages covered.

Another question was whether to limit coverage only to female-headed house-holds when other very poor women expressed interest in taking part in activities or joining the village-based groups and organizations being formed under the project. Except for the SEWA project, in which the question did not arise, the decisions were mainly left up to the members of the women's groups and organizations to decide according to the principle of freedom of association.[3] In Nepal and Bangladesh, the decision was positive. In eastern U.P. as mentioned above, all women were free to join the organization, but economic activities were limited to the primary target group.

At the field level, simple baseline surveys were carried out in the initial phase in order to identify female heads of households, to understand their conditions, needs, skills and interests, and later to measure the impact of project activities.

Problems and Constraints Faced by
Female-Headed Households

All women, especially those from the poorest groups, face severe constraints in gaining access to development resources and attaining remunerative and sus-tainable employment, but women who provide the sole or primary source of support for their families face additional problems and constraints. In order to design activities which are effective in addressing their needs, it is important to understand these constraints.

One of the most formidable constraints is the common middle-class perception of women as housewives and dependents, as providing at most a minor supple-ment to the main household income. Conventional programmes for women tend to channel them into poorly remunerated activities, often those seen as an extension of their domestic roles such as stitching. Home-based workers are perceived as women filling their leisure time, and are not perceived as the vulnerable and exploited army of workers that they are. In eastern U.P., a bank official in charge of a subsidized credit scheme which could be given only to one member of a household, i.e. the household head, refused to acknowledge that a woman could be the head of a household. In India, despite a national policy identifying female-headed households as a special target group for development assistance, there has not been an operationalization of this policy at the state or local level.

Because women have little access to the more remunerative employment opportunities, the female-headed household is likely to be among the poorest in the community. The female-headed household, on average, has fewer earners than a male-headed household, and most of these earners are likely to be women and children who almost inevitably earn much less than an adult male would. This results in below average per capita income for the household. Insufficient income leads to child labor and poor performance at school if, indeed, the child has been able to enter school at all or has not already dropped out. It is the girl child who drops out first. In order to feed the family, women tend to work excessive hours. Their domestic family maintenance tasks such as fuel and water collection may also require long hours of arduous work, and daughters are often assigned these tasks, again limiting their opportunities for education or training.

Female heads of households tend to receive reduced economic and psychological support from their kinship groups and the community. Divorced and abandoned women tend to be blamed for their husbands' departure. Among Hindus, women who outlive their husbands tend to be blamed for their deaths and their lives are affected by numerous superstitions and taboos. Other members of the husband's family often succeed in expropriating property and assets that according to law or custom should have come under the women's control. Patrilineal systems of descent and inheritance mitigate against the possibility of women accumulating many assets of their own.

In South Asia, it is men who usually deal with outsiders and participate in public affairs, so women who head their households have little experience and few skills to do this when they are left alone. Where *purdah* (seclusion) concepts are strong, women experience social constraints on taking part in marketplace activities or negotiating transactions with outsiders. Public and private transport, and wholesale markets, are governed by men's rough and ready modes. A woman trying to deal with all of these spheres on her own is extremely vulnerable, not least of all to sexual harassment or exploitation. Male relatives or friends, if asked to undertake such activities on behalf of a woman who heads her own household, may not always keep her best interest in mind.

Of particular importance is the almost total absence of formal demand structures to represent the interests of women. Ideally, the family and kinship groups are the traditional structures supposed to do this. But for a female head of household, the reverse may even be the case. Since women, on average, have significantly lower levels of education and literacy than men, they also have less access to information. Therefore, a female head of household is unlikely to even know about available development programmes or resources, much less how to go about gaining access to them.

What To Do?

While it is not possible to go into detail here about the ILO projects that have succeeded in reaching and providing significant assistance to female-headed households in South Asia, it may be worth summarizing the key elements of the approach that has been evolved in order to demonstrate how some of the formidable constraints discussed in the preceding section can be overcome, or at least reduced.[4]

Employment and Income: The first priority and the key motivator for women who carry the responsibility for family survival is nearly always to improve their employment, income and conditions of work. Therefore, the project's initial activities focus on enhancement of income. This involves combining strategies which attempt either to (a) improve income and working conditions in work in which the women are already engaged, (b) provide additional sources of employment and income, particularly during slack seasons, or (c) where necessary and feasible, provide new or alternative opportunities for employment. Group-based savings and credit schemes provide crucial support to these efforts.

Organization: Organization of women into village-based groups, whether informal or formally registered, is the key to developing support groups and demand structures outside the family and kinship group, efficient transfer of information, and training in leadership and other specific skills. Savings and credit transactions are undertaken at regular weekly meetings. Executive and management committees, and affiliations with other similar groups at higher levels, provide visibility and often make these small groups a force to be reckoned with. Participatory methodologies and the principle of democratic functioning lead to increased confidence and leadership skills, which ultimately enable women to increasingly deal with outsiders and take part in the public sphere of activities.

Appropriate Training: Skill upgrading and skill development, training in the use of new technologies, and management and leadership training are essential elements in enhancing income and employment on a self-sustained basis. Constraints on women's time, mobility and educational background all have to be taken into consideration in the design and location of training.

Appropriate Technology: Low-cost technologies which are suitable to local conditions are promoted with two objectives: to reduce the time and labor required by household tasks, and to enhance the productivity of income-earning activities. The former includes such things as ball- bearing grain grinders, increased water sources, pressure cookers and improved cookstoves, while the latter includes improved machines for making rope and leaf plates, rustic storage facilities for seed potatoes, and bicycles for transport.

Social Development: In order to enhance the overall quality of life of female-headed households, health services, literacy and education, improved child care services, and sanitation need to be promoted. These services are often obtainable through various governmental and non-governmental programmes, and the women's organizations can act as a pressure group to channel such resources into their own community.

Resource Mobilisation, Linkages and Self-reliance: In order to ensure long-term sustainability, short-term projects must promote the mobilization of local resources, the building up of assets by their women and their organization, and linkages to locally available development programmes and resources. Leadership and organisational development are also critical to ensuring long-term sustainability and self-reliance.

Replication: Small pilot projects are valuable in demonstrating methodologies and activities that are appropriate, low-cost and effective. However, the ultimate objective must be to promote widespread replication if large-scale impact is to be made on the situation. In addition to direct replication of a project or components, special attention must be given to influencing policies from the grassroots to the national level.

Conclusion

In this paper I have attempted to outline the steps which can be taken to design and implement projects and activities to address the constraints faced by female-headed households in the South Asian context and improve their situation. Because the problem and constraints, as well as the opportunities, are likely to vary in different social, economic and political contexts, I have focused on the approach rather than on specific activities. Several thousand female-headed households have already benefitted from the programmes described above. It is now time to see how similar efforts can be promoted in other parts of the world, and how these efforts can progressively move to a larger scale.

Notes

1. The views expressed here are purely those of the author and do not necessarily represent the official policy or view of the ILO.

2. This section draws upon my early analysis in Singh 1988; see also and Kumari 1989.

3. Special attention is paid to supporting international labor standards in all ILO technical cooperative activities. The relevant standard in this case is Convention 87 concerning Freedom of Association and Protection of the Right to Organize. Also of importance are conventions 141 on Rural Workers' Organizations, 131 on Minimum Wage Fixing, 18 on Equality of Treatment (Social Security) and 100 on Equal Remuneration.

4. For elaboration of this approach, see Andrea M. Singh, "An ILO Programme for Rural Women in South Asia: An Approach Paper" (Unpublished) and Maithreyi Krishnaraj 1990.

References

Acharya, Meena and Lynne Bennett. 1981. *The Rural Women of Nepal: An Aggregate Analysis and Summary of 8 Village Studies.* (Vol.II part 9 of The State of Women in Nepal Series). Center for Economic Development and Administration, Tribhuvan University, Kathmandu, Nepal.

Bennett, Lynne. 1981. *The Parbatiya Women of Bankundol.* (Vol. II part 7 of The Status of Women in Nepal Series. Center for Economic Development and Administration, Tibhuvan University, Kathmandu, Nepal.

Empowering Women: Self-Employment Schemes for Female-Headed Households. 1989. Terminal evaluation report, ILO, Geneva.

Kelles-Viitanen, Anita. 1988. "Female-Headed Households: Guideline for Data Collecetion and Targeting Strategies". Unpublished paper presented at National Workshop on "Female-Headed Households and the Development of Guidelines for Their Participation in Development", ILO, New Delhi, 26-28 April, 1988.

Krishnaraj, Maithreyi. 1990. "Background Paper" for ILO's Programme on rural Women in South Asia, presented at ILO Regional Workshop on Self-Employment Schemes for Rural Women, New Delhi 19-21 Sept.

Kumari, Ranjana. 1989. *Women Headed Households in Rural India,* Radiant Publishers, New Delhi.

Self-Employment Schemes for Female-Headed Households. 1990. Terminal project report ILO Geneva.

Saxena, D.P. 1977. *Rural Migration in India: Census and Consequences.* Popular Prakashan, Bombay.

Singh, Andrea Menefee-. 1983. "Rural-Urban Migration of Women: Some Implications for Urban Planning," in Alfred de Souza (ed.). *Urban Growth and Urban Planning: Political Context and People's Priorities,* Indian Social Institute, New Delhi.

Singh, Andrea. 1988. "Female-Headed Households: An Overview of its Concept and Application to Poverty Alleviation." Unpublished paper presented at the National Workshop on "Female-Headed Households and the Development of Guidelines for Their Participation in Development", ILO, New Delhi, 26-28 April.

Van der Kemp, Oda. 1988. "Planning for Female-Headed Households: An Overview of the issues" an excellent review and synthesis. Unpublished paper presented at the National Workshop on "Female-Headed Households and the Development of Guidelines for Their Participation in Development", ILO, New Delhi, 26-28 April.

Youssef, Nadia and Carol Hetler. 1984. "Rural Households Headed by Women: A Priority Concern for Development." Working Paper, ILO, Geneva.

13

Policy Planning for Single Female-Headed Families: What Is Needed in the United States

Anna Lou Dehavenon and Anne Okongwu

Introduction

There has been a steady rise in the number of single, female-headed households in the U.S. during the past two decades (Suro 1992). By 1990, they represented 16.5 percent of all American families (U.S. Bureau of the Census 1990). This increase occurred simultaneously with two other trends that also altered the nature of family life: (1) the increased labor force participation of women, including mothers with children under eighteen (by 1986, 62 percent were working: Taeuber and Valdisera, 1986); and (2) a decline in the economic position of women and children, so that by 1990 children were the fastest-growing segment of the poor. As a result in the U.S. as in many other parts of the world, women as the most economically and socially vulnerable population segment are charged more and more with insuring the economic support of their households, while also assuming primary responsibility for preparing their children for adult roles.

These changes in the structure and organization of family life stimulated a resurgence of scholarly and public policy interest in female-headed households. Statistics reveal a high correlation between mother-headed households and poverty, and between poverty and the low academic achievement of children. These raised serious concerns about the implications of these trends for the future, economic competitiveness of the U.S.

As noted in the Introduction, it is important to place American families in a broad international context in order to understand the range of factors leading to the steadily increasing number of women with dependent children in the labor force and their concentration in low-paying service sector jobs (Taeuber and Valdisera 1986; Woody 1989). Viewing them this way sheds light on the effects on families of the shift from an industrial to a service economy, the reorganization of the occupational structure, and the reduction of blue and white-collar jobs (Newman 1989; Philadelphia Inquirer 1991). In addition, it views the escalating poverty rates among all types of U.S. families within the wider international field.

This chapter first locates single-parent families in the U.S. within the context of certain statistical parameters and concepts of family. A discussion of the current status of these families follows. We conclude with recommendations for changes on the macro- and micro-levels of government to improve the quality of life and the life chances of female-headed families in the U.S. The recommendations are based on government documents, research on the family over the past decade, and the research and direct intervention strategies which we, the authors, have carried out previously.

Single Parent Families in Context

Qualitative and quantitative research has shown how viewing the family as a bounded, self-sufficient unit, isolated from the public domains of work and the state, obscures the role of the requirements of labor-force participation and the eligibility criteria for state subsidies in determining the organization of domestic structure and the content of family roles (Corcoran, Duncan and Hill 1983; Kamerman 1983; Rapp 1987; Wallerstein and Smith 1991). Research also shows that the range and types of government subsidies, social network exchanges, and other income-generating strategies families use are important variables in determining their quality of life in complex, industrial societies like the U.S. (Dehavenon 1991, Okongwu 1986, Stack 1975).

This approach contrasts sharply with research which is based on the theory that single-parent, female-headed families are deficient and that it is this deficiency which makes them poor, thus creating the illusion that family structure (rather than inequality) is the primary cause of the high rates of poverty in many mother-only families. Explanations of the escalating poverty among female-headed families which focus on gender relations as the cause of their declining economic condition distort the ways in which race and class interact with gender in determining the degree and distribution of poverty among families headed by women (Stallard, Ehenrich and Sklar 1982). Gender relations rather than the trilogy of race, class and gender become the central issue (See Baca Zinn 1987 and Burnham 1985 for a fuller discussion of this problem).

These differences in perception of the causes of the greater poverty in female, single-parent families have important consequences for public policies and intervention strategies. If the structural difference of female-headed families from the "ideal" nuclear family with its traditional sexual division of labor is perceived as the principal cause, the re-establishment of the two-parent family takes priority in policies to solve the problems of poverty (Moynihan 1965; Murray 1984; Wilson 1987). On the other hand, when the causal role of the interaction between race, class and gender inequalities (and the effects of these on access to education, training and stable employment in the primary labor market) is recognized, this interaction is given greater causal weight, particularly in regard to single-parent families headed by Black women. Intervention strategies are then directed toward eradicating the barriers of inequality and preparing mothers for incorporation in the primary labor force. We take the latter perspective to make the policy recommendations which appear later in this chapter.

Single Female-Headed Families: Statistical Parameters

Viewing the family in terms of its interaction with the labor market and the state permits inquiry into the ways in which single-parent families at different socioeconomic levels fulfill basic family economic functions, by integrating state subsidies with formal and informal income-generating strategies and the transfer of important services, information, and material resources through personal social network systems. This line of inquiry also provides a deeper understanding of the wide ranges of variation in the standard of living, and the current and future life chances of these families.

Current population statistics reveal that over the past two decades (1970-1990) the proportion of all U.S. households headed by females increased from 10.8 percent to 16.5 percent (U.S. Bureau of the Census 1990). There was also a decrease in the number of middle-income families and an expansion of those living in poverty (Havemen 1988; Congressional Budget Office 1989; Phillips 1989; *U.S. News and World Report*, January 11, 1988).

In 1989, the poverty rate for a family of four was $12,675. Female-headed households with dependent children were represented disproportionately in the growing poor population: more than half (51.7%) were headed by a woman with no husband formally present (op. cit.). The median incomes of White, Hispanic, and Black female-headed families were $18,946, $11,745, and $11,630, respectively. It is significant that the racial/ethnic distribution of poverty among female-headed families was also uneven: 73.4 percent of Black families in poverty were maintained by a woman, as compared with 46.8 percent of Hispanic families and 42.1 percent of White families (op. cit.).

Female-headed families living in poverty received income from a number of sources: 41.6 percent worked: 8.8 percent were full-time, year-round. Of the non-working mothers, 66 percent cited family responsibilities as the reason for not being in the paid labor force.

The implications of these statistics for the quality of life of a large segment of American families generated a resurgence of interest among social scientists and policy makers in the study of female-headed households, particularly those on public assistance. Given the impact of poverty on the health, social welfare and life chances of poor families, this is an appropriate focus.

However, not all poor families receive public assistance. In 1989, 43.2 percent of poor families were maintained by a married couple (op. cit). Therefore, singling out the difference in family structure as the principal cause of poverty in female-headed families, and focusing on those who receive public assistance, does not adequately address the scope of rising poverty among all women and children. Nor does this focus include the women and children who live below the poverty line in male-headed, two-parent families and in female-supported families in which both the mother and father are present.

Some of the misconceptions about the relationship between female-headed families and poverty relate to faulty assumptions concerning those on public assistance, particularly to the generalized acceptance of the assumptions embodied in the theory of a "culture of poverty" and the Moynihan Report (Moynihan 1965; see also Lewis 1966). These assumptions have resurfaced in current discussions of the causal role of a hypothesized "underclass" in the rise in female-headed families (Maxwell 1992; Murray 1984). For example, it is widely believed that families receiving public assistance comprise a permanently unemployed population that does not actively seek work (Mead 1989). In reality, 50 percent of those on AFDC leave within two years, and 85 percent leave within eight years (Ellwood and Summers 1986). Furthermore, many families alternate between public assistance and low-paying work, thus placing themselves and their children at high risk of hunger and homelessness, unless they have relatives or friends who support them in the interim periods between receiving income from one or the other of these two sources.

When poor parents work, most take jobs in the secondary labor sector which is characterized by low wages, irregular work hours, no job security, few opportunities for advancement, and limited work-related benefits--particularly family health insurance. It is their membership in this labor segment that forces many low-income parents to try to obtain income from public assistance (Bennett 1979; Susser and Kreniske 1987).

Given the reality of the disproportionate concentration of women in low-level, service-sector jobs (Taeuber and Valdiseria 1986), it is important to pay closer attention to marginally middle-income, female-headed families whose incomes are above the poverty line but below median family income. Policymakers have generally ignored this group. Because they have "more serious economic problems than other women workers, [e.g.] higher unemployment, lower educational attainment and more children to rear, on average" (Taeuber and Valdisera, 1986:9), these families are at risk of falling below the poverty line and joining those on public assistance.

Furthermore, when the parents in these families work, their income is often above the official poverty level. As a result, they are not eligible for important government supports in the form of health and child care and food stamps, etc. This often leads to serious problems when the mother's low wages and job-related benefits do not meet the family's needs (Okongwu 1990). For example, job-related health plans with full family coverage require some mothers to make partial payments of as much as $80 per month. This represents a significant hardship for marginally middle-income, working mothers who are already having difficulty supporting their families. The combined effects of inflation, a stagnant minimum wage, expanding debt, the high costs of housing, and the need to juggle a variety of strategies to meet basic household expenses force many of these families to live on the cutting edge of poverty.

The declining condition of poor and marginally middle-income, female-headed families is also intricately connected to socio-economic shifts which became more pronounced during the 1980s: inflation, the acceleration of the segmentation and internationalization of production, reductions in social welfare spending, and increased military spending which in combination with tax cuts led to huge federal deficits. All these trends contributed to the increased vulnerability of an expanding racially/ethnically diverse population of female-headed families, and the proportion of American children living in poverty.

To narrow the gap between theory and practice, some of the knowledge from the research described in our Chapters 3 and 6 provides the empirical base for policy relevant recommendations. These are addressed to both public and private agencies which sponsor programs for families whose annual incomes are less than $25,000. This research was undertaken collaboratively with the staff mem-bers of several private agencies serving families living in New York City on incomes within this range. Most of the recommendations also apply to other programs elsewhere. Here we focus on those located in New York City, as an example of how they apply on a local level, and because that was where the research was done. Our overall goal is to contribute to the strengthening of family income and to provide individual families with a greater understanding of why they are poor and single-parented, and what they can do about it.

Intervention Strategies at the Macro-Level of the State

This discussion suggests the need for intervention strategies at the macro-level of the state to improve the standard of living and life chances of female-headed and other low-income families. As compared with other advanced industrial societies, the U.S. does not provide adequate subsidized support to families. The need is demonstrated by looking briefly at the dilemmas faced by low-income families who live in New York City.

Between 1979 and 1990, the city's poor population increased from 1.4 million to 1.8 million, and the poverty rate grew from 20.2 percent to 25.1 percent (Community Services Society of New York City 1992). The poverty rate among female-headed families also increased, by more than 10 percent. By

1990, 65.3 percent of all female-headed families were poor, and the number of poor children reached 762,244. Sixty-four percent of poor children lived in female-headed families, and 69 percent lived in households that did not have a wage earner.

By 1992, almost a half million households received public assistance (Human Resources Administration 1992). Most had children, and the parent was most often a single mother. Many who were eligible for public assistance did not apply because of the onerous application procedures and the shame of being on "welfare". In 1990/1991, less than two-thirds (59.3%) of all poor families received any form of public assistance. As of March 1991, the basic AFDC grant in New York City for food, clothing and all expenses other than rent for a median family of three had increased only 61 percent since 1969 (from $179 to $291), while the increase in the Consumer Price Index during the same period was 278 percent (Dehavenon 1992). Similarly, the public assistance shelter allowance had only increased 35 percent since 1975. In 1991, the fair market rent for a two-bedroom apartment was $625, more than twice the allowance of $287 received for rent by the median AFDC family of three (Krueger, 1991).

The labor force participation of all groups declined from the beginning to the middle of the 1980s. In 1991, it reached an 11-year low. Nor did those who worked full time at the minimum wage earn enough to support a family. Because of inflation and the government's failure to raise the minimum wage, the earnings of a full-time worker now provides an average family with an income which is $2,300 below the poverty level.

In the 1960s and 1970s these earnings were enough for a family of three to rise out of poverty (Greenstein 1991). This gap between income and the costs of basic life necessities is the principal reason why newly forming families have only two housing options at the present time: either to live doubled up in someone else's apartment, or to ask the city for emergency shelter. It is estimated that New York City families with annual incomes under $25,000 cannot rent apartments at current market prices (Dehavenon 1991).

Chapter 3 proposes recommendations at the three levels of government. These underscore the need for increased government support for subsidized jobs and job training, adequate public assistance grants, subsidized housing, and safe healthy emergency shelters (see also Okongwu 1990). The recommendations also emphasize that unemployed fathers should be included when their families receive these subsidies. Finally, the minimum wage should be increased to a level which enables those who work full-time to earn a living. Eligibility for the federal, low-income health insurance program (Medicaid) should be expanded to include quality health services for all those who lack employer paid medical insurance (See also Okongwu 1990:87). For these changes to be made, and to enhance the ability of parents to care for their children and insure that the next generation of the labor force can meet the challenges of the 21st century competitively, a major shift would have to take place in our national political priorities.

On another level, the implementation of the 1988 Family Support Act (the "welfare reform bill") should be modified to meet the needs of the families in each state. Programs designed to bring mothers into the labor force should take into account their individual work histories and academic and skill levels. The goal should be to prepare mothers for permanent entry into the labor force with secure jobs which have adequate fringe benefits and career mobility opportunities. Simultaneously, mothers should be assured quality day care for preschool children and care and academic support for school-age children. Failure to address both aspects of their labor force participation would lead a significant segment of the AFDC population to continue to vacillate between public assistance and work. Such failure would also contribute to the low academic achievement of low-income children, and would leave them as adults at the lower end of the occupational structure for which there will be fewer and fewer employment opportunities.

New York City's version of the Family Support Act requires AFDC mothers with children 6 years of age or older to be evaluated for participation in the Begin Employment Gain Independence Now program (BEGIN). The program is intended to support mothers in pursuing the training or employment they need to become economically independent. Other AFDC recipients are encouraged to participate in the program voluntarily.

Education and training programs suited to the actual needs of the New York City job market are fundamental to the success of any program which promotes the employment which would enable low-income women to remain independent of public assistance (Passell 1991). Therefore, early evaluation of job skills and suitable remediation are as essential as specialized training for specific, real job options. Thereafter, continued on-the-job training should be provided as needed.

The children of mothers currently in the BEGIN program are eligible for only six months of "transitional" day care when their mothers start working and stop receiving AFDC. We recommend that working mothers be provided with the option of licensed day care (at income-based fee levels) and structured after-school programs to keep their children until they can reasonably be expected to pick them up.

Some mothers in the program (those who chose to fulfill their BEGIN requirement by studying at a four-year college to prepare for more secure positions in the primary labor segment) do not now receive day care allowances for their children. We recommend that these mothers receive the same day care support as other BEGIN families, and that their four-year college strategy be encouraged rather than discouraged as under present policy, since they will provide the city and industry with the labor pool they require. The money these mothers receive for school books is currently counted as income for the purposes of calculating the family's AFDC budget. We recommend that this requirement (which decreases their public assistance grant) be dropped.

Nationally, under the Family Support Act, mothers who become employed receive income support and Medicaid for only six months. We recommend that both benefits be provided until mothers' income from work equals 185 percent of the poverty level, and they have obtained employer-paid health insurance for themselves and their families.

Interventions at the Micro Level
of Local Private and Public Agencies

Low-income families are increasingly dependent on private agencies to take up the slack of the decreases in state subsidies during the 1980s and 1990s. Given the inadequacies in public programs, the role of these agencies is more important than ever before. While they provide services to much smaller numbers of families than public programs did in the past, their support often enables families to remain intact. For example, young, newly-forming, low-income families in New York City today, who do not have relatives or friends with whom to share housing and child care, can survive at best with great difficulty without the support of the private agencies. We now briefly consider two programs (one private, one public) which taken together are excellent examples of what the mothers in all single-parent and other low-income families need to have in order to realize their own family, school, and work goals. The authors have each worked closely with one of these agencies over a number of years.

The Little Sisters of the Assumption Family Health Service

For 30 years the Little Sisters of the Assumption Family Health Service in East Harlem has offered a range of health and other services which help families "heal, grow and develop" (Little Sisters of the Assumption 1991). These services are provided through four programs in which the same family may participate simultaneously.

For example, 465 families received comprehensive, coordinated, home health care services in 1990. These included skilled nursing, home health aide services, social casework, physical therapy, pastoral ministry, health promotion and guidance, and maternal and child outreach services. The latter services identify and address the problems facing individual women and their children longitudinally as they experience childbearing, infancy and childhood. These services are comprehensive, intensive, and targeted to high-risk families. In 1990, 23 families included a member with AIDS. The families are all dealt with as part of a community, and enough staff time is allotted to build close individual relationships based on mutual respect.

In 1990, 29 families participated in the agency's "Grandmother Program" in which older community resident mothers with grown children receive training and professional guidance which enables them to help young parents to develop the confidence and competence to care for their own children. The grandmothers often become role models (even surrogate mothers) to young parents who may never have experienced a consistent, nurturing relationship during childhood.

In 1990, 45 families participated in the agency's "Family Life Program" which has the goal of integrating families into a network of support groups within the agency and within the wider community of school, work and church. This program is based on the assumption that good health involves functioning well socially, emotionally and independently within a society. The activities include working with an educational consultant, completing high school equivalency, learning English as a second language (where necessary), and participating in parenting classes, in teen or youth groups, running rummage sales, special trips, and presentations. While mothers participate in these activities, their children are cared for in a developmental play room supervised by the "grandmothers" and an early childhood development specialist.

The agency's fourth program provides advocacy and emergency services to families who come to the agency in need. On a daily basis, staff care for people who knock on the door with any or all of the problems associated with lack of education, unemployment, loss of entitlements, hunger, poor housing, homelessness, violence, and drugs. In addition to getting help with their most immediate problem, families are given support and guidance, referral to other programs within the agency or other community resources, and education and encouragement (through role-playing) to enable them to interact independently with the public agencies on which their survival depends.

Families are also educated about their legal rights and the need to work for systemic social change. In November, 1990, 120 signed a petition to City Hall asking for continued budget support rather than cuts for social programs. In 1990, between 1,200 and 1,400 households of individuals and families received help through 3,000 visits to this program. To summarize, the Little Sisters Family Health Services Agency is an example of how to provide very vulnerable families with the comprehensive support they need over time to raise children and realize goals as members of their families and the larger community.

The SEEK Program (Search for Education, Elevation, and Knowledge) at Queens College

The SEEK program is funded by New York State and New York City. From its inception in 1966, it has provided a unique opportunity for economically and academically disadvantaged students to enter one of the senior colleges of the City University of New York and to receive the financial, academic, and personal support necessary to earn a B.A. degree. The City

University, as an institution that is primarily dependent on public funding, has been seriously affected by the recent fiscal crises of the state and city. The results include the imposition of tuition increases and a reduction of study services. For low-income students attending a commuter college, these changes (combined with the increased costs of public transportation, books and other academic supplies) make attending college and preparing for work in the primary labor market difficult. These challenges are compounded when the student is a female single-parent who must juggle academic work with child care and a part-time job. Long-term experience working with these students shows that a comprehensive program which is sensitive to the special needs of mothers with children (and is also knowledgeable about--and creatively integrating--the public and private services available to students in this category) can enable them to realize their career goals.

There is a SEEK program at each of the ten campuses of the City University. The program has the same entrance requirements and core components at each site. There are variations, however, in the organization of the program and support services offered to students. This discussion focuses on the SEEK program at Queens College.

Students must have a high school or General Education Diploma, meet the financial guidelines, and have less than an 80 percent average on graduation from high school to be eligible for the SEEK Program. They must also show that they have lived in New York City for at least a year. Upon acceptance in the program, students take an assessment test to determine their proficiency in math, writing, and reading. The results are used to place them in classes that will strengthen the basic academic skills they need to function effectively in college courses and realize their academic goals. The program's eight components consist of 1) academic personal and vocational counseling, 2) financial aid counseling, 3) remedial and developmental courses, 4) tutoring, 5) Committee on Academic Standing, 6) SEEK Learning Center, 7) book stipend, and 8) financial aid.

Upon entrance to the program, students are assigned an academic counselor and a financial aid counselor, both of whom provide services to the student until he or she graduates or leaves Queens College. The academic counselor meets with the student regularly and provides academic, personal, and vocational counseling. In addition, the counselors help the students with program planning and monitor their academic progress through contacts with the faculty in remedial and developmental courses and the SEEK Learning Center. The financial counselor assists students in preparing financial aid forms, approves emergency loans, and advises them on all financial matters pertaining to their education. The Learning Center, in addition to providing students with tutoring services, offers workshops which include study skills and writing. Furthermore, the Center enables upper-level, academically strong students to enhance their skills and earn money by training them to work as tutors for the Center. The teachers of SEEK courses extend their role beyond the classroom by working with students individually, meeting with counselors, and offering workshops and other academic services. The Committee on Academic Standing monitors the academic progress of the individual student closely, and works with all the other components of the program to support the student's success. The program at Queens College currently serves approximately 1,000 students.

In addition to the programs' services, students are able to use all of the college-wide student services, including the campus day care center. To summarize, the SEEK program is an example of a viable avenue for low-income, female, single parents to realize academic and career mobility for the following reasons:

1. It creates the necessary academic supports for those who have not been adequately prepared to compete successfully in a college setting. This is done through careful evaluation of the student's academic skills and provision of the needed course and tutoring services.
2. It provides the student with both academic and financial counselors who can work with them towards realizing their academic goals while financing their education.
3. The stipends (book allowances, emergency loans for academic needs, and opportunities to increase their income through working as tutors or in work/study) create crucial financial supports for students.
4. Day care on campus enables mothers to bring their pre-school children to school with them and to feel comfortable in classes knowing that their children are receiving quality child care.

The multifaceted SEEK program has enabled many single parents to earn B.A. degrees and enter the work force, or graduate school. Without this type of support, these mothers would not have been able to provide their families with a secure economic base.

Some Other Local Level Supports for Female, Single-Parent Families

There is also a need for closer integration of services for low-income single-parent families between public and private agencies. Information on the range of services, eligibility criteria, and the agency's program goals should be updated regularly and centralized. In this way, direct service providers could gain quick access to information on specific services and make appropriate referrals to them. In many instances the needs of female single-parent families are themselves multifaceted. For example, a family may need affordable housing, child care for preschool and school-age children, and employment counseling. Through comprehensive planning and the integration of public and private services, strategies could be developed to simultaneously meet the total needs of individual families before they experience a crisis. The creation of an information clearing house and hotline could serve as a means for meeting this need. Direct practitioners could quickly gain needed information on the services available in the family's community and work with the mother to utilize these services to meet the family's short- and long-term needs.

Another problem confronting middle-income and low-income mothers is stable, adequately paid, employment opportunities which have career mobility. As noted above, most single mothers who work have low-level, low-paying service-sector jobs. Given this reality, more attention needs to be given to the development of comprehensive long-range programs building on the SEEK model to enable mothers to enter the primary labor sector. For example, such a program would:

1. Carefully assess the skills, education, and work history of the mother in relation to labor force needs;
2. Examine the family's current living arrangement, including housing and child care;
3. Review the projected occupational structure with special attention given to employment growth sectors;
4. Work with the mother to develop realistic short- and long-range goals and the strategies for realizing them; and
5. Provide academic training and family supports in concert with other public and private agencies that will enhance the realization of these goals.

An important component of this type of program should be the linkage with actual jobs in the public and private sectors. These jobs should permit mothers to move up the career ladder relative to the rate of growth in their labor force preparation.

In this discussion, we have stressed the importance of integrating services in the public and private sectors to develop localized strategies which meet the actual needs of families. Too often, they fall through the cracks because of the fragmentation of service delivery. In crises they may find help to address their most immediate needs, e.g. hunger and homelessness. This kind of help rarely leads to the long-term viability of the family. There is, therefore, a need for holistic interventions, like the examples presented here, to address the most immediate needs of female, single-parent families, while also building towards their long-term health and stability.

Closing the Gap Between Theory and Practice Further: Some Direct Intervention Strategies

Researchers in the social sciences are with increasing frequency becoming involved in activities designed to improve the quality of life of the populations they study. For example, an anthropologist doing research on the provision of community-based health services to the aged used his research skills to write proposals for a community-based health unit and his research findings to advocate health care for the elderly (See Sanjek 1987). Mencher used her research on poor rural women in agriculture in India as the basis for applied work for an international agency working in another Asian country. This agency was interested in the recommendations she would make for expanding avenues of credit for poor women in the rural areas in a developing country. In addition to doing longitudinal studies of the causes of hunger and homelessness, Dehavenon is a monitor in New York City's Emergency Assistance Units (city offices where homeless families wait for emergency shelter placements for the night). She has used her observations in expert witness testimony in court actions brought on behalf of homeless and other low-income families. During the past decade, some of her policy-relevant recommendations have been implemented by the city and state. These are examples of the ways in which anthropologists close the gap between research, theory and direct practice.

It is to build another bridge between the insights and information gained in scientific research and the direct intervention strategies agencies use in their work with individual families that the following micro-level recommendations are proposed. As was shown above, social historians and social scientists have actively re-examined the nature and organization of American family life over the past two decades. Unfortunately, many of their insights have not filtered down to policy makers, direct practitioners and the low-income families they are intended to serve. Misconceptions concerning the organization of family life and the content of family roles continue to be generally accepted.

The Myths and Realities of Family Life

Direct practitioners should therefore share with female, single-parent families the fact that there has always been a wide diversity in how American families are organized. In addition, it is important for them to know how the content of male, female and children's roles within the family has been conditioned by wider economic, social and political forces. The "ideal" nuclear family division of labor (with the father as the sole breadwinner and the mother as homemaker) was actually experienced by a small segment of the population. These facts provide the broader context needed to explore contemporary family life. Importantly, this would include questioning the conception of female-headed families as necessarily deficient or problem-ridden in order to help more mothers to feel comfortable with the differences in role content embodied in their own lives. This could enable them to be more flexible and effective in shaping their human resources and meeting their families' needs. We now present some examples of strategies for sharing these kinds of information with single-parent mothers through the public and private agencies with whom they work directly.

Small group discussions provide a useful forum for mothers to explore a range of topics that directly affect their lives as single parents. In this context they are able to develop relationships with other mothers facing similar problems. Most importantly, it provides a place and a time for them to share information and express feelings of frustration and concern as well as those of joy and success in relation to situations that they face in their daily lives as women, workers, and primary care providers. What follows are some suggestions of topics and goals for small group discussions.

Small Group Discussion 1. *The Re-examination of "Ideal Models of Family Life"*. This group topic can be used to stimulate discussion among the mothers as to what they envision as the "normal" American family, and the content of men's and women's roles within "healthy" families. These perceptions of family life can be discussed in relation to their own families and other families they know. Information drawn from contemporary social history and social science literature on the family can be shared with the group. Drawing on their own experiences and this new information, single mothers can usefully examine the myths and realities of family life in relation to their own forms of family composition and organization. In this way they will be able to see that there has always been a wide range of diversity among American families, and thus move away from the perception that single-parent families are necessarily deficient. They can also begin to see the linkages between their own family experience and wider social, political and economic forces.

Family Social Network Systems

Single mothers often feel that they alone are responsible for basic family functions and that if they are unable to be self-sufficient, they are not adequately fulfilling the parental role. In reality, families are not isolated units. Rather, each one is embedded in a complex kinship-friendship network system which provides for exchanges of a wide range of material resources, services and information. These exchanges contribute substantially to family members' standard of living and life chances. Helping mothers conceptualize this reality enables them to better understand and effectively utilize their social networks and the bundle of resources exchanged through them.

Small Group Discussion 2. The importance of social network systems. In this group discussion mothers can examine the range of human resources they draw upon to provide economic support for their households, and help with child care, child rearing and domestic activities. In this way they will be able to see the differences in patterns of support within the group, and the roles that family members and friends play in helping them to carry out these responsibilities. In this process it proves useful to have the mothers do inventories of their own social network systems by mapping out the composition and patterns of exchanges that are transferred through them. As a group the mothers can share information on how these exchanges influence their standard of living and lifestyle.

In the course of this discussion, mothers can re-evaluate the content of family and friendship roles within their network system as they come to understand the critical role that these relationships play in their everyday functioning. For mothers who have limited network systems, this process provides a context to explore ways to expand their networks and to see the importance of reciprocity in maintaining positive network systems. This exercise also provides an opportunity for mothers to discuss some problems that can occur as a result of unfulfilled expectations, based on their idealization of the content of family members' roles. For example, grandmothers may refuse to babysit, but may be very willing to give other types of assistance. Anger resulting from their refusal to help with childcare can result in closing off a needed source of assistance in other areas.

Employment

Given the importance of labor force participation and location in the occupational structure, employment counseling is a very important aspect of working with both employed and unemployed single mothers.

Small Group Discussion 3. How to Better Negotiate the Labor Market. Developing long-term occupational mobility strategies can be very important for single mothers. In this respect it becomes necessary for mothers to carefully assess their skills and employment histories in relation to the needed requirements for their long-term career goals. The development of short-term goals and plans to realize these can be very helpful in this process. In some instances, structuring these plans within a buddy system enables both mothers to support each other in the realization of their goals. It is also important for mothers to carefully assess the formal and informal fringe benefits attached to jobs in making employment decisions.

a) The importance of knowing how formal and informal fringe benefits are attached to jobs and how they relate to making better employment decisions. For example, one job may offer higher pay, but have fewer fringe benefits, and less time flexibility, while a lower- paying job might offer a fuller benefit package and more occupational mobility which could better meet the family's ongoing needs and the mother's long-term career goals.

b) How to develop long-term occupational mobility strategies and the short-term goals to realize them. In some instances, structuring these plans within a buddy system helps both mothers support each other in relation to their long-term goals.

Political Action

It is important to remember that single mothers are often short of time and under pressure. Thus, they may not have the time to attend meetings or take part in demonstrations. However, it is important that they be informed of pending legislation and the impact of political change on their families.

Small Group Discussion 4. How to Be Active in the Political Process. Agencies can sponsor discussions on the implications of pending legislation on families, women and children. In small groups mothers can discuss these issues and the positions that their representatives have taken on issues relating to the well-being of families, women and children. They can also compose letters to their representatives which speak to their particular concerns.

Agencies can assist mothers in these activities by developing a short clear newsletter and a mother's chain hotline in which each mother calls one other mother to quickly give her information about an event or proposed legislative change. Further, they can encourage mothers to register to vote and circulate petitions in response to pending legislation that will affect them.

Although it is often difficult for single mothers to attend meetings and demonstrations, the development of an alternating child care system, in which one mother attends a meeting and shares information with the mother who cares for the children, can enhance political participation. In this way each mother is better able to become more actively involved.

In addition to group discussions, agencies can also assist female single-parent families by providing information about state and city subsidies and the eligibility criteria for particular entitlements. This can be done through regular circulation of newsletters which list services and eligibility criteria. It might also be possible to develop a chain telephone hotline for communicating certain types of information quickly.

State Subsidy Information

If mothers are not aware of the eligibility criteria for particular entitlements or services, they cannot use them.

Small Group Discussion 5. Expanding Knowledge On Public and Private Entitlements and Services. This can best be accomplished by: a) Circulating newsletters which list service and eligibility criteria regularly; and b) Developing a mothers' chain telephone hotline for communicating the same kinds of information.

Conclusion

In this chapter, we have discussed some of the major problems confronting low-income and marginally middle-income female, single-parent families in the U.S. We described some of the major limitations in current programs designed to meet the needs of families. We argue that more attention needs to be given to their current condition. We concluded with policy-relevant recommendations at both the macro- and micro-levels that could prove useful in alleviating the declining economic and social position of all low-income families.

References

Baca Zinn, Maxine, and Stanley Eitzer. 1987. *Diversity in American Families*. New York: Harper and Row Publishers.

Burnham, Linda. 1985. "Has Poverty Been Feminized in Black America?" *The Black Scholar* March/April, pp. 14-24.

Community Service Society of New York. 1992. *Poverty in New York City, 1991: A Research Bulletin*. New York.

Corcoran, Mary, Greg Duncan and Martha Hill. 1986. "The Economic Fortunes of Women and Children: Lessons from the Panel Study of Income Dynamics," in Barbara Gelpi, Nancy Hartsock, Clare Novak, and Myra Strober, eds., *Women and Poverty*. Pp. 7-23 Chicago: University of Chicago Press.

Dehavenon, Anna Lou. 1992. "From the Nature of Cultural Things to the Causes of Hunger and Homelessness in New York City in the 1990s," in Maxin L. Margolies and Martin F. Murphy, eds., *Science, Materialism and the Study of Culture*. In preparation.

_____. 1991. *No Room at the Inn: An Interim Report with Recommendations on Homeless Families with Children Requesting Shelter at New York City's Emergency Assistance Units in 1991*. New York: Action Research Project on Hunger, Homelessness and Family Health.

Ellwood, David and L. Summers. 1986. "Poverty in America: Is Welfare the Answer or the Problem?" in Sheldon Danziger and Daniel Weinberg, eds., *Fighting Poverty*. Cambridge: Harvard University Press.

Greenstein, Robert. 1991. Testimony as Director of the Center on Budget and Policy Priorities before the Committee on Ways and Means of the U.S. House of Representatives. March 13. Washington, DC.

Harrison, Bennett. 1979. "Welfare Payments and the Reproduction of Low-Wage Workers and Secondary Jobs." *Review of Radical Political Economics*. Summer, pp. 1-16.

Haveman, Robert H. 1988. "New Policy for the New Poverty," IRP Reprint Series, No. 582. University of Wisconsin, Madison.

Human Resources Administration. 1992. Monthly Report for April. New York.

Kamerman, Sheila. 1986. "Women, Children and Poverty: Public Policies and Female-Headed Families in Industrialized Countries," in Barbara Gelpi, Nancy Hartsock, Clare Novak and Myra Strober, eds., *Women and Poverty*. Pp. 41-63. Chicago: University of Chicago Press.

Krueger, Liz. 1991. Personal Communication. New York.

Lewis, Marilyn. 1990. "Single Parent Homes Continue to Increase." *Philadelphia Inquirer*, September 13: 47.

Lewis, Oscar. 1966. "The Culture of Poverty." *Scientific American* 215: 19-25.

Little Sisters of the Assumption Family Health Services. 1990. *Annual Report for 1990*. New York.

Maxwell, Andrew H. 1992. "The Underclass, Social Isolation, and Concentration Effects: The Culture of Poverty Revisited." Unpublished Manuscript.

Mead, Laurence. 1989. "The Logic of Workfare: The Underclass and Work Policy," in William Julius Wilson, ed., *The Ghetto Underclass: Social Science Perspective*. Annals of the American Academy of Political and Social Science. Vol. 501. January, pp. 156-169.

Moynihan, Daniel P. 1965. *The Negro Family: A Case for National Action*. Washington, D.C. Office of Policy Planning and Research, U.S. Department of Labor.

Murray, Charles. 1984. *Losing Ground*. New York: Basic Books.

Newman, Katherine. 1989. *Falling From Grace: The Experience of Downward Mobility in the American Middle Class*. New York: Vintage Books.

Okongwu, Anne. 1986. *Different Realities: A Comparative Study of Nineteen Black and White Female Single Parents in Philadelphia*. (Dissertations.) Ann Arbor: University Microfilms nternational.

_____. 1990. *Female-Headed Families in New York City: A Comparative Study of Black and White, Low and Marginally Middle Income Families*. Unpublished UNESCO Report.

Passell, Peter. 1991. "When Children Have Children." *New York Times* September 4. P. D2.

Phillips, Kevin. 1989. *The Politics of the Rich and Poor*. New York: Harper Collins.

Rapp, Rayna. "Urban Kinship in Contemporary America: Families, Classes, and Ideology," in Leith Mullings, ed., *Cities of the United States*. Pp. 219-242. New York: Columbia University Press.

Sanjek, Roger. 1987. "Anthropological Work at a Gray Panther Health Clinic: Academic, Applied, and Advocacy Goals," in Leith Mullings, ed., *Cities of the United States*. Pp. 148-175. New York: Columbia University Press.

Stack, Carol B. 1975. *All Our Kin: Strategies for Survival in a Black Community*. New York: Harper and Row Publishers.

Stallard, Karin, Barbara Ehrenreich, and Holly Sklar. 1983. *Poverty in the American Dream: Women and Children First*. Boston: South End Press.

Suro, Roberto. 1992. "For Women, Varied Reasons for Single Motherhood." *New York Times*. May 15. P. A12.

Susser, Ida and John Kreniske. 1987. "The Welfare Trap: A Public Policy for Deprivation," in Leith Mullings, ed., *Cities of the United States*. Pp. 51-68. New York: Columbia University Press.

Taeuber, Cynthia and Victor Valdisera. 1986. *Women in the American Economy*. U.S. Bureau of Census, Current Population Reports, Series P-23. No. 146. U.S. Government Printing Office,

Washington, DC.

U.S. Bureau of Census, Current Populations Reports, Consumer Income Series, P-60, No. 160. *Poverty in the United States: 1986*. U.S. Government Printing Office, Washington, DC.

U.S. Bureau of Census. 1990. Current Population Reports, Series P-60, No. 168. *Money Income and Poverty Status in the United States 1989*. U.S. Department of Commerce, U.S. Government Printing Office, Washington, DC. 1990.

U.S. Congressional Budget Office. 1988. *Children and Families in Poverty: The Struggle to Survive*. Hearing before Select Committee on Children, Youth and Families, U.S. House of Representatives, February 25, 1988.

U.S. News and World Report. 1988. "America's Hidden Poor." Jan 11:18-24.

Wallerstein, Immanuel and Joan Smith. 1991. "Households as an Institution of the World Economy," in Rae Lesser Blumberg, ed., *Gender, Family and Economy*. Pp. 225-242. Newbury Park: Sage Publications.

Wilson, William Julius. 1987. *The Truly Disadvantaged: The Inner City, The Underclass, and Public Policy*. Chicago: University of Chicago Press.

Woody, Bette. 1989. *Black Women in the New Services Economy: Help or Hinderance in Economic Self-Sufficiency?* Working paper No. 196, Wellesley College, Center for Research on Women.

14

Conclusion:
Pulling It All Together

Joan P. Mencher and Anne Okongwu

Introduction

The cross-cultural examination of female-headed/female-supported households presented in this book enables researchers to (1) explore the range of factors leading to the emergence of female-headed households; (2) examine the impact of variations in religious, ideological, and cultural traditions in defining the content of male, female and children's roles, and family organization; (3) examine the impact of socio-economic factors and the particular ways in which structures of inequality manifest themselves at a given point in time; (4) examine the critical role of class or differential access to income in a wide variety of societies and circumstances as they condition the life chances of children, women and even some of the men in these households; (5) examine the role of race and/or caste as it impinges on the lives of young women and men during their formative years; (6) look at differences in the role of the state in providing supplemental support for some female-headed/ female-supported households; (7) examine how each nation is integrated into the world economic system, which in turn influences the resources held by the state and available to female-headed as well as male-headed households, and the possible strategies available to each for survival.

Factors Leading to Emergence of Female-Headed Households

The different articles point to a wide variety of factors that may lead to the emergence of female-headed households, including:

1. *Early marriage of girls to men considerably older than themselves* (noted for Bangladesh, India and Egypt). One of the obvious consequences of such marriages is that women with young children are more likely to be widowed. In each of these contexts there are some cultural norms that restrict the range of strategies that these mothers can use for their family's survival. For example in India, widow remarriage is not an available option for higher caste women. There are varied restrictions on types of employment outside the home suitable for women, family norms that make it difficult for widowed women with property living alone with their children, and cultural attitudes that look down on women in female-headed households. The paper on Egypt also notes that widows may choose not to remarry because they wish to protect their children from a step-child status, if they cannot leave their children behind in the mother's natal home or do not wish to do so.

While widows and divorced women in Islamic countries such as Egypt and Bangladesh may have more control than married women over their own lives and the lives of their children, they may be too poor to afford education for their children because of the lack of any male income, unless education is not only free but includes such state subsidies as noon-feeding, uniforms and books. The long-term implications for the future of these children must be noted by policy makers.

2. *War or political unrest* (refugees, for example, in Africa). Though this book only deals with refugee women in one part of Africa, this is a factor influencing the incidence of female-headed/female-supported households in many parts of the world, from Cambodia or southeast Asia to parts of Central America such as El Salvador, etc. This is a situation that should be investigated further. Clearly cultural norms also play a part, since it may be easier for women who have lost husbands to function alone in some settings than in others. In the Cambodian instance a female head of household must still be soft-spoken, search out friends or relatives to help with male tasks such as plowing the fields, and do many things she was never trained to do such as patching roofs, making ax and knife handles or driving oxcarts. The Mozambiquan refugee women are still required to carry out family reproductive tasks such as food preparation, washing clothes, etc. However, all of this must be done in a context where water is much further away, firewood is difficult to obtain and family members, particularly children, are more frequently ill.

Nonetheless, what many women suffering from the effects of war or political unrest share in common is the loss of male income as well as male socio-psychological and physical support. In addition, they have often lost their own traditional modes of generating income and have become ever more dependent on both the state (where they currently reside) and on international agencies.

3. *Differential mortality rates among males in some sectors of the society as a result of the intersection of several stuctures of inequality creating greater vulnerability to unemployment, involvement in illegal activities, and incarceration* (the United States, Jamaica). This is particularly striking in the case of the United States where poor black males have disproportionately high

rates of unemployment, death, and incarceration. The kinds of services, job training and education available to inner-city males is so grossly inadequate that they are in effect often structured out of formal sector employment. For Jamaica they are structured out as a result of the nature of the international division of labor and the lack of job opportunities for men at home which force many to migrate, get involved in illegal activities, or drop out of day-to-day family living. Many of these men may also be more vulnerable to early death because of lack of health care, especially preventive care.

4. *Desires to escape from oppressive structures emanating from the sex-gender system in particular contexts* (Brazil). Castro in particular notes that some poor women in Sao Paulo may be heads of household because of choice and not only economic constraints, and that female heads of households are not always worse off than women with husbands. Abused women in the United States represent another example of women choosing to live alone with their children. In addition, Blumberg mentions the increased frequency of upper-middle-class women in the United States choosing to be single mothers and the sole supports of their children.

5. *The role of the state in its eligibility criteria acting to separate poor men from poor mothers and children in order for the latter to gain access to life sustaining goods and services* (the United States). Dehavenon notes for the United States that the structure of state subsidies is such that poor men may see their children better taken care of if they absent themselves than if they are visible. This is especially true when semi-educated males cannot obtain wages sufficient to provide basic subsistence for their families.

6. *Cultural attitudes to marriage and consensual unions and the processes involved.* Cultural attitudes that do not totally disown a female for bearing a child out of wedlock are operative in a wide variety of places, including the United States, Mexico, the Caribbean and both Central and South America. This may be sharply contrasted with both rural Africa and most parts of Asia, where girls tend to be married off and sent to their husbands soon after reaching child-bearing age.

7. *The effect of the general economic climate* (e.g., the ways in which the oil boom and bust affected Curaçao, the effect of the current recession in the United States). Abrahams describes the end of the oil boom in Curaçao as a case of interrupted capitalist development that was characterized earlier by a mixed economy of tourism and manufacturing. Increasingly people pushed out of the labor force had two alternatives: migration to the Netherlands, where there is relatively good state support even for female-headed households (despite some degree of racism); or remaining on the island where state supports are inadequate. On the island greater numbers of people are involved in the informal economy, and there has been a sharp increase in the number of female-headed households in all socio-economic classes.

8. *The effect of migration.* Migration sometimes involves males, sometimes couples or families, and sometimes women alone. In the case of Egypt, many parts of Africa both under colonialism and today (such as Malawi and Mozambique), parts of the Caribbean such as Jamaica, and in Brazil, male migration has had the effect of creating large numbers of *de facto* female-headed households. In some of these cases the women may be left alone for years on end, having to manage their households as best they can. While male remittances can sometimes raise the socio-economic status of these households, in many instances males send very little home and the women may face considerable hardship. This is particularly severe where they lack authority to make any decisions related to household productive assets (e.g. where they cannot get a loan for seeds or fertilizers for the land they are cultivating).

Migration also sometimes involves women migrating without males to urban areas. Sometimes they may leave children at home with relatives or friends, and in some instances they may migrate before they bear children. Female migration from urban areas is mentioned by Castro as a factor leading to an increase in urban female-headed households.

9. *Polygamy* (in parts of Africa). In many parts of Africa polygamous households represent a significant part of the population. For certain purposes, polygamous, non-coresidential unions, where women provide the basic subsistence needed for themselves and their children, have been considered to be female-headed (in terms of some but not all of the criteria for headship).

Cultural Factors

Along with well-known and well-documented economic factors, a large number of cultural factors influence the incidence of female-headed/female-supported households and their impact. They or society also influence the way women experience the status of being a head of a household and the extent to which the crossing of roles is feasible. Cultural attitudes towards female sexuality, towards control over children etc. also play a part. Cultural factors also affect such variables as how women with "purse-power" allocate funds compared to males. For example Blumberg demonstrates the impact of purse-power on the allocation of funds for female and male education.

Religion is one of the powerful forces influencing the extent of female-headed households as well as the autonomy of women who find themselves without husbands. Wherever there are strong fundamentalist religions (and this includes at least some sects in all of the world's major religions i.e. Islam, Hinduism, Buddhism, Christianity or Judaism), women tend to be epected to be under the power of some male, and female-headed households are a rarity which tend to be stigmatized. Under such circumstances divorce on the part of women is rare, and if divorced, a woman must then be under the authority of her father or brother. The bearing of children out of wedlock is severely sanctioned (sometimes the woman is killed), and young widows are expected to remarry. Only elderly widows are to be found in some orthodox religious groups. Where young widows do not remarry (as in the case of young high and middle caste Hindu widows) they may be forced to live with their late husband's relatives as a kind of household servant (though this is slowly changing nowadays).

Even among the less orthodox sects of the traditional religions there is considerable variation in the extent to which female-headed households are tolerated or accepted. The cases of Bangladesh and Brazil bring this out clearly.

Traditional patterns of sex-role allocation also play a part in the incidence of female-headed households as well as in the extent to which they suffer disabilities. That is, cultural definitions of what women can and cannot (or should not) do are also relevant to the functioning of female-headed households. Thus, the article on Bangladesh points out that while poor landless (or practically landless) female-headed households may be found in villages, if a woman is left land by her husband, his relatives are likely to incorporate her and her children into their household in order to control the use of the land. However, in the Bangladesh instance, the marriages of children and any major family decisions are controlled by the extended kin even in the case of poor households.

In the case of India, this tends to vary by region as well as the age of the woman, her caste, her age, as well as class. Mencher found more younger female heads of household in southern India than in the north. There was also a tendency to find more among poorer socio-economic classes than among land-owning ones. Even then, there were some land-owning female-headed households found both in Tamil Nadu and Kerala.

The proportion of female-headed households in any given society is clearly mediated by cultural as well as socio-economic factors. What we see if we look cross-culturally are a myriad of different forms within a wide variety of cultural contexts. The one paper presented at the symposium from which this book results that is not included was a paper from Taiwan (presented by Rita Gallin). It was not included because the only female-headed households were single-person households. That is, the Taiwan case was at the extreme where women could only live in "female-headed" households if they never married or had children.

Clearly ideology is very important in family formation even if it is not the only factor. Ideology includes beliefs about control over children, about rights and access to resources as well as their deployment, about what happens to female-owned land if there is any, about female sexuality and its acceptability (i.e. if unmarried mothers are tolerated and how they are viewed), about what is permissible for females to do if males are missing.

Another factor which depends on context is how many workers are needed to generate subsistence for a given household. Obviously this depends on the dependency ratio, i.e. the number of people who do not or cannot work (children, aged and disabled). But it also depends on the income of each working person, i.e. the relationship between each working person's income and what it can buy in the market. In all situations, the more people working, the more the income coming into the household. This holds true among the wealthy and middle class as well as among the poor. But for the poor it can make the difference between survival and disaster. In this connection, culturally defined spending priorities also play an important role in the viability of female-headed households. Are men expected to spend a significant proportion of their incomes on male status-producing activities such as drink, dress, gambling, or other women? Does each household have to spend money on religious activities? Does a man or a woman have to support other dependents such as parents? Are men expected to make major economic contributions to public rituals or to political activities?

Networks

All of the articles deal with the importance of networks, either directly or indirectly, and their effects on the incidence of female-headed/female-supported households and their economic well-being. In some parts of the world such as Bangladesh, female-headed households with any assets are uncommon because a woman left widowed with small children and possessing assets is customarily absorbed into the household of her husband's kin and loses control over those resources; whereas if she lacks any appreciable assets she is much more likely to be left as a separate economic unit. A similar situation may be found in India and in most of east Asia and the middle east. The situation in Brazil and the United States is different in that there are some (though proportionately fewer) female-headed households with assets.

The article on Jamaica examines the critical nature of social network systems and discusses the variations in the size of networks as women age. In Curaçao networks are also critical, particularly in obtaining referrals to housing, for jobs and essential subsistence goods. However, the article by Abrahams notes that the resources held by these networks have decreased. For African refugees often their very survival depends on their networks. These networks not only transmit goods and services, but also information about lost relatives and about conditions in the new setting and home community.

Blumberg also notes the importance of networks in many other parts of the world and even points to their importance for middle-class female-headed households in the United States.

Regardless of whether the female-headed household has assets or not, their ability to mobilize networks both for day-to-day living and in times of emergency is even more important than it is for households with two parents. This is not to deny the importance of class and the fact that the poor must make more extensive and intensive use of their personal networks to survive. Those who are slightly better-off are also dependent on their networks, though perhaps more for services than for material goods. How homogenous or heterogenous the networks may be vary from society to society, and this variability relates to the degree of rigidity of class location within the society.

The kinds of assets that flow through the networks in which female-headed households are embedded come from family, friends, and state agencies. For the United States these are discussed in detail by Okongwu. Network analysis presents a new way of looking at how they are constituted, the types of resources, services and information transmitted through them, and the ways in which these articulate with the state to either expand or restrict the viability of female-headed households. This analysis points out how women belonging to different cultures, different classes and ethnic groups, at different points in their life cycle or at different periods of transition in the world economy, respond differently to economic and other pressures.

Policy Considerations

Many of the articles in this book also make a number of culturally or societally relevant policy suggestions. A review of these demonstrates the importance for policy makers to give close attention to the particular sets of parameters operating within a given context, that is, the importance of framing policies that are context-specific. On the other hand, all of the articles point to the importance of *improving the status of women and empowering them* as well as upgrading their skills and access to education, credit, and other facilities, and the direct consequences of meeting all these needs for the health and well-being of their offspring, both male and female.

It is clear that this is an issue that will increase in importance over the next several decades, not one that will simply disappear. Both national and international agencies will have to deal with the issues involved and develop appropriate strategies for intervention. This applies to both so-called developed societies as well as Third World societies. In the area of adequate supports for families, countries such as the United States and some European countries are seriously lacking appropriate family supports, especially for female-headed households.

Questions and Future Directions

The articles from this book also point to a number of questions that remain to be answered and to new lines of inquiry.

They raise questions about the differential functioning of female-headed versus male-headed households in terms of access to resources, decisions about children including health, diet, education and future options. We need more detailed studies about the relationship between "purse-power", "decision-making authority", and the ways in which state resources can be utilized. We need to become more sophisticated in our research in looking at the ways in which constellations of factors operate. One of the implications that emerges sharply from the consideration of these studies is the importance of taking a wide range of variables into account in both our understanding of the consequences of female-headed households and in planning policies for these households.

The articles show that an understanding of survival patterns of female-headed households must include an awareness and understanding of cultural as well as economic factors, and must take into account both national and international policies. And they point to the need to avoid the kinds of stereotyping of female-headed households (as destroying male children, as necessarily leading to generation after generation of poor women bearing children out of wedlock, or as being better for children in every way) that have clouded rather than clarified policy planning.

About the Contributors

Eva Abraham is employed at the Anthropological-Sociological Institute of the University of Amsterdam. She has conducted extensive research in the Dutch Caribbean and the Netherlands on women, the family, ethnicity and medical anthropology.

Nana Apeadu is a Queen Mother from Ghana. She is a widely travelled spokesperson and consultant on problems of refugee women and children in Afri;a. She is President of Pan-African Human Rights, Inc., executive member of the Women's Commission on Refugee Women and Children in New York, and a member of the NGO working group on refugee women in Geneva. She has a Master's degree in Anthropology from Hunter College.

Rae Lesser Blumberg is Associate Professor of Sociology at the University of California, San Diego. Her research interests focus on the theory of gender stratification and gender and development. Her publications include *Stratification: Socio-Economic and Sexual Inequality*; *Making the Case for the Gender Variable: Women and the Wealth and Well-Being of Nations*; and "A General Theory of Gender Stratification in Sociological Theory" (1984). She has conducted field research on development and/or gender in more than a dozen countries around the world, most recently in Equador, Guatemala, Nicaragua, and the Dominican Republic.

Mary Garcia Castro teaches at the Department of Sociology and in its Masters program at the Universidade Federal Da Bahia (Brazil). She is currently conducting research on the interaction of race, gender, generation, and class in the production of political female leaders such as union leaders. This research is sponsored by an award from the Brazilian government (CNPQ). She has conducted studies on working women in Latin America for the ILO in Colombia and Brazil. With Elsa Chaney she published *Muchachas No More: Household Workers in Latin America and the Caribbean* (Temple Un. Press 1989). Her doctorate in sociology is from the University of Florida.

Anna Lou Dehavenon is Adjunct Assistant Professor of Anthropology in Community Medicine at the Mt. Sinai School of Medicine (CUNY), and the founder and director of the Action Research Project on Hunger, Homelessness and Family Health. She received her doctorate in Anthropology from Columbia University.

Deborah D'Amico earned her doctorate in Anthropology from the Graduate Center of the City University of New York in 1986. She has taught anthropology, political economy and women's studies at undergraduate colleges of the City and State Universities of New York and with the graduate faculty of the New School for Social Research. She has written on issues of class, race, gender and education and has participated in curriculum revision projects aimed at the inclusion of scholarship by women and people of color. Dr. D'Amico has worked as an applied anthropologist in the fields of cultural awareness training and adult education. Currently, she is the Deputy Director of the Consortium for 82Worker's education, an organization of unions which provides education services for adults.

Mahmuda Islam is a feminist sociologist currently employed as Professor at the University of Dhaka, Bangladesh. She has a doctorate in Sociology. She is the author of a number of books including *Women, Health and Culture; Folk Medicine and Rural Women in Bangladesh; and Bibliography on Bangladesh Women with Annotation.* She has written extensively in the field of women and development in both national and and international journals and bulletins, and is an active member of numerous women's organizations and both national and international forums.

Sohair Mehanna is an Assistant Director of the Social Research Centre of the American University in Cairo. She received graduate training at the Fletcher School of Law and Diplomacy of Tufts University. She has conducted extensive research experience throughout Egypt during the past thirty years and has published the results of this research widely.

Joan P. Mencher is Professor of Anthropology at Lehman College of CUNY and the City University of New York's Graduate Program in Anthropology. She has worked in South Asia for more than 13 years starting in 1958, including approximately 4-½ years each in Kerala and Tamil Nadu as well as shorter periods elsewhere in India and Sri Lanka. Her research has included work on women and the family, on agriculture and agricultural development, and on health. She has published extensively on this research including a book *Agriculture and Social Structure in Tamil Nadu.* She has also worked as a WID consultant for UNFPA and UNDP and as a consultant on agriculture for the World Bank.

Anne Francis Okongwu is an anthropologist currently working as Assisstant Professor in the Department of Education at Queens College of CUNY. She has lived for extended periods of time in Nigeria. She has worked intensively on problems of female-headed/female-supported households in both Philadelphia and New York City, and has carried out a study for UNESCO on female-headed households. She received her doctorate in Anthropology from the Anthropology Program at the City University of New York.

Andrea Menefee Singh is an anthropologist currently working as Director for East Africa of the International Labour Organization. She has worked as head of Women's Programming for ILO in India, and has carried out research in India on women's issues for over 20 years. She has written extensively on this research. She received her doctorate from Duke University.

Lucie Wood Saunders is a Professor of Anthropology at Lehman College of CUNY. She received her doctorate in 1959 from Columbia University. She has been working in Egypt since the early 1960s along with her colleague Sohair Mehanna. She has published extensively on her work in Egypt.